STENDHAL

By Joanna Richardson

THEOPHILE GAUTIER: His Life and Times

PRINCESS MATHILDE

VERLAINE

ENID STARKIE

STENDHAL

JOANNA RICHARDSON

LONDON
VICTOR GOLLANCZ LTD
1974

Copyright © 1974 by Joanna Richardson

ISBN 0 575 01870 4

Printed in Great Britain by
Lowe & Brydone (Printers) Ltd, Thetford, Norfolk

Contents

Illustrations follow page 160

STENDHAL

PREFACE

STENDHAL IS ASTONISHINGLY modern. He did not consciously attempt
to be avant-garde, but he belongs, in a curious way, to the present
age. He was a fierce individualist. He needed tradition, he respected
certain conventions, but "the done thing," so he wrote, "is the great
misfortune of the nineteenth century." He found it difficult to conform. Indeed, he was the embodiment of paradox and insubor-
dination. The very tone of Stendhal is provocative. It draws the
reader into a state of complicity. His style and his technique
proclaim a subversive temperament. Stendhal was bourgeois and
provincial; he longed to be aristocratic and Parisian. He was a rebel
and an outsider; he longed to find room for himself at the top. He
had no conventional religion, but some maintain that his atheism
was an attitude rather than a conviction. He never married, but he
believed that true passion was the privilege of an elite; he needed
love and even domesticity. He was French by birth, but he asked
that on his tomb should be the words "Arrigo Beyle, Milanese."

"Really, from his twentieth to his fiftieth year," wrote a critic in
Stendhal à cosmopolis, "Stendhal did not consider himself French."
Yet though the Milanese agreed to give his name to a street in
Milan, and though they set his bust in La Scala, they could not call

him Milanese without reservations. And though the road from Parma to the Charterhouse is named after Stendhal, it does not bind him, wholly, to Parma. An undistinguished street in Grenoble has long since borne his name, but this certainly does not bring him closer to his native town. Mérimée, who knew him well, said that despite his claims to be cosmopolitan, he was completely French in mind and heart. "He was French by his spiritual parentage," insisted Paul Hazard, "French like the Voltaire whose bust grandfather Gagnon had set on his mantelpiece. . . . He was French in his mania for criticising France, in his vanity, in all his ways, French to the very marrow of his bones." Yet perhaps Mérimée and Hazard would have come nearer the truth if they had added that he was European. This, alone, makes him a figure of the 1970's, indeed, a timeless figure.

Stendhal was considered one of the formative influences on French Romanticism. And yet he did not wholly belong to the Romantic world. He was born seven years before Lamartine, fourteen years before Vigny, nineteen years before Hugo, twenty-seven years before Musset. He belonged to a different generation. He alone, among the French Romantics, had been born before the Revolution. As a child in Grenoble he had seen something of the bloodshed, the bitterness and suspicion it aroused. Hugo's father had been one of Napoleon's generals; Stendhal himself had retreated from Moscow with the Grande Armée. He alone, among the Romantics, had seen Napoleon face to face; he alone had spoken to Byron. He was already a veteran, a man of experience, when the others were youths, or still in infancy. One of his great merits, as Paul Léautaud said, was that, before he wrote, he had lived.

He brought to the Romantic movement not only experience, but—it must be said—a strong strain of bourgeois prudence. In money matters, for example, he was no sentimentalist; he would never have borne with the later hardships of Murger's Bohemia. Beyle was more bourgeois than he cared to admit, and so it is that he can usher us better than anyone else into the bourgeois nineteenth century. The heroes of his novels are closer to us than Chateaubriand's René or Byron's Manfred. Today he seems to us to have come from an almost mythological past, yet he appears more modern than many of his successors.

Above all, he brought to the Romantic movement an intellect

that belonged to the eighteenth century. To the lyric, Catholic and royalist Romanticism of 1820 he brought a Romanticism that was liberal, prosaic and rationalist. He brought to the Romanticism of sensibility the Romanticism of the intellect. As a faithful disciple of the Ideologists he attacked the classical theory of ideal beauty. Ideal beauty? He did not know what it meant. Condillac had forbidden him to believe in any innate idea. Art knew no eternal laws, and the dogmatism of the Classics, in 1820, was to him a monstrous error.

The disciples of Condillac defined language as an algebra, and in fact, Beyle wrote like an algebrist. The Romantics were passionate; he presented the phenomenon of analysis in action and in passion. His tone—as Léautaud said—was so true and his accent so sincere that it sometimes seemed one was hearing a voice and not reading words. Writing was usually for Stendhal the pleasure of reliving his life and re-creating the mechanism, the atmosphere and the facts in literature.

Stendhal represents a special form of Romanticism, and in his works, in the 1820's and 1830's, we have the point of departure for Realism and Naturalism. Taine's famous theory of *la race, le milieu, le moment* owed much to Stendhal's scientific appraisal of the human heart in *De l'Amour*. Taine, like Stendhal, treated feelings like a naturalist and a physician. We may find the influence of Stendhal in the scientific precision of Zola; we may find it too, perhaps, in the interior monologues of Proust and Joyce (Marsan observed that Stendhal used the technique in *Armance*). Howard Clewes, in 1950, declared that the broad shadow of Stendhal was "discernible across the pages of all modern French literature. . . . It was with Stendhal that the contemporary novel began."

Whatever his significance in literary history, we still have much to learn from him as a man. Professor F. C. Green maintained that his greatness derived "from a quality rarely encountered in imaginative literature—the unswerving respect for truth." It does not matter, perhaps, so much that he saw his epoch as an Ideologist, an abstract logician, rather than an observer of reality. What matters is that he observed himself. His most interesting novel remains the story of his life. His profession was, as he said himself, that of observer of the human heart.

"It is possible that everything has been said about Stendhal, and even about Stendhal the novelist," wrote Henri Jacoubet in 1933.

"He has had more biographers than anyone," Jules Dechamps continued, thirty years later. "We know the very walks he took, we argue about quarters of an hour." "It is virtually certain," said Yves du Parc in 1959, "that, apart from some lost books of the *Journal*, all Stendhal's works—except for a few corrections—are known to us to-day. But . . . two paths remain open. We need to rediscover a good many of his letters, scattered in the four corners of the world, and numerous works in which his *writing mania* led him to scribble countless annotations." The scope of such research is enormous (he had at least 300 correspondents), but the prospect of discoveries is dim. Another difficulty remains: the distinction of the critical work about him. Stendhal has inspired a cult. The Stendhal bibliography is alarmingly large. It is also dauntingly perceptive.

How, then, can one justify yet another book about him? One can, I think, explain it by the fact that the last serious life to be written in English, the work of Professor F. C. Green, of Cambridge, was published more than thirty years ago, and in the last thirty years many contributions have been made to Stendhal studies. It is time to take account of them. Besides, all writers of Stendhal's standing may be reassessed by successive generations. It is time to consider what he means to us today.

JOANNA RICHARDSON

London
July, 1973

PART I

Grenoble
1783–1799

One

GRENOBLE IS SOME 400 miles southeast of Paris; it is not far from the borders of Switzerland, and it is very close to the northwest border of Italy. It was the native town of Hugues de Lionne, the statesman who negotiated the Treaty of the Pyrenees for Louis XIV. It was the birthplace of Cardinal de Tencin, Bishop of Lyons (and uncle of d'Alembert). It was in Grenoble, in 1715, that Etienne Bonnet de Condillac was born: philosopher, chief of the sensualist school and author of the *Traité des sensations* and the *Logique*. It was in Grenoble, in the rue des Vieux-Jésuites, that Marie-Henri Beyle, later known as Stendhal, was born on January 23, 1783.

All his life he was to show the warmth of nature, the dilatory manner of the south; all his adult life he was to look beyond the frontiers of France. "This inhabitant of *Cosmopolis* had *the national honour* at heart."[1] So Paul Bourget was to maintain when Stendhal's monument was unveiled in Paris. Whatever Stendhal felt about honour, he was not instinctively drawn to his native country. "Gautier thought himself an Oriental," Maurice Barrès emphasised. "Stendhal considered himself a Milanese, an Italian."[2]

He came of bourgeois stock. His paternal great-great-grandfather, Jean Beyle, had been a draper in Lans. His great-grandfather, Joseph

Beyle, and his grandfather, Pierre Beyle, were *procureurs* at the Parlement of Grenoble. On his mother's side, his great-grandfather, Antoine Gagnon, had been an army surgeon; his grandfather, Henri Gagnon, was a doctor. The ancestors of Henri Beyle were respectable, solid Dauphinois.

Henri's father, Chérubin-Joseph, was an advocate at the Parlement of Grenoble. He seems to have had his share of provincial virtues and weaknesses. He was rigidly in favour of the established order—the Bourbon dynasty—and content to attend to his property, his building and his cattle. He was diligent, but he had no business sense. Henri's mother, Henriette-Adélaïde-Charlotte Gagnon, was twenty-five when he was born. She gave birth to a daughter, Pauline, in 1786, and to a second daughter, Zénaïde-Caroline, in 1788. She died in childbirth on November 23, 1790; she was thirty-three, and her son was seven.

It is no exaggeration to say that the whole of his life—certainly his emotional life—was changed by her sudden and premature death. As a small child, he had been devoted to her. If we are to believe his *Vie de Henry Brulard*, his devotion had been intense, and she had returned it wholeheartedly.

> My mother, Madame Henriette Gagnon, was a charming woman, and I was in love with my mother. . . .
>
> I wanted to cover my mother with kisses and I wanted there not to be any clothes. She loved me passionately and often kissed me, and I returned her kisses with such fervour that she was often obliged to move away. I abhorred my father when he came and interrupted our kisses. I always wanted to kiss her on her breast. Let people deign to remember that I lost her in childbirth when I was seven years old.
>
> She was plump, she was very fresh, she was very pretty, and I think that she was rather below the average height. She had a nobility and a perfect serenity about her features; she was very lively, and preferred to run and do something herself rather than give orders to her three maids. She quite often read Dante's *Divine Comedy* in the original. . . .
>
> She died in the flower of her youth and beauty.
>
> My psychological life had begun.[3]

More than forty years later, in *Vie de Henry Brulard*, Henri Beyle was to recall now, the morning after her death, he was told to kiss his father. "I felt an aversion to my father and I felt repugnance at kissing him."[4] A moment later the Abbé Rey arrived: tall, cold, and disfigured by smallpox. Henri claimed that he already disliked him because of his priesthood.

> The Abbé Rey kissed my father in silence. I found my father very ugly, his eyes were swollen and he was constantly being overcome by tears. . . .
> "My friend, this is God's will," said the abbé, at last; and, said by a man whom I hated to another whom I hardly liked, the words made me think deeply.
> People will consider me unfeeling, I was still only astonished by my mother's death. I didn't understand the word [death]. . . . I began to speak ill of God.[5]

Next day the family assembled for the funeral. Chérubin wrapped a black woollen cloak round Henri's shoulders. When the child saw the coffin, draped in black, he suddenly understood the meaning of death, and he was overcome by despair. In the parish church of Saint-Hugues he was choking with tears. "I have never been able to look, dispassionately, at the church of Saint-Hugues and the cathedral nearby," he remembered in 1832. "The mere sound of the cathedral bells, even in 1828 when I went back to see Grenoble, gave me a dull, empty sadness, a sadness without affection, the sadness that borders on anger. . . . With my mother, there ended all the happiness of my childhood."[6]

The figure who stood out most clearly, after his mother's death, was her father, Dr. Gagnon.

> I have [wrote Henri] the clearest and most distinct memory of my grandfather's round and powdered wig, it had three rows of curls. He never wore a hat.
> It seems to me that this dress had helped to make him known and respected by the [common] people, from whom he never took money for his medical services.
> He was the doctor and friend of most of the nobility. . . .
> He was, and had been, for twenty-five years, . . . the promoter of

every useful enterprise, indeed of every enterprise which ... one
might call liberal. They owed the library to him. ...[7]

Until Henri left Grenoble, Dr. Gagnon was to be his virtual father
and his close friend.

After the death of his daughter, the doctor withdrew into silence.
He had—said Henri—loved no one in the world except Henriette
and her son. He was irritated by his surviving daughter, the
temperamental Séraphie; he had "a sort of aversion" for his son, the
feckless and engaging Romain.[8] Dr. Gagnon was restrained in his
manner. He gave his son board and lodging and a handsome
allowance, and Romain bought embroidered coats and kept actresses.

Dr. Gagnon was a necessary figure in Henri's youth; indeed one
wonders how the child would have developed without the help of this
wise and much loved man. For Henri, who had idolised his mother,
felt a compensating hatred for his father. It is tempting to see this as a
classic example of an Oedipus complex. During his mother's lifetime,
he had resented his father's presence; after her death, one suspects
that he resented his father's existence. Chérubin was incurably mid-
dle-class; he lacked the "Spanish" fire and grandeur which Henri
found in his great-aunt Elisabeth Gagnon. He was alien to all the
literary ideas which Henri used to discuss with Dr. Gagnon. It is hard
to believe that Chérubin earned the loathing which he inspired in his
son; but this loathing was real, and it was to embrace all his family. If
Henri could have disowned the Beyles, he would have done so with all
his heart.

In *Vie de Henry Brulard* he left a blistering impression of his father.

> Joseph-Chérubin Beyle [was an] advocate in the Parlement, he
> later became an ultra and chevalier de la Légion-d'honneur, assistant
> to the mayor of Grenoble. ...
>
> He was an extremely unpleasant man, constantly considering the
> acquisition and sale of property, excessively cunning, used to selling
> to peasants and buying from them, an arch-Dauphinois. ... He was
> also extremely wrinkled and ugly, and confused and silent with
> women, who were none the less essential to him. ...
>
> It would have been difficult for him to love me. ... He clearly saw
> that I had no love for him, and I never spoke to him unless I had
> to. ... I saw very little of him. ...

After I left [Grenoble], at the end of October, 1799, I was nothing to my father except a demander of money, and the coldness grew unceasingly, he could not say a word that did not displease me. I thought it loathsome to sell a field to a peasant and haggle for a week in order to gain 300 francs; that was his passion. . . .

Never perhaps has chance brought together two people more fundamentally antipathetic to one another than my father and me.[9]

In *Vie de Henry Brulard,* Henri recorded that he hardly remembered the years from 1790 to 1795. They had left him only a sense of sorrow and disgust. He was always scolded for everything; his only protector had been Dr. Gagnon, and since the doctor hated scenes, he avoided doing battle for him. Aunt Séraphie, who had taken a marked dislike to Henri, was well aware of the fact.

A fortnight or so after his mother's death, he and his father went back to their melancholy house. Chérubin—who was clearly capable of love—was stricken with grief. He locked up the room in which she had died. It was to remain locked for the next ten years. He dismissed his servants and took his meals at Dr. Gagnon's. If the doctor accepted his company, he did so, Henri later surmised, out of concern for the child. Dr. Gagnon and Chérubin were united only by their sorrow. On the death of Mme. Beyle, the family had cut all social contacts, and to crown Henri's misery, they remained in permanent isolation.

M. Joubert, thin and scruffy, taught the child the rudiments of Latin, but he was clearly more sympathetic than his appearance suggested. As a man Henri found the Coliseum sublime because it was a living reminder of the Romans whose history had filled all his childhood. However, in December, 1792, Chérubin engaged the Abbé Raillane as Henri's tutor. The abbé, a Provençal, was small and tight-lipped. It would have been difficult to find "a more arid soul, a soul more inimical to everything that is honest, more devoid of any feeling of humanity."[10] More than forty years later, meeting an amenable woman, it suddenly occurred to Henri Beyle that her nose was like the Abbé Raillane's. Thenceforth he could not bring himself to look at her.

Since his mother's death, Henri had been unhappy and withdrawn. During the "terrible tyranny" of the Abbé Raillane, he grew sombre and full of hatred for all the world. He was forbidden, to his regret, to play with other boys; Chérubin was afraid to see him consort with common children. Henri's most frequent companions were the thirty or so canaries which the abbé kept in a cage beside his bed. Chérubin raised no objection, though the smell was intense, and the birds woke the child at dawn every day.

Henri's misery and misanthropy (the word was not too strong) increased every day. A year after his mother's death he had another cause of distress. His father—so he considered later—fell in love with his sister-in-law, Séraphie Gagnon. Henceforth he was her slave, and "two devils," in Henri's words, "were let loose in my poor childhood." Chérubin and Séraphie went for long walks in the country. They took Henri with them to preserve appearances in Grenoble; as soon as they were outside the town, he was sent on far ahead. Séraphie, who was violently jealous of the child, was always persuading Chérubin to scold him. Caroline, Henri's younger sister, was her father's favourite, and she told tales about him.

Chérubin, so Henri said, was a man of enthusiasms. He now had a passion for agriculture; this was to be followed by his passion for building and finally by his passion for administering Grenoble for the benefit of the Bourbons. His current passion for agriculture took him twice a week to his small property south of Grenoble. The ground was arid and stony, but every self-respecting bourgeois had to have his property. Chérubin's house at Furonières, in the commune of Claix, was two leagues from Grenoble, and Henri often walked there on his Thursday holidays; grudgingly he tramped round the fields with his father and listened to his plans. Sometimes they spent a night or two at the house, and August and September were always spent there. Henri was consoled only by the library and by his discovery of a forty-volume edition of Voltaire and an illustrated edition of *Don Quixote*. "Just imagine the effect of *Don Quixote* in the midst of such horrible misery!"[11] Chérubin, shocked by the boy's amusement, threatened to take the book away. It was small wonder that Henri had a passion for revolt, a mania for antipathy.

And with this passion for revolt went a timidity which one may also trace to the uncertainty and unhappiness of his childhood. In *Les Grands Timides*, Dugas has suggested that Henri's life was an unremitting struggle against his timid nature. He was timid because he did not know what he really wanted. His timidity was mistrust of himself. So it was that he tried to create himself a character, but there again he failed. His ideal was constantly changing; everything tempted him but soon disappointed him. He was permanently unsettled.[12]

In 1789, when Henri was six, the Revolution had burst upon France. The Beyles had become more legitimist—more devoted to the Bourbons—than ever. When Louis XVI was being tried, Chérubin followed his trial in the papers as if he had been an intimate friend.

> When the news of the condemnation arrived [Henri recorded], my family were in absolute despair. "But they'll never dare to carry out that infamous sentence," they said. "Why not," I thought, "if he was a traitor?"
>
> I was in my father's study in the rue des Vieux-Jésuites, at about seven o'clock in the evening. It was quite dark. I was reading by the light of my lamp and separated from my father by a very large table. I was pretending to work, but I was reading *Mémoires d'un homme de qualité* by the Abbé Prévost (I had discovered a copy worn with time). The house was shaken by a mail coach which arrived from Lyons and Paris.
>
> "I must go and see what those monsters have done," said my father, rising to his feet.
>
> "I hope that the traitor has been executed," I thought. Then I reflected on the extreme difference between my feelings and those of my father. . . . I was judging the case between my family and me when my father came back. . . .
>
> "It's all over," he said, with a heavy sigh, "they have murdered him."
>
> I was overcome by one of the most intense feelings of delight which I have ever known.[13]

Three months later, on April 21, two representatives of the people arrived in Grenoble; soon afterwards they published a list of the political suspects of the department. Those who were merely suspects were to be kept under observation; those who were notorious were to be arrested. Chérubin found himself listed among the notorious; on May 15 he was imprisoned for the first time. He spent at most forty days in prison, but he remained on the list for twenty-two months.

There were other ominous reminders of the political ferment. In 1794, when Henri was eleven, the anticlerical movement reached Grenoble, and—as in other cities—the *bataillons de l'Espérance* were organised. Instead of receiving religious instruction, the local children were drilled and paraded and held public meetings. They were prepared for patriotic service and trained to combat the alleged antirepublican activity of the clergy. "I longed to join these battalions which I saw filing past," Henri recorded in *Vie de Henry Brulard.* "I see today that they were an excellent institution, the only one that might uproot *priestery* in France. Instead of playing at chapels, the children's imagination turns to war and grows accustomed to danger."[14] A former priest, the Abbé Gardon, was in charge of the Battalions of Hope. In his childish hand, Henri forged a letter purporting to be from Gardon to Dr. Gagnon; the letter invited the doctor to have his grandson enrolled. The hoax was discovered, and Henri was forbidden to dine at table for three days. "I prefer," he said, grandly, "to dine alone, rather than dine with tyrants who constantly scold me."

One tyrant was soon to disappear from his life. In August, 1794, the Abbé Raillane was replaced as his tutor by Joseph Durand. But it was clearly Dr. Gagnon who gave the boy a love of learning; he helped him to write his Latin verse, he told him about his exploits at school, and Henri longed for school, for there at least he might talk to children of his own age. He was soon to have this pleasure. An Ecole centrale was established, Dr. Gagnon was a member of the organising committee, and he had M. Durand appointed a professor.[15] On November 21, 1796, the Ecole centrale opened its doors, and that day Henri entered it as a pupil.

The reality of school was far inferior to the wild ideas which he had formed in his imagination. "Everything surprised me in this liberty I had so longed for, the liberty I had now attained at last. The delights I found were not those I had dreamed of. The pleasant, noble, gay companions whom I had imagined were not to be found, instead there were very self-centred and mischievous little boys."[16] Throughout his life, reality would nearly always fail to match his dreams.

As one might expect, he was hardly popular with his schoolfellows.

They did not appreciate his haughtiness or his ideas of Spanish nobility. They left him out of their games—which, moreover, he did not know how to play.

The Ecole centrale had given him a taste of liberty, and he began to grow more resilient. On January 9, 1797, Aunt Séraphie died. Now that Séraphie had gone, Chérubin spent more time at Claix, and Dr. Gagnon's house became more serene. When Henri came home from school in the evening, he was no longer afraid of interrogation. Often, on the way home, he spent half an hour at the Jardin de Ville, where, on summer evenings, under the chestnut trees, all the youth of the town would assemble. Gradually he began to emerge from his cocoon.

It was in November that Virginie Kubly arrived at the Théâtre de la Ville. Henri never spoke to her, but, watching from the pit, he was soon infatuated with her. "She was a slim young woman, quite tall, with an aquiline nose, pretty, slight, well made. . . . Her expression was serious and often melancholy. Everything was new to me in the strange madness which suddenly took command of all my thoughts. All other interests disappeared for me."[17] He had discovered life through books, and through books alone; one does not do so with impunity. He was destined, by his education, to feel only cerebral passions, and the influence which formed his idea of love also fixed his conceptions of the world. From the ideas of novelists and poets, the only ones within his reach, he created imaginary destinies and an illusory society.[18]

Virginie Kubly played in comedy, and she sang in comic opera. Henri knew little of real comedy. But on the eve of his fifteenth birthday, he wanted dramas about the misfortunes of love. In *Claudine de Florian,* Virginie played a country girl who had been abandoned with an illegitimate child. For several months this drama remained a success in Grenoble, and for several months it gave him exquisite pleasure. "I didn't dare to utter Mlle. Kubly's name; if someone mentioned her, I felt a curious movement near my heart, I was on the point of falling. There was a kind of tempest in my blood. If someone said *la Kubly* instead of Mademoiselle Kubly, I felt a movement of hatred and horror which I could scarcely control."[19]

The fact that she sang led him to love music ("perhaps my strongest and most expensive passion"[20]). One day he asked someone where she lived; it was, he considered, later, perhaps the bravest action which he had then performed. When he felt especially courageous, he used to walk down her street, with beating heart.

> I should perhaps have fallen if I had met her. I felt wonderfully free when I reached the end of the rue des Clercs and I was sure that I should not encounter her.
>
> One morning, walking by myself at the end of the avenue of massive chestnut trees in the Jardin de Ville, I caught sight of her at the other end of the garden. . . . I was nearly ill and I finally *took flight,* as if the devil were after me. . . . I had the good fortune not to be noticed. Observe that she did not know me at all. That is one of the most striking features in my character, I have always been like that [so he was to write in 1835]. The happiness of seeing her close to, five or six yards away, was too much.[21]

Nearly forty years later, he was still to remember the look of the playbill, with her name on it. In his devotion, he had walked from poster to poster, reading her name again and again.

On April 15, 1798, Virginie Kubly left Grenoble. For a long while he could not bear to go to the theatre.

> When I came back to life [he wrote] after several months of Mlle. Kubly's absence, I found that I was another man.
>
> I no longer hated [the thought of] Séraphie, I forgot her; as for my father, I wanted only one thing: not to be near him. I observed, with remorse, that I did not have a *drop* of tenderness or affection for him.
>
> So I am a monster, I said to myself. And for many years I found no answer to this objection. In my family they talked all the time, till it made you sick, about affection for relatives. What these good people called *affection* was the continual vexation with which they had honoured me for five or six years. I began to suspect that they were mortally bored and that, being too vain to take up again with the society which they had imprudently left at the time of a cruel loss, I was their resource against boredom.
>
> But nothing could move me any more after what I had just felt. . . .
>
> The moral tempest from which I had suffered for several months had made me more mature, I began to take myself seriously.
>
> "I must make a decision and get out of this quagmire."
>
> I had only one possible means: mathematics.[22]

He persuaded his family to let him have extra tuition in mathematics. He worked with single-minded application. In September, 1799, at the end of his third year of studies, he was awarded a first prize. The way was clear for him to go to Paris and try to enter the Ecole polytechnique; as a *polytechnicien,* an official career would be open to him. On October 30, 1799, he left Grenoble, "that town that I abhorred and still hate, because it was there that I learned to understand men."[23]

He travelled with M. Rosset, an acquaintance of his father's, to Lyons and Nemours, and at Nemours, some twenty leagues from Paris, they learned of the events of 18 Brumaire (November 9). Napoleon Bonaparte had engineered a coup-d'état, and he had become First Consul. He had supreme authority in domestic and foreign policy, and he could rule as a dictator. Henri Beyle, wrote Pierre Brun, "belonged to the generation which trembled under the Terror, and aspired with all its strength to the reestablishment of order."[24] Henri Beyle, countered Léon Blum, needed a disordered life. "For the development of a Stendhal, this state of incoherence was the chosen milieu, just as it was later to be for the Stendhalian generations."[25] Perhaps neither statement was wholly true. When Henri Beyle learned of 18 Brumaire, he understood little about it, but he was "enchanted that young General Bonaparte should make himself King of France."[26] It was an event which destroyed the hopes and beliefs of Grenoble, now far behind him. It appealed to his romantic imagination. Bonaparte was a parvenu. He had shown what might be achieved. Now Beyle and countless contemporaries were fired to make triumphant careers.

On November 10, M. Rosset left him at a hotel at the corner of the rue de Bourgogne and the rue Saint-Dominique. It was conveniently near the Ecole polytechnique, where Henri was to sit for the entrance examination.

PART II

In The Emperor's Service
1800–1814

Two

THE ECOLE CENTRALE at Grenoble had failed to match his dreams of school. Paris proved to be another disillusionment. The surrounding countryside seemed ugly, for there were no mountains. He disliked the capital itself, and his dislike increased every day. No doubt it owed something to the fact that he was alone, uncertain of himself and far from rich. He left his hotel and took a cheap room.

He seems to have had only one introduction from his family. Soon after his arrival in Paris he called on Noël Daru. It was the first formal visit he had ever paid. Noël Daru was seventy, a cousin of Dr. Gagnon's. He was a Grenoblois, a self-made man who had acquired a substantial fortune. He had bought a house, 505, rue de Lille, on the corner of the rue de Bellechasse, but he modestly chose to occupy a small apartment over the carriage entrance. One apartment in the house was let to Mme. Rebuffel, the wife of Daru's cousin Jean-Baptiste Rebuffel. Jean-Baptiste called every day on his wife and daughter Adèle, but he lived in the rue Saint-Denis with his mistress. Jean-Baptiste welcomed Henri warmly. Daru received him with touching expressions of devotion to Dr. Gagnon. Mme. Daru was prudent and polite; her prudence had no doubt helped to form the character of her elder son, Pierre, who was soon to be secretary-general at the Ministry of War. Her second son, Martial, had "neither mind nor wit, but he had a good heart, it was impossible for him to hurt anyone."[1]

Henri was to form such opinions later; in December, 1799, he was far from seeing things so dispassionately. He was in an emotional state.

> What I see today very clearly [he was to write in *Vie de Henry Brulard*], and felt very confusedly in 1799, is that on my arrival in Paris two great objects of constant, impassioned desire had suddenly turned into nothing. I had adored Paris and mathematics. Paris without mountains inspired me with a distaste so profound that it almost verged on nostalgia. Mathematics were nothing to me, now. . . .
> I was tormented by these changes. And, of course, at sixteen and a half I couldn't see the why or the wherefore.
> In fact, I had only loved Paris out of disgust with Grenoble.
> As for mathematics, it had simply been a means. In November, 1799, I had even begun to hate it because I was afraid of it. I had decided not to be examined in Paris.[2]

Looking back, many years later, he could not understand why his father had not compelled him to sit for the examination. Perhaps he had trusted in Henri's evident passion for mathematics. But Henri was desperately afraid that he would be obliged to enter the Ecole polytechnique, and he waited impatiently to learn that the course had begun. Once it had done so, he was safe. In *sciences exactes* one could not embark on a course at the third lesson.

He was physically frail, with an appetite for happiness which was only an enormous need for relaxation. In his attic, overlooking the Invalides, he became ill with anxiety. He was always to fuss about his health. Young and innocent, he now fell into the hands of a dubious army surgeon. This doctor prescribed "black medicine, which I took," he wrote, "alone and abandoned, in a room which had only one window seven or eight feet up, like a prison."[3] He no longer knew what he wanted. He decided that he needed a woman, but the thought of a prostitute filled him with horror. In his nervous state, he could not eat. Finally M. Daru brought the famous Dr. Antoine Portal to see him. Henri learned afterwards that he had been in danger of dropsy of the chest. He was delirious, and he spent three or four weeks in bed, with a nurse in attendance.

Then Noël Daru, well disposed and concerned, gave him a room on the second floor of his house: a large room, looking over four gardens. Even Henri was satisfied. It was, he thought, the proper setting for a dramatist, and he determined to write plays. For mathematics, as he had said, had simply been a means of escape from Grenoble. Virginie Kubly's admirer was now comfortably settled in Paris and free to write masterpieces for the theatre.

He was a far from gracious tenant at the rue de Lille. He did not object to living at M. Daru's, but he was mortally bored to be obliged to dine there. He disliked Parisian cooking; he disliked the Darus' apartment. He had to accept an etiquette which he disdained. His family had not taught him the social obligations to which he was now obliged to conform. He had been intent on his own thoughts; now he had to consider his relationships with other people. These relationships depressed him. He felt that he had an infinite capacity for loving and being loved; he longed to meet warm responsive human beings. He had believed that only the occasion was wanting. Now he found himself awkward and inferior in a society which he considered dull. How would he fare in a fashionable salon? Society hurt his self-esteem; it made him constantly afraid of being judged and being derided.

He had another cause for anxiety. Noël Daru clearly wanted to know why he had not entered the Ecole polytechnique and why, if he had failed this year, he was not preparing to enter at the next session. "My family leave me more or less free to decide," Henri explained. "So I observe," came the answer.[4] M. Daru's irritation was understandable.

Occasionally Pierre Daru would dine at the rue de Lille. In 1800 he had just been appointed to the Ministry of War. Sometimes he kept the family waiting for an hour or two before he arrived, looking "like an ox exhausted by its labours." Often he returned to his office later in the evening; in fact, remembered Henri, they were secretly preparing the campaign of Marengo.

Noël Daru saw his opportunity. Early in 1800, he informed Henri bluntly: "My son will take you to work with him at the Ministry of War."[5]

Just after his seventeenth birthday, bewildered and untrained, Henri Beyle was given a desk at the ministry. The first time he had to copy a letter, he made a mistake in spelling. He later marvelled at the kindness which the Darus had shown the conceited and ignorant youth that he had been. Meanwhile, the kindness continued. Noël Daru had given him medical attention, board and lodging; Pierre had given him a clerical post. Now Martial, a quartermaster, or commissary of wars, suggested that Henri might soon acquire the same attractive uniform.

Henri said nothing of his occupations, let alone his dreams, in his letters to his sister Pauline. It was hardly to his credit that his first letter to her was written five months after he arrived in Paris. Nonetheless, he exhorted her to write to him every week, and he began to take a brotherly interest in her. Constantly, in his correspondence, he urged her to form her taste for the theatre, to tell him which pieces of music to send, to read Miss Edgeworth on education, to study Plutarch, Racine and the tragedies of Voltaire. He explained to her that to write good letters "one must write exactly what one would say to the person if one saw them. . . . One must never repeat an opinion, even the Pope's, without having considered it. . . ."[6] His sister Caroline was rarely mentioned; perhaps he had not forgiven her, even now, for her telltale behaviour as a child. But Pauline, at least, was not to vegetate in the provinces. "Cultivate your mind a good deal," Henri exhorted her, "and leave the manual work to human machines."[7]

On May 7 he was finally swept into the Napoleonic saga. He left Paris to join the reserve army in Italy. He entered the field of war as a future writer. In *Vie de Henry Brulard* he was to record how he crossed the Saint-Bernard and how he came under fire for the first time.

Early in June, at the small Italian border town of Ivrea, he had an even more momentous experience. He heard the *Matrimonio segreto* of Cimarosa. Music was suddenly revealed to him. Years later he was to write that nothing purified him of the company of fools as music did. It became dearer to him every day.

Everything was divine in Cimarosa.
In the intervals of the pleasure I said to myself: And here I am,

thrown into a crude career instead of devoting my life to music!! . . .

My life was renewed, and all my disappointment in Paris was buried forever. . . .

The evening at Ivrea destroyed the Dauphiné in my mind forever. . . .

To live in Italy and to hear such music became the basis of all my reasoning.[8]

He was soon to discover the part of Italy that he loved best. He fell in love, at first sight, with Milan, and that love was to be intensified by the love which he was to feel for two women whom, in time, he came to meet there. "My reason tells me," he wrote, "real beauty is places like Naples and Posilipo, it's the country around Dresden, the crumbling walls of Leipzig, the Elbe . . . at Altona, the Lake of Geneva. . . . My reason tells me that, but my heart feels only Milan and the *luxuriant* countryside around it."[9] Henceforward he was betrothed to Italy.

On a sparkling morning early in June, 1800, Henri Beyle rode into Milan for the first time. It was the eve of the Battle of Marengo; but the Italians already looked to the French to liberate them from Austrian domination, and Henri Beyle was welcomed as one of the conqueror-liberators. In the Corsia del Giardino he met Martial Daru, who took him to his headquarters at the Casa d'Adda. They rode into a splendid courtyard; Martial's servants took his luggage and led away the horses, and Martial's servants brought them *côte-lettes pannées*—veal cutlets fried in breadcrumbs. For several years the dish was to remind Beyle of Milan.

> For me this city became the finest place in the world [he confessed towards the end of his life]. I don't feel the charm of my native land in the least, and for the place where I was born I feel a repugnance which borders on physical nausea (seasickness). From 1800 to 1821 Milan was the place where I perpetually longed to live.
>
> I spent some months there in 1800; it was the finest time in my life. . . . Only my reason tells me, even in 1836, that Paris is better. In about 1803 or 1804, in Martial's office, I avoided looking at an engraving which showed Milan cathedral in the distance, the recollection was too tender, and I found it painful.[10]

On June 29, 1800, writing to Pauline, he described the cathedral and the opera. He confessed that he had acquired a better opinion of the Italians than the one which was generally held in France. He had, he said, been far from expecting "the charming amiability of the women in this part of the world."[11] There, no doubt, was one of the chief reasons why he fell in love with Milan. In Italy he found a warmth and naturalness which he had not known in France, a sensuality to match his own. In Paris he had been liberated from his provincial family; in Milan, for the first time, he was free of his inhibitions, he discovered his real nature. He felt able to be himself.

It was, one surmises, in Milan, a few months after his seventeenth birthday, that he was initiated into sex. He later claimed that he had forgotten the circumstances, but that seems unlikely, especially as they left an unpleasant legacy.

> In those days [writes Henri Martineau] the same remedy was used for blennorrhagia and syphilis. The ailments which he later complained of, headaches, erratic fever, disorder of the stomach, fits of congestion, accompanied him more or less all his life. Most of them may well have been sequels of the Milanese ailment, and they would suggest that he suffered from the second of these afflictions. And so today we may surmise that Stendhal's death from apoplexy . . . was a result of his first imprudence.[12]

On this first visit to Milan, Beyle discovered his manhood. He also found a romantic love which eclipsed any passion that he had felt for Virginie Kubly.

> One cannot clearly see the part of the sky that is near the sun, and for a similar reason I shall find it very difficult to give a rational account of my love for Angela Pietragrua. How can one give even a fairly rational account of so many follies? Where should one begin? How can one make this at all intelligible? I am already writing badly, as I do at great moments of passion, and yet I am writing about things that happened thirty-six years ago.[13]

Angela Pietragrua was six years older than himself. Her parents, the Borronis, were drapers in Milan; her husband, Carlo Pietragrua, was an employee at the Office of Weights and Measures. She came of humble stock, she was clearly not a model of fidelity; but she was sensual, sultry and magnificent. She seemed to Henri Beyle to have a kind of grandeur, the nobility of soul for which he longed. He was too timid, too aware of his insignificant status, to declare himself, but while he satisfied his immediate physical needs with other women, Angela Pietragrua already satisfied a deeper need: a need for a goddess in his imagination.

Henri Beyle had had no military training, but on September 23, presumably through the influence of Pierre Daru, he was appointed a provisional second lieutenant in the 6th Dragoons. He accepted his commission with the nonchalance which he was so often to show in his career. He felt in no haste to join his regiment. He remained at general headquarters in Milan, where he found time to be bored at a ball and to send advice to "la citoyenne P. Beyle" about her education. On November 22 he eventually joined his regiment and arrived with it at Bagnolo, "a nasty little Cisalpine village three leagues from Brescia. We have absolutely no provisions at all," he told Pauline, "and the worst thing is that the colonel cannot give us permission to go to Brescia because we expect to attack at any moment."[14] The local populace hated the French, and any Frenchman who ventured out alone would be shot.

Late in December he found himself, conveniently, on a mission to Milan. A carnival was in full swing; the city was jubilant with bells and resplendent with decorations. On February 1—again, one must presume, through Pierre Daru—the raw young subaltern was appointed aide-de-camp to General Claude-Ignace-François Michaud. At the end of the month he joined him at Mantua.

On April 18, 1801, Beyle began to keep the journal which has come down to posterity. He intended it to be, literally, a daily record of his life: an intention which he failed to fulfil. But he was to keep it, sporadically, until October 31, 1823, and it illuminates his career, his ambitions and his nature. Now, in Milan, he watched the manoeuvres of the second Polish legion. They had come from the army of the Rhine and were on their way to Florence. The cavalry, in blue jackets piped with crimson, their lances adorned with small tricolour flags, paraded before three Napoleonic generals. Next day, in Milan, the first stone of the *foro Bonaparte* was laid.

In her provincial isolation, Pauline must have marvelled at her brother's adventurous life. Yet he himself appeared to be more interested in *dolce far niente* than he was in the Italian campaign. He hardly seems to have been aware of military duties. In Milan he played lotto at the café. In Bergamo he read Voltaire and a critical edition of the campaigns of Julius Caesar. His syphilis still troubled him. He suffered from recurrent bouts of fever and noted his condition and his cures. He took abortive lessons on the clarinet, and he translated a play by Carlo Goldoni. On July 12 he recorded his stream-of-consciousness and his persistent ambition to be a dramatist.

> I have slight bouts of fever every evening at eleven o'clock.
>
> Let us make haste to enjoy ourselves, our moments are numbered, the hour I have spent in grieving has nonetheless brought me nearer to death. Let us work, because work is the father of pleasure; but let us never grieve. Let us consider sensibly before we make a decision; but, once we have decided, let us never change. With persistence, one succeeds in everything. Let us give ourselves talents; one day I should regret the time that I have lost. . . .
>
> I believe, for example, that one day I shall do something in a theatrical career. My mind, which is constantly occupied, always makes me look for instruction, which can justify my hopes. . . .[15]

The journal records Henri Beyle's trend of thought; it illuminates the workings of his mind. It also removes any lingering doubts about his potential gifts as a dramatist; Beyle lacked humour, he lacked the ability to create a plot, he saw his characters merely as embodiments of virtues or weaknesses, set in the situation which would test them most. He considered his theatre with his intellect, as a scientist might consider an experiment; he did not approach it with his heart.

On September 18 he left General Michaud to rejoin his squadron of the 6th Dragoons. At Saluzzo he fell seriously ill. Some weeks later he urged Pauline to send him shirts and stockings. "It is diabolically cold in this country, and a poor convalescent needs to be well covered."[16] He continued to study life, to analyse himself, with the maturity of a man of fifty. He also discussed his nature with a doctor. "It seems," he concluded, "that my usual malady is boredom. A good deal of exercise, a good deal of work, and never any solitude, will cure me. M. Depetas [the doctor] told me that I had some symptoms of nostalgia and melancholy."[17]

It was a convincing diagnosis, but no doubt his melancholy was assuaged at the end of December, when he went home, on convalescent leave, to Grenoble.

·Three

"AT SEVEN O'CLOCK in the evening she was practising a Haydn symphony. She was to play it that evening at Mme. Périer's."[1]

The unnamed musician was Victorine, the nineteen-year-old daughter of Joseph Mounier. Her father had been a member of the Convention nationale, the most memorable of the Revolutionary Assemblies. Her brother Edouard (one day to be a *conseiller d'état* and a peer) was a childhood friend of Henri's in Grenoble. Eager, impressionable, too timid to declare his love for Angela Pietragrua in Milan, Henri conceived a violent passion for Victorine. Like his passion for Virginie Kubly, it was an *amour de tête:* a love that existed entirely in his imagination. But it existed there, so intensely that it was to last for years. This love for Victorine Mounier, wrote Paul Arbelet in *Trois solitaires,* was without question his finest love. "None of his loves, at least, belongs to him so much as this one. His imagination provides everything, and the heroine almost nothing."[2] It was characteristic of him that even now, he chose, instinctively, to abandon himself to this idealised passion. In his journal he might coolly note the most effective way to seduce a woman. But he kept such physical necessities apart. The inflexion of a word, an unexpected gesture put him in a heaven of happiness or in a very hell of despair. He remained romantic at heart; he needed, perhaps unconsciously, a nostalgic, melancholy love.

In the spring of 1802 Victorine left Grenoble for Paris. On April 5 he followed her.

There was a further reason for his journey to Paris. Throughout his life he was to show only an erratic regard for the duties imposed on him by his career. He had now decided that a military career did not suit him, and he intended—war or no war—to resign his commission. There was no financial need to keep it, for his father gave him an allowance. He was drawn to literature; he dreamed (for he was just nineteen) of becoming a great poet. He sketched out plans for tragedies and an epic poem. He prepared himself, with his usual diligence, for his future.

> If you mean to do something you must work, and work with a purpose. The morning seems to me suitable for that. I think I could go to bed at ten when I come out of the theatre. In that case, I could get up at six; and, from six to ten, I should have four hours of good work. . . . I could take a room near the Tuileries and go for half an hour's walk every morning to wake myself up. . . . When I don't want to go to the theatre. I shall also be free from five to six for a walk, and from six to ten for work. . . .[3]

The journey to Paris may have been intellectually fruitful, but it had not brought him closer to Victorine. On May 15 she left, with her family, for Rennes. Her father had just been appointed prefect of Ille-et-Vilaine.

"So much for the promises of friends!" Henri wrote to her brother, on June 6. "When you said good-bye, you swore you would write the day after you got to Rennes, and the days go by, and nearly a month has passed. . . . I see inconstancy every day, but I do not yet understand it, in friendship or in love; when you have once seen one another, when souls have grown aware of one another, is it possible to change?"[4]

It was indeed possible. Or perhaps one should say that in Henri's imagination passions could easily coexist. He did not cease to remember Victorine, even to dream of her. Within two months of her leaving for Rennes, he had once again fallen in love. In July he noted: "I am in love with Adèle. She gives me a thousand marks of preference. She gives me a lock of her hair."[5] Once again he had become enamoured of the impossible. Adèle Rebuffel, it will be recalled, was a distant cousin of Henri Beyle's. She lived with her mother, a tenant of Noël Daru's, in the rue de Lille. She was fourteen.

Henri now found himself in a situation more fraught with possibilities than any drama which he might have planned. On August 24 Adèle confessed that she had long been in love with someone else. The next day he spent the evening with mother and daughter and struck a Byronic pose. "I looked extremely sad. I developed my violent character. During the last hour I had a conversation *à double entente* with Adèle and Mme. Rebuffel. The latter arranged a meeting for next day at half past one."[6] The next day, on leaving, he kissed Adèle. On the evening of August 27 he arrived to be greeted warmly by M. Rebuffel. "Then he went," recorded Henri, "and I had Mme. Rebuffel."[7]

Madeleine was old enough to have been his mother; she had probably made the advances to him. No doubt she was glad to take revenge for her husband's constant infidelity. Henri's account of the episode was hardly impassioned, but the following day, presumably to make himself appear more romantic, he arrived in his subaltern's uniform. The gesture was ironical, since he had now resigned his commission. However, that evening he escorted mother and daughter in the Bois de Boulogne. The dual romance continued for months. Sometimes he feigned coldness, sometimes indifference. He noted Adèle's behaviour as though she alone existed for him. On November 11 he recorded, clinically: "I have had Mme. R. since the beginning of Fructidor"—since the end of August. He had become more worldly since the day he had first arrived at the rue de Lille.[8]

He also remained strangely romantic. Throughout the summer, in his letters to Edouard Mounier, he had tried, obliquely, to express his love for Victorine. No doubt Edouard was intended to show the letters to his sister.

"What is the use of knowing that the sun goes round the earth, or the earth goes round the sun, if, by learning these things, I lose the days I was given to enjoy them?"9 So Henri asked Pauline, on the first day of 1803. He himself was determined to enjoy his existence. He was twenty and unattached, and a little of the gold dust of the Bonaparte epic had rubbed off on him. He was plain, but intelligence shone in his eyes, his talk was animated; he was eager to learn and he was, above all, eager to please—and that was the surest path to social acceptance. As an unembittered young man he must have been engaging.

He had a room, now, at the hôtel de Rouen, in the rue d'Angivilliers. It was on the sixth floor, looking over the Louvre. "Every evening," he told Pauline, "I see the sun, the moon and all the stars go to rest behind those colonnades which witnessed the great century. I imagine that I can see the ghosts of the great Condé, Louis XIV, Corneille, Pascal, hidden behind those massive pillars, and watching mankind, their descendants, as they pass."10

He wrote repeatedly to his sister. "I am constantly afraid of dying before I have given you my experience."11 He did not tell her of his love affairs, but otherwise he confided his most intimate feelings to her. Pauline's answers filled him with pleasure. "I see that we are made for one another," he replied. "We have the same spirit."12

His relationship with Pauline was eminently happy; for Caroline he continued to show complete indifference. With his father, his relationship was as strained as ever. Their scale of values kept them apart. Chérubin gave him an allowance. He was naturally worried that Henri had resigned his commission; he was even more concerned that he made no attempt to earn his living. Henri felt it prudent to reassure him.

> I was very sorry indeed, dear Papa, that I could have given you some cause for dissatisfaction [March 3]. I beg you to believe that it is absolutely unintentional and I assure you that I haven't a feeling or a thought which might offend you in the very least. . . .
>
> I don't know how I could have made a mistake in my accounts for Fructidor so as to forget a sum of 100 francs in the expenses. But, except for some books, I have certainly bought nothing since I've been in Paris. After my two masters who cost me 40 sous each a lesson, I have no pleasure but the theatre. I only go to the pit which costs 44 sous. . . .13

A fortnight later, to Mounier, he wrote in different terms:

I have énjoyed myself here like a god. If you were here I should procure you the prettiest acquaintances in the world. Every Tuesday I go to a house where Mme. Récamier comes. They play music; the mothers play *bouillotte*, the daughters play forfeits, and we nearly always end with dancing. On Fridays I go to the Marais, to a society of the *ancien régime*, where they call me M. de Beyle; they talk a good deal about the religion of our fathers, and the delightful Abbé Delille recites his poems to us when we have drunk. On Saturdays, the most delightful of my evenings, we go to M. Dupuy's, where there are scholars of every colour, every tongue and every land. Mlle. Duchesnois [the actress] often comes there with her master Legouvé! They talk Greek there, *Greek;* do you feel the power of that word? If you were here, you would shine. Really I don't know how you can live in Rennes.[14]

By May 1 he was again in financial difficulties, and again he was obliged to write to his father. He owed money to his landlord and to his restaurateur. He thought it would be advisable to go and economise for five months at Claix; this would enable him to enjoy Parisian society next winter.[15]

On June 24 he arrived in Grenoble, where he was in fact to stay for nine months. "Come to Grenoble," he exhorted Mounier. "We should rove about the mountains, we should shoot. . . . This countryside delights me, and it is in harmony with what romanticism still remains in my soul."[16]

He remained romantic. On the last day of July, writing, yet again, to Mounier, he made an illuminating confession. He had hoped to find a woman who understood love as he himself understood it. He had come to regret that he had created a dream figure which he had been seeking for five years.

I want to use all my reason and dispel it [he explained], and it always returns. I have given this dream a name, and eyes, and a face. I see her constantly, I sometimes speak to her, but she never answers, and, like a child, when I have kissed my doll, I weep because she has not returned my kisses. I see now that only great things can distract me from this terrible state of perpetual longing for something which one knows doesn't exist, or which, if it does exist, by some unhappy

chance, does not respond to my passion. Since Love, as I have conceived it, cannot make me happy, I began some time ago to love
glory.[17]

Such emotions would have inspired many pages of Proust.

He did not regret his return to Claix, for he had chosen provincial
isolation as a means of fostering his future. It would enable him to
save money for his Parisian future and to work for literary fame.
Now, on his father's estate, he turned again to literature: read
Rousseau's *Du Contrat social* and Montesquieu's *De l'Esprit des lois.*
His isolation was conducive to reading, but he made no progress in
writing *Les Deux Hommes,* the play which he intended to bring him
glory.

Four

As the new year opened, his prolonged visit to Grenoble began, predictably, to weigh upon him. In February, writing to his usual correspondent, he complained of the "pleasures" of the local carnival. "For the past month, I have abandoned myself to every possible dissipation. I wanted to forget to feel. I have found here, as elsewhere, many vanities and no souls."[1]

He was just twenty-one, but already he wrote like a disillusioned elderly man. Perhaps he was recalling some experience in Paris; perhaps he was simply striking a pose. He had, he said, little esteem for men because he found very few who deserved esteem. He had even less respect for women because he had seen most of them behave badly, but he still believed that virtue existed. Mounier thought him a ladies' man, but Henri was too well aware of the ridicule he might incur ever to be a real womaniser. And Mounier would cease to think him frivolous when he learned that while Henri had had occasion to see the woman whom he loved, he had never told her that he loved her. It was another oblique reference to Victorine.

I have every reason to believe that she has never noticed me [wrote Henri], or that, if she has done so, she has forgotten me completely.

I've sometimes thought of going in search of her and saying: "Do you want me as your husband?" But apart from the fact that the proposal would have been ridiculous and, as you say, I should have been refused, I don't think I am worthy to make her happy. I am still too fiery to be a good husband, and I should blow my brains out if I believed that she could ever think: "I should have been happier with another man."

My father made me promise, when I left him for the first time, six years ago, that I shouldn't marry till I was thirty.

Actually I had no ambition except for her; what reason should I have, then, to get a position? I am completely disgusted with women, none of them will ever be my mistress again. . . .

I feel that I should have an ardent love of glory, if I managed to cure myself of another love. There are military glory, literary glory, the glory of the orators in the republics. I have renounced the first because one has to stoop too far to reach the top, and it is only there that people see your achievement. I am not a scholar, so we must forget the second. There remains the third career, where character can partly make up for talents. . . .[2]

It became increasingly clear that he would not further any career by staying in Grenoble. He left on March 20 and travelled, by way of Geneva, to Paris, where he arrived on April 8.

His trunk had been delayed on the way; he found it impossible to work. Four days later he wrote, in frustration, to Pauline:

I haven't settled down at all yet, I'm wasting my time, because the plans for study are in my trunk. . . . I want at least to benefit from the last moments that remain to me; I must get an occupation, and I can see nothing but the army. It is sad to sacrifice the whole of ones life to a prejudice. I shall come back a soldier; of all occupations, it is still the one that bores me least. I could make myself independent in one way, but by putting myself in harness in another. This morning I gave *déjeuner* to a man who returned my visit and let me understand that, if I wanted, I should be given a certain young lady. . . . The young lady is eighteen; she is pretty, tall, well made, she has three hundred thousand francs today, and she will have five hundred thousand in ten years. I am loved by the family, they have an excessively good opinion of me. There is the trap, but I shan't be caught in it. I should be rich, but the slave of every custom; I should have a fine *hôtel,* but not perhaps a dovecot where I could read Corneille and Alfieri in peace.[3]

He was still determined to write for the stage. He still went assiduously to the theatre. He waited for his luggage with increasing impatience. "I am longing for my trunk to arrive [April 17]. Then I shall be able to work. I am tired of my obscurity."[4] His trunk was not to reach him for another week. As soon as it arrived, he continued to work on his play.

He fed his mind on the theatre; he had now been presented to Mlle. Duchesnois, and she looked upon him with favour. He saw her, with Talma, in *Andromaque*. "She was vexed with the public, who did not recall her; she also felt that Talma had eclipsed her."[5] A few days later he saw Mlle. Mars "perform like an angel" in comedy. "I am as happy as a god," he told his schoolfriend Louis Crozet on June 7. "I've found an excellent subject for a comedy."[6] He broke off *Les Deux Hommes* to think about his latest idea.

Beyle was driven by love of glory, but he did not spend all his time in the Bibliothèque nationale or in his new room at 500, rue de Lille. On June 26 he urged Mounier to come to Paris. "Come soon, we shall be very gay. At the moment, everyone goes to Ranelagh on Thursdays; you waltz a little, and go on to Frascati . . . I've got an idea: couldn't you come for his Majesty's coronation?"[7]

The First Consul was soon to be crowned Emperor. As Beyle had recognised, the time for being republican had passed. On July 14, the fifteenth anniversary of the fall of the Bastille, he and some friends found themselves outside the Tuileries. "We saw Bonaparte perfectly, he passed fifteen yards away, on horseback; he was on a fine white horse, in a fine new uniform, a plain hat, the uniform of colonel of his guards, shoulder knots. He saluted a good deal and smiled. The theatrical smile, where you show your teeth, but your eyes do not smile."[8]

In these summer months of 1804, Beyle's journal reflects his intensive interest in the theatre, in particular, his devotion to Shakespeare. On August 21 he went to the tragedian La Rive to begin a course in acting. For he was not only intent on writing for the theatre, on learning the craft of drama, but he wanted to gain more poise and more assurance. He still felt like a timid provincial; he wanted to gain Parisian airs. His self-consciousness was itself enough to make him awkward and artificial. As Jules Lemaître was to observe, the journal shows us a man of action gradually paralysed by a matchless analyst.[9]

Beyle was not only awkward, he was also aware of his plainness.

He was short, and possibly, even now, he was overweight. His face was distinctly plebeian: his jaw protruded; his nose (to judge from the portrait by Boilly) was too thick; his cheeks were too fat. Only his eyes were remarkable; they were small, but they had an intense expression, an irresistible penetration. He was glad when La Rive assured him of his powers of attraction. "La Rive told me (and he says what he thinks) that I have something which naturally draws people to me."[10] Beyle had the assertiveness of the insecure.

He remained uncertain of himself, uncertain of his prospects, plunged into self-indulgent Romantic gloom. "The doctors have advised me to seek distraction," he explained to Pauline. "They have told me that otherwise I should die of melancholy."[11] He wanted to work, but he felt no interest in anything. He needed to be among people he loved.

> All that I love is in Grenoble, or eighty leagues from here [he told his sister]. I can write only to you, the other may have forgotten me: that is what makes me melancholy. . . . A mad idea is going through my head: before I go back to Grenoble, I should like to go incognito to the town where she is, and fill myself, there, with the pleasure of seeing her. It is a romantic way of behaving, but it will give me much pleasure.[12]

The girl of whom he was dreaming now was Victorine, in Rennes. He desperately needed a figure on whom to focus his dreams. In his next letter to Pauline he was already reflecting, nostalgically, about another figure in his past: "I knew in Italy a woman called Angelina whom I loved beyond all expression."[13] On December 31, after a visit to the theatre, he added: "This isn't the happiest day I could imagine, I should have seen the play with Victorine beside me, loving me as I love her, and with my fortune assured, for example, an income of 6,000 francs."[14]

In fact, the last day of 1804 was significant for Beyle. It began to distract him from his barren nostalgia, from his useless and persistent dreams. It brought a real woman into his life: the actress Mélanie Guilbert, known in the theatre as Louason or Mélanie Sainte-Albe. Born in Caen in 1780, she was now nearly twenty-five. She had Greek features and fine blue eyes; she was graceful and rather thin. He had met her at the actor Dugazon's, where—dissatisfied with La Rive—he was now learning acting and declamation. His thoughts soon turned towards her. "I took Louason home [February 3, 1805]. I almost want to attach myself to her, it would cure me of my love for Victorine."[15] The next day, in his journal, he made the characteristic reflection: "I think of Mélanie, and this memory charmed me like the pleasure itself."[16]

Mistresses arose in his mind, hovered in his imagination; sometimes they came and went in reality. One woman remained a perpetual object of love and concern: his sister Pauline. Henri respected her honesty, her persistent innocence, her energy of spirit—they were the qualities which he sought in a mistress, in a potential wife. "My divine Pauline," he wrote, and, again: "I love you with all my soul, I shall never love a mistress as much as you." And yet, as Del Litto says, in his preface to the correspondence, Beyle was not revealing a neurosis. If he wrote to Pauline like this, it was because she had no real consistency. She was a creature forged by his imagination.[17]

The comment is true. There is a world of difference, for example, between these letters and those that Keats was to write to Fanny Keats, only a few years later. Keats was talking to his sister, taking part in her life, marvellously adapting himself to her way of thought; Keats was entertaining, teaching, consoling and looking after a lonely girl in the care of a strict guardian. He was talking to her alone and—as he always did—without the least shadow of public thought. Henri Beyle is not simply thinking of his correspondent, he is using his letters as a *déversoir,* writing with an eye on posterity. "Don't lose my letters, they will be useful to both of us: to you, because you will later be able to understand what you did not at first comprehend; and to me, because they will give me the history of my mind."[18] Rarely, one feels, has a correspondent been so coolly introspective. In July, 1804, he suggests: "Perhaps you would do well to make a notebook and copy my letters into it, leaving room for comments."[19]

Yet while he wrote for posterity, he wrote, in the present, for Pauline alone. "Does anyone see the letters I write you [February 14, 1805]? Give me an answer, and do not trust appearances. If you have suspicions, put these Italian words in your letter: *Il grande Alfieri;* if not, don't."[20] In the same letter he told her, eagerly, of his pleasure in gaining knowledge of the world. Their correspondence was, to him, a delectable conversation; to her he confessed his social triumphs with disarming honesty. "Yesterday I had a delightful day [February 26]; all things considered, it was the finest day of my life. Of course you know how ugly I am; women whom I had offended paid me compliments on my appearance; I wore knee breeches and stockings, a bronze coat, with superb cravat and frill! Huh! I'm a coxcomb to tell you that, but I think aloud with you."[21] The most enduring pleasure, as he once observed, was to be satisfied with oneself.

Until now, he assured Pauline, society had been a distraction from his studies; it had now become his object, since Chérubin kept him in financial straits. Questions of finance and commerce were often in his mind, but he needed money from his father if he was to establish himself in business. His aversion to his father remained implacable. He would often refer to him as "the Bastard," he would calculate how much longer his father would persist in living and depriving him of his inheritance. If he had to approach him, he preferred to do so through another member of the family, even through a friend, and now, in April, 1805, his former schoolfriend Fortuné Mante visited Dr. Gagnon and Chérubin in Grenoble. On April 11 he reported that Dr. Gagnon was gravely concerned about Henri's attitude to his father, his transparent lack of trust. He had assured Mante that it was quite unjustified. Henri and his father, he said, were both independent, and this prevented any lasting relationship between them. A recent letter from Henri had moved Chérubin to tears. Dr. Gagnon and Chérubin were both concerned about the young man's contempt for religion. Dr. Gagnon had then talked about Henri's sisters, "especially about Pauline. . . . *Pauline believes in her brother as she does in God the Father;* and when someone contradicts her with a certain authority, her great argument is: *That is Henri's opinion.*" Dr. Gagnon, reported Mante, "would like you to cultivate these happy dispositions and that is one of the reasons why he wants you to come back. He reproaches you for liking only your elder sister, for he believes the younger one loves you quite as much."[22]

Dr. Gagnon had assured Mante that Chérubin was devoted to Henri, but he was afraid to show his feelings because he wanted to keep his authority over him. It would, so Mante discovered, be impossible for Chérubin to give Henri the 30,000 francs he wanted to establish himself in commerce. He had too little credit to borrow the money, even if he wished. Dr. Gagnon considered that Henri had no need to try to earn money. Chérubin apparently meant to leave him Claix and the house; this would easily bring him in an income of 15,000 livres which he could spend as he chose.

A few days later Henri suggested to Pauline that she might learn banking with him in Marseilles. In Paris there were a score of women who ran banks with much profit. "You can do the same, and also enjoy the freedom you want so much, and the charms of the most agreeable society."[23] Henri was always conscious of Pauline's loneliness in a family where no one appreciated her intelligence or her capacity for affection. His advice was well meant; but she remained sad, and her unhappiness disturbed him.

> I am very worried, my Pauline, by the tone of sadness and brevity in the letter which brought me the hundred ecus. You want a kind of life which is not without its troubles. Happiness comes from ourselves, position has little to do with it. . . . We shall seek together for means of happiness. I think that if we correct certain faults in ourselves, and acquire an independent fortune, we shall find it. I may soon be at your feet, perhaps in a month and a half. Love keeps me here, but I must tear myself away, and the longer I stay, the weaker I become. I see so well how little intellectual knowledge affects the decisions of the heart! I have sought to understand the passions all my life; perhaps I see them quite well in people who are absolutely indifferent to me, all the same they carry me away like a child.[24]

He had never ventured to declare himself to Victorine Mounier, and she had shown no interest in him. Faced with this barren dream, Henri had now fallen in love with Mélanie Guilbert—or Louason. He was paying constant court to her, and as she had just obtained an engagement at the theatre in Marseilles, he decided to go there with her. He would learn the import and export trade with Charles Meunier, the firm where Mante was already employed. "He would not be Henri Beyle," wrote Arbelet, in *Stendhal épicier*, "if he did not interrupt the wise pursuit of his destiny by some wild escapade."[25] He thought of commerce as an adventure story, just as he dreamed of seeking his fortune in America or of setting sail for Pondicherry. His fantasy invested his plans with the glamour of a dream. On April 30 he told Pauline that he would soon visit Grenoble on his way to Marseilles, "where I hope to find what does not create happiness, but helps it."[26]

On May 4 Mante reported from Marseilles that he had seen "Loyson, pupil of Mlle. Clairon," billed as a coming attraction at the theatre. He added a warning (not unexpected during the Napoleonic Wars): "It is very difficult to find a place in commerce. Really, *nothing is happening.*"27

Four days later, undeterred, Henri left Paris with Mélanie. They parted company at Lyons. Mélanie continued her way to Marseilles where her friend Joseph Blanc de Volx, an author and would-be dramatist, had given her an introduction to the general secretary of the department of Bouches-du-Rhône. Henri went to Grenoble, to try to persuade his father to give him some capital.

In Paris, he had felt assured of her. In Grenoble, he soon became a prey to his imagination and his fears.

> You must have a very bad opinion of yourself, or of me [she answered on May 23], to regret and even blush at what you wrote. Is it a crime, then, to say what you think? Or don't you believe what you told me? . . .
>
> To judge from your letter, I can't hope any more than you will be here for my first night. It will take place towards the end of next week. I must confess that the moment alarms me, and I'm growing more nervous about it every day. I should like to be surrounded by the people I love. I need to be reassured, because I am nothing by myself, if people don't keep up my courage a little.28

Mélanie's letter gave a clear promise of love, a clear statement of need, but Henri found in it only reasons for desolation. Psychologists often fail to understand reality. He was always carried away by his imagination, especially when his thoughts were melancholy. On June 18 he began a long letter to her.29 The letter which began as a gentle reprimand for Mélanie's silence became a cry of desperation. As Henri wrote, as he recalled the letters which she had sent him, he contrived to persuade himself that she did not feel even friendship for him. On June 20 he pleaded:

> Help me, I beg you, to cure myself of a love which no doubt you find importunate—a love which can therefore only bring me misfortune; deign to tell me once, openly, what you say implicitly in all your letters. Now that I read them soberly and in succession, I think that

you must have been astonished that I have taken so long to understand a language that was so clear.[30]

Mélanie's answer was perhaps a passage which he copied out:
"How could my letter have made you sad? I don't think I've said
anything to upset you. . . . Why don't you tell me if you are coming
to Marseilles soon?"[31] This fragment has been provisionally dated
June, 1805; on June 22 she wrote again, with brisk conviction: "What
with one final letter and another, I think I shall write you enough to
make a substantial book. . . . That shows a very poor understanding
of my interests, especially if my letters are to delay your journey. But I
am not urging you to make this unless your family think it a good
idea. I believe they do, according to what I hear from M. Mante. He
comes to see me sometimes to talk about you."[32]

Mante was diligently playing the part of the go-between: judging
Mélanie's feelings and reassuring Henri, who remained in a turmoil
of doubt and despair. "Don't worry, you happy idiot," Mante admonished him on June 27. "Mélanie loves you, loves you very
much. . . . The first thing she asks me when I go to see her is: 'Have you
any news of Beyle?' . . . Good-bye. I promise that Mélanie loves
you."[33]

On July 22, having reached an agreement with his father, Henri
left Grenoble. On July 25 he arrived in Marseilles. He lodged in the
same hotel as Mélanie. The next day he assured Pauline: "I feel the
most intense happiness that I have ever felt in my life."[34]

Five

For the rest of 1805, while he continued his honeymoon with Mélanie, Beyle worked diligently for Charles Meunier. During the Napoleonic Wars, on the eve of the Battle of Trafalgar, import and export were a hazardous business, but he copied letters, visited the Customs, the Office of Weights and Measures and the Exchange. "If you don't send me money every month, and linen," he told Pauline, on August 8, "I shall be obliged to borrow at any price. For I have only commerce as a means of earning my daily bread, . . . and in the meanwhile I need to be clothed and fed." And in a second letter that day, he added: "I'm asking you again for shirts. . . . I'd rather have two a fortnight hence than six in two months' time. . . . Write me a four-page letter."[1] "I shall write to you freely," Pauline told him. "Write to me often, my only friend."[2]

Henri wrote to her often; he urged her to study the depths of her heart and mind and to tell him exactly what she felt. He had, he said, been reading a book by Mme. de Staël: *De l'Influence des passions sur le bonheur.* Mme. de Staël had thought herself a person of remarkable sensibility when in fact she was not. She had abandoned herself to passions, and she had been surprised not to find in them the happiness that they gave to passionate souls. "Once or twice a year," he wrote, "one has these moments of ecstasy when the whole soul is happiness. She had imagined that that was happiness and she had been sad not to find it so. A little study of human emotion teaches one the rarity of this delightful state." Ecstasy could not endure without producing pain. Unlike Mme. de Staël, he had cured himself of the wish to be more passionate than nature allowed. He added a significant comment: "Mme. de Staël does not feel the happiness of loving. She always wants to be loved in return. She does not feel that one can have pleasure in loving as a person of feeling loves the sight of the Apollo Belvedere."[3]

He himself was profoundly happy. Mélanie did not only love him, she had—so he believed—the nobility which he needed in a mistress.

> I did not think [he told Pauline] there could be so fine a nature. You have no idea of Mélanie. She is Mme. Roland with more graces. . . . My happiness would be assured if I had an income of 15,000 francs. . . . I hope to have them one day and then nothing will be able to compare with my happiness.
>
> Since I have been so happy, I have had only one anxiety, and that is not seeing you as happy as you deserve. . . .
>
> Good-bye. When shall we be able to live together in Paris, you and Mélanie, my daughter, Mante and I? Oh, how happy we should be, my good Pauline! I should so like you to get married—to Mante, for example. What would you say to that, if we could arrange it?[4]

The letter was wise, but it was strangely innocent. Beyle's appreciation of books, his theoretical understanding of people, remained more mature than his everyday understanding of humankind. The idea of a possible marriage for Pauline came from Mélanie; the idea of a *ménage à cinq* suggests his own impulsive enthusiasm. He had already told his sister about Mélanie's illegitimate daughter, the child whom he now considered his own. An eager idealist, he praised his mistress' noble nature; he chose to forget that she had had a past.[5]

He remained an idealist, warm, honest and spontaneous to those whom he loved, but even now, at the age of twenty-two, he planned his social behaviour with cynical calculation. "Until now," he told Pauline, "there has not been an action in my life in which I have pretended, except for certain deceits with women, and certain mysteries to amuse the foolish. At present, I do not want to be spontaneous and honest except with Mélanie, you, Bigillion, Mante and Crozet. With everyone else I don't want to lie, I want to say only what is suitable." Pauline must learn, as he did, to tolerate the foolish, but, more important, to cultivate and exploit their goodwill. She must learn to assess mankind at their true worth. She could not be happy, now, in Grenoble, but she must benefit from her time of slavery. One day Henri and Mélanie, Pauline and Mante might live together in Paris, moving in a society which included Talma and Destutt de Tracy. Such people could be themselves only when they were among their equals.

> So let us try to make ourselves their equals [Henri instructed his sister], and then, with an income of 15,000 francs, I promise you that we shall be the happiest family in France. . . .
> Mélanie is burning to know you. Your souls are so alike that you will love each other. . . . She used to be unhappy for a fortnight every month, she thought that she would always be unhappy. Young, and full of trust, she had been exposed to all the baseness of the world. She had been betrayed by a friend whom she adored, and by everyone. She thought that all souls were as base, and she felt that she could not be happy unless she were passionately loved by a soul like her own. She was in complete despair. . . . She thinks now that she has found [happiness] and she is losing the habit of misery. She is still in poor physical health, and this takes a little longer to cure than the ill health of the soul. But I hope that both will be all right in the end.[6]

Henri's idyll with Mélanie continued throughout the summer. One August day they set out with a picnic: two partridges and a pâté, peaches, grapes and a bottle of Bordeaux. A league away, across the arid country round Marseilles, past the dusty olive trees, they found a little valley; a river ran past a small estate, where the trees and grass seemed magically green.

> There is a château with high towers [Henri told Pauline], but it is so surrounded by a mass of chestnut trees that one can only see the towers above the treetops. The château really seems like a castle in a fairy tale. . . . It does not inspire sombre thoughts: the towers are not heavy or black enough; it does inspire melancholy. And here they have planted a pretty little avenue of plane trees which are perhaps five or six years old. . . . I seemed to hear a work by Cimarosa, where,

among great, terrible and sombre themes, the grand master of the heart's emotions had set a pretty, gay little tune.[7]

In this sudden, lyrical passage, Beyle did not merely recall an August day in the country with his mistress; he did not only record his abiding love of Cimarosa. His awareness heightened by love, he found the deep relationship between the senses: the moment when sight came near to sound, when sensations appeared to converge and to be identified with one another. He was later to equate the emotions caused by love with the emotions roused by music; more than once, in his letters, his journal and his novels, he was to associate music with passion. But here he is also on the verge of the theory of *correspondances:* the theory to be explored by Gautier, Baudelaire, Rimbaud and Verlaine. As early as 1805, he is approaching a theme which will be familiar to French writers in the mid-nineteenth century and become a cardinal theory of Symbolism.

When Beyle wrote to his sister, he was often ponderous. Yet no doubt she was heartened and enlightened by his letters. She showed her love for him by ensuring that he received his linen and letters of credit (he still chose to write to her, rather than approach his father, *le Bâtard);* she showed her romantic nature, her concern for self-improvement, by reading Shakespeare and Ossian. "If you knew how I want to know Mme. Louason," she told Henri on September 4, "how happy I should be if I could live with her all my life! The people around me make me understand how I should appreciate this happiness."[8] "The tone of your letters is perfect," Henri answered, "because it is extremely natural. They give great pleasure to someone who loves you very much and to whom I read certain passages."[9]

Beyle remained intensely concerned about his sister's welfare. No one could doubt his devotion to her. And yet, for all this, he showed a masculine lack of perception, a masculine want of tact. He assured her, repeatedly, of his own overflowing happiness; he reminded the lonely, frustrated girl of his own continual satisfaction. "I am happy here, my dear. I am tenderly loved by a woman whom I adore with passion."[10] Pauline was trying, in solitude, to improve herself, to please the brother whom she admired. But Mélanie was to him an object of constant admiration: "She has a fine soul. Fine is not the word, it is sublime. At times I have the misfortune to be jealous of it."[11] A woman with so noble a soul deserved Pauline's devotion; and

Henri made extraordinary demands of his sister for this woman she had never seen and even for this woman's natural daughter.

> As she is less rich than you, I am going to buy a sheet of stamped paper to make my will and give everything to her and after her to my daughter. I am quite sure that I haven't much; but I shall then have done all that I can. If all this produced nothing, if I came to die and if one day you were rich, I commend this tender soul to you. . . . Even if you are not rich, let your tears upon my ashes be a tender friendship for Mélanie Guilbert and for my daughter.[12]

Pauline responded, as he knew she would.

> My Henri, don't be afraid that I shall forget my promise. My will is made. I am nineteen and six months; I don't know if I'm old enough for it to be valid. . . . My plan is to copy it out again every six months. I say this to give you peace of mind and because I don't want you to be at all worried, and I want you to be happy. If I survived you, I should divide all that I possessed into three equal parts; I shall do all I can to make two-thirds independent, and these will belong to your friend and your daughter.

She added, with astonishing delicacy: "Good-bye, don't be sad anymore. As long as I have something or I can work, your friend, whom I am burning to know, and your daughter, will not lack anything. It seems to me that I shouldn't tell you this; don't talk about it to Mme. Mélanie, she doesn't know me, and it might worry her. All the same, I love her."[13] Henri answered brusquely: "I was talking about your friendship for our daughter, not about your will at all. It is your care I want for her, if we should die before her. She is called Mélanie, too; at the moment she is *en pension* at Neuilly, near Paris."[14]

The letters continued to make their way from Marseilles to Grenoble. Often a letter from Grenoble arrived in Marseilles. Dr. Gagnon admonished his grandson for his unjust complaints about Chérubin Beyle. Chérubin, wrote the doctor, must never know about Henri's liaison. "It is absolutely essential that your father should not know of this event; it would legitimise his complaints all too well, and you would lose his trust."[15] Early in October the unhappy Chérubin urged Henri to go into partnership with Mante. "I care about nothing, nothing on earth," Chérubin insisted, "except my children and my extreme desire to make them happy."[16]

On November 15 Henri gave Pauline some significant news. Ten days earlier he had begun to read the *Logique* of Destutt de Tracy. He had so far read only half, but he felt "an astonishing revolution" in all his ideas. He had once been hampered by his vague memory of facts; now he was learning how to verify recollections and make judgments. He was making "sublime discoveries." He was schooling himself as a student of humankind. The *Idéologie* was to be a cardinal book in his intellectual development, and seeing a blank space at the end of his letter, he added: "I cannot leave a blank without talking about the *Idéologie*. It teaches you *not to make any contradictory wishes,* and therefore sets you on the road to happiness."[17]

Projet d'éléments d'idéologie, by Antoine-Louis-Claude, Comte Destutt de Tracy, had been written for the Ecoles centrales of France. It is curious that a work which was designed for classroom use should have had so deep an effect on a man who was nearing his twenty-third birthday, but Henri discovered it at a time when he needed to clarify his ideas and to plan his future. Destutt de Tracy appeared at the psychological moment and organized the mind of Henri Beyle. "Locke is, I think, the first man who tried to observe and describe human intelligence as one observes and describes the properties of a vegetable or mineral." So Destutt de Tracy wrote in his preface. Henri Beyle was to observe and describe the intelligence and the heart in the same manner. "The only useful thing is to study the facts; that leads us to understand them and to gain the greatest possible advantage from them." This was to be Henri Beyle's incessant preoccupation. Destutt de Tracy discussed the art of using all ones faculties in the way most conducive to happiness; and here, in words that Beyle himself might have written, he laid down Beyle's philosophy.

> The art [of seeking happiness] consists [he wrote] entirely in avoiding the formation of contradictory ideas, for these are sure to bring us unhappiness; in preserving ourselves from physical ills, for these bring real pain; and finally in ensuring ourselves the

benevolence of those who are like us, and making ourselves satisfied with ourselves, for these are real advantages.

For the moment, simply remember that just as we should know nothing unless we had the faculty of judgement, so we should do nothing unless we had the faculty of determination.[18]

Henri Beyle—at this moment in his career—did not lack determination. Destutt de Tracy seemed to direct him in his search for happiness, to guide him in *la chasse au bonheur*.

Henri wanted infinite happiness for himself and Mélanie and for Pauline. Pauline depended on the love of her absent brother. At one o'clock on the morning of December 5, while the snow fell heavily on Grenoble, she settled down to write to him.

> My soul is peaceful like everything around me. Oh, my dear, how long I have suffered! Don't let's talk about that anymore. My dear Henri, you believed that I did not love you any more and I had not the strength to undeceive you. I love you as much as ever, and if I did not have at least you to love, what should I do in this world? . . .
>
> And yet I should like to give you a reason for my silence. My dear, I have none at all. I feel such horrible spleen that I am doing hardly anything. For four days, I have sworn to myself that I would get out of this lethargy one way or another. I have the choice between a pistol or reading; my dear, how I feel the lines of André Chénier! Twenty times as I handled pistols I felt a violent urge to empty them into my heart. I should free myself of the burden which oppresses me. I am surrounded by empty souls which are killing me.[19]

"Spleen takes the energy from the soul, . . . and so one must control it by firm resolutions," Henri answered. "That is the infallible remedy. . . . Promise yourself that you will never go to bed without writing half a page to me. I will indicate the subject for your work. . . . Follow my example, master yourself."[20]

Henri himself had much to learn about humankind, and Destutt de Tracy was not his only source of wisdom. On December 28 Dr. Gagnon sent a letter of advice. Henri might well have profited from his counsel and his affectionate criticism.

> As a rule [wrote Dr. Gagnon], you should mistrust your own judg-

ment, because it is often premature. The relations you have with certain men have inspired you with too general a scorn and contempt. . . .

I now see your reasons for wanting to live in the capital, but I also see that you have taken the longest and most uncertain way to attain a fortune and all that you desire. It seems to me that you have a more certain means of going back to Paris, and of being in a good position there, and that is approaching Daru again: he is fond of you, and he might employ you in the administration.[21]

Dr. Gagnon's counsel was soon to have effect. Henri detested provincial life. He hated Grenoble, and after five months' stay, he was growing weary of Marseilles. On January 4 he wrote to Edouard Mounier: "Not the slightest amusement here, not even social pleasure. . . . What a place to be in, when you have lived in Paris!"[22] "I am growing at least as impatient as you, my dear fellow," Dr. Gagnon wrote on January 8. ". . . I want to do everything to force [Pierre Daru] to do what he has so many reasons for doing. . . ." And Dr. Gagnon added, with the authority born of affection:

> I always find two things in your letters which take away three-quarters of my pleasure in receiving them: these are your unjust prejudices against your father and your threat of Louisiana. I have told you what I think on these two heads a hundred times, and I am sorry that you show so little attention. My judgment is surer than yours, because it is cool and disinterested; and yours is just the contrary. As for your delirium about New Orleans, . . . I warn you that, as long as I live, I shall use all the influence I may have on your father's mind to prevent him from favouring this plan by giving you a single ecu.[23]

The letter was astringent and wise, and it was effective. On January 14 Henri wrote to Martial Daru. His letter was transparently diplomatic. "You abandon me in my exile, my dear cousin. . . . But however provincial one may be, one can love, and I feel this every day when I think of you."[24]

It was indeed necessary to plead to Pierre Daru in favour of Henri Beyle. Daru must have been offended and angered by Henri's casual resignation of his commission in 1802. However, Dr. Gagnon had written him a letter which seems to have been a model of tact. "What did I not say [this to Henri] in those three and a half close-written pages! I did not actually say what I wanted, . . . but I think I have clearly indicated a post as *auditeur* at the Conseil d'état."[25] It was an ambitious demand. The *auditeur* belonged to the administrative elite: he was a promising young functionary preparing for a position as counsellor.

Dr. Gagnon wrote to Pierre Daru; his son, Romain Gagnon, sent a letter to Martial.[26] The whole family for once united to speed Henri on his career, and Chérubin assured him: "If M. Daru would act, we are all persuaded that you would be going more in the direction of your destiny."[27]

"Mélanie rushes into unhappiness, and would even find the art of making herself unhappy with an income of 30,000 livres and a husband who was *conseiller d'état.*"[28] So Henri told Pauline on February 6.

He was not only weary of Marseilles, he was also weary of his mistress. She had failed in the theatre, he had failed in commerce, and their professional bitterness seeped into their private lives. They both chafed at provincial isolation. For Henri, the glamour of physical love had vanished long ago; he now felt oppressed by Mélanie's possessiveness, by the constant demands she made of him, by the "slavery" in which she kept him. Mélanie was still devoted to him, and she hoped that the relationship would be permanent. He himself wanted to end the affair, but he was too timid to do so. He asked Louis Crozet, in Paris, for advice.

> The affair you mention is very delicate [Crozet replied]. . . . If she loves you, the question is simply this: are you to bring despair to a woman whom you esteem, a woman who loves you, a woman with [so sublime] a nature? It seems to me that to leave her suddenly is to make her irrevocably unhappy. . . . In fact, it comes down to this: either you want to leave her or you don't; if you do, you must prepare it so that she can fill the void that you will leave in her life. Why shouldn't she come and make her debut at the [Théâtre-]Français?
>
> There, my dear fellow, is all I can say. . . . I've known for a long while that you were tired of her. I had seen it in your letters and I didn't dare to tell you.[29]

Perhaps this letter fired Henri with the courage which he needed; perhaps he gave Mélanie Crozet's comments on the state of the Théâtre-Français. Even the presence of Talma did not improve the performance of the lesser actors, and Mlle. Georges hardly made her appearance nowadays in the theatre, except as a spectator. "It therefore seems to me," Crozet added, "that the theatre must really need new actresses. So urge on Mlle. Louason. Such a character as hers can only love glory."[30] It was perhaps the dream of glory at the Théâtre-Français which led her to leave for Paris on March 1.

Six

Once Mélanie had left Marseilles, Henri felt predictably lonely. Next day he wrote to her. On March 4 he had a letter from her, dated from Aix; it gave him "the sweetest pleasure."[1] "Write to me," he told Pauline, "I need it most violently. . . . Mélanie's departure plunges me into the darkest misery."[2] Mélanie was scarcely happier, as she made her way across France; on March 6 she reported from Lyons: "Slush, icy cold, and unbearable travelling companions; that is all we have had on the way, except for much fatigue. . . . In six days we shall be in Paris. I shall leave for the country next day, and then I hope to write to you at some length."[3]

If she wrote, there is no copy of her letter among his papers. On March 11 he noted: "Solitude often saddens me, Mélanie's faults are beginning to fade."[4] She had planned to be away for a fortnight; but the fortnight passed, and she did not return. His feelings fluctuated. Now that she had gone, he became physically aware of other women. He recorded a visit to a Mme. Tivollier, and a crude advance he had made to her. He assessed her possibilities.[5]

His journal records the feelings which have escaped his published letters: the vicissitudes of his feelings for Mélanie. It was characteristic of Henri Beyle that his emotions should become intense now that she had gone. He was bored and lonely; as usual, he also suffered from his imagination. He had wanted to leave Mélanie; he was jealous, now, that she might have found some other lover.

Boredom begins to make me feel Mélanie's absence [March 25] On Sunday I was absolutely inaccessible to all pleasant feelings. . . .
  The slavery in which Mélanie kept me often weighed on me, the unconstraint in which her departure leaves me is tedious. . . .

26, Wednesday.
Mélanie doesn't write to me at all, I don't know what that means; but her last letter, which was the first of any length, was cold. Is she simply piqued, or has she ceased to love me? . . .

Thursday [March 27]
. . . I had a letter from Mélanie today, five pages but still cold. . . .

30 March 1806
. . . I passionately wanted to be loved by a woman who was melancholy, thin, and an actress. I have been, and I haven't found continual happiness.
  It is, I believe, because this continual happiness is a chimera, and I haven't got the sense to get all the happiness I can from my position. In general, I have an infinite lack of wisdom; in fact, I do not know what I want. On the whole: Paris, *auditeur,* eight thousand livres, received in the best society, and having women there.

That day he recorded advances to two women in Marseilles; a few paragraphs later he made a delicate and Stendhalian observation: "It seems that my memory is only the memory of my sensibility."[6] On April 23 he recorded a night with another woman. On May 3: "I should die if no one loved me. . . . Mélanie is angry, too."[7] He analysed his feelings; he also wrote to Mélanie, expressing his doubts and his suspicions. On May 21 she answered, fervently:

What, I don't love you, and I make a rival read your letters! Oh, my dear, you know all too well that my heart is too full of you ever to belong to another. But this heart of mine needs to be completely reassured about your own. . . .
  Let us see in a while which of us can take care of the other, and let us never part again. Let us at least have this sweet consolation in our misfortunes. . . . I propose to accept an engagement at Naples, in spite of my weak chest, and if you don't obtain anything from your family,

well, then you leave them and come with me and our dear child. . . .
   Good-bye, my dear and dearest friend. Believe that I love you and
that I shall love you until the last day of my life.[8]

On May 27 Henri replied. He was on his way to Grenoble. Pierre
Daru had been appointed councillor of state and quartermaster
general of the Grande Armée, Henri's ambition had been rekindled,
and he had now determined to reenter his cousin's good graces. On
June 1 he wrote with pleasant frankness to Martial: "My dear
cousin, . . . Do you think that M. Daru would take an interest in me?
Does he think I've matured a little since I gave in my resignation?"[9]

   Mélanie was still in Paris. She knew that Henri was in Grenoble.
She assumed that his future would soon be decided, and she grew
increasingly anxious about the part that she herself would play. "I
want to say how happy I am to see you nearer to me [June 2]. . . . I
expect you will spend a month at your father's and then come on to
Paris. Oh, my dear, how I need to see you! How I need you to love
me!"[10]
   If he answered her, his letter does not seem to have survived. On
June 10 she wrote again, with pardonable indignation. Her letters
have been described as the letters of a tragedy queen, but she could
not help being an actress and, perhaps unconsciously, playing a part.
Now she was really disturbed and hurt; she was genuinely concerned
about her professional future. She felt betrayed. And since she still
cared for Henri, she tried to rouse his jealousy.

   Although all my behaviour must have proved to you how dear you
   are to me, although I have repeated it to you time and time again, you
   have still thought that M. Blanc de Volx was drawing me to Naples,
   since he had become influential. These ideas don't surprise me, my dear,
   and I readily forgive you for them. I see that you cannot know my
   heart. About M. Blanc, I have always forgotten to answer the questions you put to me to find out his position.
   He is now director and inspector general of customs. They say it is
   a well-paid position. He wrote to me, three days ago, that he had
   engaged me at the theatre in Naples for 5,000 livres from now till
   Easter. He assures me that next year I shall have at least 8,000 livres

and he urges me to accept what he has done. . . . I am going to write a letter to M. Blanc in which I ask for a little time for reflection.[11]

It was a last attempt to mend the relationship; it showed a touch of the tyranny which Henri had resented. One day he would come to count Mélanie among his four great loves, but that time was not yet. Now, in 1806, he felt no passion for anyone or anything.

But if his emotions were dormant, his ambitions had been stirred. On July 10 he returned to Paris and again paid court to the Darus.

He plunged into society with the eagerness of a Parisian returning from exile. He rigorously schooled himself for his future.[12] He was so busy cultivating those who might serve his purpose that he hardly had time to keep a diary; he could only keep a list of the plays that he had seen.

One of them, the tragedy *Gaston et Bayard*, had, he noted, delighted Mélanie. They were now seeing each other again, though—for Henri, at least—their relationship seems to have been a matter of convenience rather than renewed devotion. On August 22 he noted: "From five to eight with Melanie in the Champs-Elysées; she is piqued, and hardly says a word."[13] She was piqued, no doubt, because she was no longer the centre of his existence. He led a pleasant life with more sophisticated friends; he was spirited because he found himself in Paris and because he had hopes for his future. He found occasional pleasure with Mélanie, but she must have recognised that she would henceforth be insignificant. Once, when he was vexed by the events of the day, he noted that he had found relief with her. "The relief would," he wrote, "have been complete if I had been in love with a woman who slept with her husband. This tragic character into which I have fallen pleases Mélanie more than my ordinary character. Once you have persuaded an affectionate woman that you have brilliance, you must try to have this tragic and loving nature."[14] No relationship could last that was so insincere.

Seven

On October 16 he left Paris. His immediate ambition had been fulfilled. He had as yet no title, but he was going to Prussia with Martial Daru, now *inspecteur aux revues de la Garde impériale.* Two days later, from Metz, he exhorted his sister: "Have a little patience. My destiny is about to change. That will enable me to support you."[1] On October 27, in the wake of Napoleon, he entered Berlin. Two days later the everobliging Pierre Daru appointed him provisional assistant to the Commissaries of Wars and ordered him to Brunswick. "We are leaving for Brunswick this evening, at last," he told Pauline on November 8. "We should be marching with His Majesty to Küstrin, Poznan and Warsaw."[2]

On November 13 he was in Brunswick; a few days later, conscious of censorship, he wrote a guarded letter to his sister, complaining of his boredom. He was spending a good deal, he had brought two coats and he was having one of them embroidered; in a month's time he would need money. He had hardly a moment to himself, he was doing the work of secretary to a prefecture six times the size of the Isère. On Christmas Day he set out for Paris. He was entrusted with a mission to the war administration.

He returned to Brunswick on February 5. Now that he had secured an administrative post, as he wanted, he was once again dissatisfied. He found the Brunswickers so dry (a favourite word), so unresponsive that he lost himself in his imagination. "My soul still has the bad habit of loving, and my reason tells me it's absurd. Except for you [this to Pauline], I see nothing worthy of love."[3]

The love to which he referred was his love for Wilhelmine, the youngest daughter of Major General Auguste von Griesheim. He had been paying court to her before he went to Paris, and on his return he continued to indulge in elegant flirtation. André François-Poncet, in his study of Henri Beyle in Brunswick, considers that the relationship was more than a flirtation. Lucien's confession to Mme. de Chasteller in Beyle's unfinished novel *Lucien Leuwen* is, he suggests, the account of a scene which had really occurred between Henri and Mina—or Minette.[4] But one suspects that—at least at first—Henri was indulging in an emotional exercise. On March 16 he explained to his sister: "There's a rather curious society here, I'll describe it to you when I'm stronger. I was doing all I could to feel some feelings for a young lady in this society; my illness interrupted this noble enterprise."[5]

He had been in bed for a week with rheumatic fever. His hands and feet were swollen, but the swelling was subsiding. Unable to sleep, he had, as usual, analysed his character. He had decided that he must eradicate his vanity. He must also create his own independent pleasures. He had resolved to take piano lessons, so that he could appreciate music better. "Every day I grow more aware of this noble art, and every day I feel more contempt for the generality of mankind."[6] Pauline, at least, must remain superior to most of humankind. She must acquire the habit of reasoning, so as not to be led astray by emotion.[7] Passion, he explained to her, was the persistence of desire, but how could marriage arouse or sustain a passion? She must look for happiness with a kind and docile husband, who would give her children she would adore. This would fill life "not with fictional emotions which are physically impossible, ... but with a reasonable contentment."[8]

On April 30 Henri wrote to her, freely, of his own continuing love for Minette. He could offer sound advice to others; he could "work on his feelings," for, as he told his sister, this was the only path to happiness. Yet when he found himself in love, he still behaved with romantic intensity, soaring from despair to exaltation, sinking from exaltation to despair. At one point he had thought of leaving Brunswick; and then Minette had grasped his hand, and they were reconciled. "I have no inclination, now, except for Minette, for this blonde and charming Minette, this soul of the north, such as I have never seen in France or Italy."[9] It was characteristic of Henri that once Minette responded, he began to grow indifferent to her. He paid court to another young woman, Mlle. de Treuenfels, whom he did not even love. Then, for the first time, he saw Minette with another suitor, who was anxious only to marry her. He himself had no wish to marry her, but he determined that Minette should love him. He could not resist the challenge, and he was quite aware that success would make him cool again. Undoubtedly, he told Pauline, "the day after I am certain of her love she will be almost unbearable to me. . . . This is my life, my dear, what is yours? Are you thinking at all seriously about getting married? I mean are you cured of believing you'll find a Saint-Preux or an Emile for a husband?"[10]

On June 17, having neglected it for a year, Henri began a new volume of his journal.

> The adventure with Mina is a lost battle. It will teach me the value of time. If she did not give me a moment of sublimity, like Adèle [Rebuffel] at Frascati, I found some highly delectable moments with her.
> *Je ne veux en aimant que la douceur d'aimer.*
> That line is almost true of my soul.

That morning he consoled himself. "Music at the *Chasseur vert,* as I came back from escorting Mlle. de Treuenfels. . . . Minette had a pretty face."[11]

He wrote in the past tense, but the flirtation continued. Once again Minette became jealous of Mlle. de Treuenfels. On June 23: "Minette constantly sought me out, I was a little timid until dinner, it produced a revolution."[12] On July 1: "Quite a happy day, this morning because of my father's money. I went to the *Chasseur vert* at one o'clock; I fired thirty-five shots at twenty-five paces: two in the bull's-eye. . . . I returned there in the evening. . . . Mlle. de Griesheim and Mlle. d'Oenhausen were there. At supper, I made the latter a little amorous, from what I could guess."[13] He was fooling with love.

He was clearly uncertain about his career. On July 8 France, Russia and Prussia had signed the Treaty of Tilsit. Peace was established at the expense of Prussia. France and Russia formed a military alliance against Great Britain. The news appears to have taken some time in reaching Brunswick, for on July 10 Henri could still write to Pauline: "It is probable, my dear, that peace will be made. At that great epoch in history, what shall I become?"[14] Next day a decree from Königsberg appointed him an assistant quartermaster—or, more grandly, titular assistant to the Commissaries of War.

He continued to enjoy his officialdom. He continued, also, to meditate about his past. He still dreamed, even now, about Victorine Mounier. Her idealised figure lingered in his imagination. Real mistresses had come and gone, but she remained his Proustian dream: the dream which he had once described to Edouard Mounier, the ideal which did not exist, but for which he longed unceasingly.

Now, in August, 1807, it occurred to him that Pauline might have met Victorine. They had mutual friends, the Malleins. Abraham Mallein was a *conseiller* at the Cour de Grenoble. Victorine might have visited them. Henri begged his sister to send him news. Pauline saw Victorine, and she wrote to him with warmth and understanding. Her letter reached him at Salzdahlum, where he was stag hunting. On September 2, at four o'clock in the morning, he sat down to answer her.

> I think you are right. [Victorine] is a very rare soul. I loved her dearly, and I've seen her seven or eight times in my life. All my other passions have been a mere reflection of that one. I loved Mélanie because she reminded me of her character. You know how much I value the smallest details about Victorine. . . .
>
> I shall think of the two of you all day. Try to discover if she loves someone in Paris or in Rennes; I almost want to say to you like the good Lord: wherever you shall be gathered together, I shall be with you.[15]

His emotional needs remained unending. A few days later, in Halberstadt, he saw Mme. Pierre Daru; she was on her way to Berlin to join her husband. She immediately inspired his devotion.

To François Périer-Lagrange, a young landowner in Grenoble,

Henri confided his personal fortunes and his financial anxieties. It
was essential, he explained, to persuade Chérubin not to undertake
new enterprises. He must perfect what he had done, not attempt to
enlarge his property. Henri was receiving an allowance from his
father. If Chérubin embarked on further ventures, Claix would have
to be sold to liquidate his debts, and Henri would have to depend
entirely on his salary. As it was, his work was physically and financially demanding. His clerical work was enormous, and he also had
to attend all of Martial's parties and entertain any friends who
arrived; he had to be available day or night and travel at least forty
leagues a week. The horses cost nothing, but he had to buy presents
and food and constantly replenish his wardrobe. "All this for a
salary of 200 livres and office expenses of 125 livres, always two
months in arrears. . . . There, my best friend, is a brief sketch of my
finances. . . . Try to get a little order into my father's activities. . . .
You exhort me to get married; prove to me that I have enough daily
bread for two."[16]

Henri could not consider marriage; he continued to record his
unsatisfactory emotional life. "I am cured of my love for Minette. I
sleep every three or four days, to satisfy my physical needs, with
Charlotte Knabelhuber, the mistress of a rich Dutchman, M.
Kutendvilde."[17]

But if Henri remained unsettled, Pauline was at last to find
happiness. She became engaged to François Périer-Lagrange. How
long this engagement had been considered has not been recorded—at
least in Henri's published correspondence. But at some time, it seems,
he had mentioned the idea to Périer-Lagrange. Now, on January 24,
1808, with genuine delight, he sent him his congratulations. "Your
letter gave me the liveliest possible pleasure, my dear Périer. You
know that I had already chosen for my sister."[18]

Considering his inadequate formal education, his youth and lack
of experience, Beyle's promotion was remarkable. He owed, one
surmises, more than he deserved to the happy accident of his relationship with the Darus. A few months earlier he had been appointed
titular assistant to the Commissaries of War. Now, on January 29,
just after his twenty-fifth birthday, he was appointed to assist the
prefect in governing the department of the Ocker. His correspond-

ence became considerable. Among his papers at Grenoble are draft letters to local and imperial dignitaries, including prefects, intendants, the Minister of Justice and the Interior and the Minister of Finance. He laboured on, doing all his official work under a portrait of Raphael. It seemed to change its expression according to the time of day, and, he wrote, "it prevents my soul from drying up entirely."[19]

He could be natural only in solitude, and in his solitude, he continued to confide in his journal. He was glad, now, that chance had taken him far from Napoleon's court, where he had wanted to be two years ago. That wish, he considered, had been much mistaken, and it should make him circumspect about embarking on marriage and about resigning his position. He was convinced, now, that he was unsuited to court life. "An independent and solitary place like the one I have today suits me much better. It is true that I'm infinitely bored." As he told Pauline, he was "exiled in the devil of a hole."[20]

Pauline alone understood the nuances of his thoughts, the endless subtleties of his emotions, and as her marriage approached, he recalled their lifelong relationship, and some of his own deepest feelings, in one of his most delicate letters.

> 26 March 1808
>
> I know quite well, my dear, that you must have a thousand things to do, a thousand duties to perform: you will hardly have time to read my letter. But it gives me pleasure to write to you; I shall have even more in reading and rereading your answer, if you have time to send one. It seems to me that, in sensitive souls, a multitude of tunes are floating, so to speak; suddenly you are affected by the feeling that they express, they come into your memory and you hum them for days on end, always finding a new pleasure in them. That theory is my story for today; a charming tune came to me on the little words *cara sorella*. I recalled in memory all the time we have spent together. How I didn't love you in our childhood; how I once beat you at Claix, in the kitchen. . . . And then all the unhappiness that poor Aunt Séraphie made us suffer; our walks along those paths surrounded by stagnant water, towards Saint-Joseph. How I looked at the slope of the mountains in the direction of Voreppe, and sighed! It was especially at twilight, in summer, when their silhouettes stood out against a pale orange sky. How I felt that name: *Porte de France!* How I loved that word France for itself, without thinking of what it expressed! Alas! that charming happiness that I imagined, I glimpsed

it once at Frascati, and at other times in Milan. Since then, there's been no question of it anymore, I am astonished that I could have felt it. The memory of it is itself stronger than all the present happiness I can procure.

There are my dreams, my dear; I am almost ashamed of them; but when all is said, you are the only person in the world to whom I should dare to tell them. I notice something rather sad; when you lose a passion, you gradually lose the memory of the pleasures that it gave you. I told you that at Frascati, at a pretty firework display, at the moment of the explosion, Adèle leant an instant against my shoulder. I cannot express how happy I was. For two years, when I was overwhelmed with grief, that image gave me back my courage and made me forget all my misfortunes. I had forgotten it for a long while; I wanted to think about it again today. Despite myself, I see Adèle as she is, but, such as I am, there is no longer the slightest pleasure in this memory. Mme. Pietra Grua [sic], that's different: her memory is bound with that of the Italian language. As soon as something in a work, in a woman's part, gives me pleasure, I involuntarily put it into her mouth. I hear it, all my feeling today began with that; I was reading an author whom I did not know and hardly esteemed: the works of Count Gasparo Gozzi. . . . I found myself crying like a child. . . . Since then, I have verified an account of 9.007. 661 fr. 07 scattered through 140 pages of a folio register; I have written a report of eight pages; nothing has been able to efface that sweet impression.

Good-bye; love me, and give me news of Grenoble.[21]

There was soon news to send from Grenoble. On May 25 Pauline was married. Before the month was over, Henri was writing to the new Mme. Périer-Lagrange: "There is one of the great affairs of my life brought to a happy issue. . . . I tremble with pleasure like a child, to think of the address which I shall have to put on my letter."[22]

On June 8 he moved to Richmond, on the outskirts of Brunswick, to be able to work more peacefully in his leisure hours, and there, in the second half of the month, he received a visit from Mélanie. Thanks to the protection of François Roger, a dramatist and future Academician, she had entered the Comédie-Française the previous year. Her debut there—like her debut at Marseilles—had been far from triumphant, and she had performed only seven times. She was now on her way to St. Petersburg, where she was to marry General de Barcoff.[23] She had kept in touch with Pauline; she knew of Pauline's marriage; she brought Henri a letter from his sister and remained to *déjeuner.* He did not record his feelings on seeing her again. No doubt his passion for her was dead. On September 19, when he next wrote to Pauline, it was to tell her about a love affair which might have been. The woman in question, whom he did not name, has been identified as Livia Bialowiska.

> Now, here's my story. Eight months ago, there was a colonel here, and I made his acquaintance by virtue of my position. He had a wife of twenty-three, infinitely intelligent, and with that nobility which I love so much in Italian women.... The husband left with his regiment, but six leagues away he died. She came back a few days later. I called on her. I thought that she received me well, in the midst of her deep grief, but she received me like everybody else. And bored, and knowing that she was bored, sure of having some pleasant moments with her, I remained four long months without calling on her again. One evening, on the promenade, chance put us side by side. She was leaving in a week, and, from that moment, we spent our lives together. She knew the same towns in Italy as I did, and almost the same people; she left, I galloped for ten leagues beside her carriage.... The day before yesterday, someone brought me a miserable little letter, on yellow paper....
>
> Isn't it very comic that, for four long months, in Brunswick, it depended only on me to see or possess a charming woman, and that I should have waited for three hundred little leagues to divide us before I thought of it?[24]

The next day, September 20, after a stay of more than three months, Henri left Richmond. He had grown weary of solitude. Besides, Richmond had been a summer residence, and he now felt the autumn chill. It was from Brunswick, on October 29, that he wrote an illuminating letter to Pauline.

> The arts promise more than they contain. This idea, this charming feeling, has just been given me by a barrel organ in a neighbouring street. It played a phrase of music two passages of which are new to me and, what is more, seem to me to be enchanting. They almost brought the tears into my eyes.
>
> Music pleased me for the first time at Novara, a few days before the Battle of Marengo. I went to the theatre; they were giving *Il Matrimonio segreto.* The music pleased me as an expression of love. It seems to me that none of the women I have had has given me so sweet and

so gratuitous a moment as the one I owe to the phrase of music that I
have just heard. This pleasure came to me without my expecting it in
any way; it filled my whole soul. . . .

All this makes me think, my dear Pauline, that the arts which begin
to please us by painting the delights of passions and, so to speak, by
reflection, as the moon illuminates, may end by giving us pleasures
which are stronger than the passions. I am astonished, every day, to
find how little pleasure the German women give me; the French ones
bore me; I place this kind of happiness for myself in Italy. If chance
gave me an income of forty thousand livres, I should go to Italy.[25]

Chance did not bring him a handsome income or an immediate
visit to Italy. But soon afterwards he was recalled to Paris. He
arrived there on December 1.

Eight

In Paris he translated a page or two of *Don Quixote,* took lessons in Spanish and dancing, strolled in the springlike weather from the Café de la Rotonde to the Café de Foy; he went to the Vaudeville, read Alfieri, attended a performance of *Cosi fan tutte.*[1] On March 28 this dilettante's existence was interrupted. He received his orders to go to Strasbourg, to await instructions from Pierre Daru. Once again he was swept into the emperor's campaigns.

When Napoleon returned from Spain to Paris early in 1809, only four powers remained at war with him: Great Britain, Portugal, Sicily and Sweden. All the rest of Europe was either under his rule or allied to him. Austria chose this moment to prepare for war against him. Napoleon's high-handed treatment of the Spanish Bourbons had made the Austrians anxious about the future of the Hapsburgs. The Austrian army had been reorganized since its defeat at Austerlitz, and it now seemed capable of dealing Napoleon a hard blow. In January, 1809, mobilization began. On April 12 Archduke Charles invaded Bavaria. He called on all German people to rise in arms and to throw off the French yoke.

On April 12 Henri Beyle left Strasbourg for Vienna. He travelled in a carriage with a commissary of wars, and as they followed the course of the Rhine, Beyle admired the sunset and the voice of his companion, who sang Italian tunes. They drove from Karlsruhe to Stuttgart. Constantly moving, constantly uncertain of what the next day would bring, Beyle found it difficult to be melancholy or introspective.

> This life enchants me [he told Pauline on April 19]. . . . The things to be done demand such speed that I am almost continually attentive. These last two days, I have done twenty leagues each morning before *déjeuner*.
> I think that tomorrow or the day after the Austrians will be beaten near Ingolstadt, for which we are leaving in two hours. I must rush into the street. I'm told that they are stealing our horses and our carriage.[2]

Beyle's prediction of an Austrian defeat was fulfilled. On April 21, from Ingolstadt, he wrote: "We had a small victory yesterday: four flags, four pieces of cannon, all the enemy positions. . . . I haven't been to bed for three days."[3] He travelled from Landshut to Burghausen. The road was covered with ammunition carts, and as their carriages passed in single file, they had time to admire the pinewoods and to observe the desolation left in the wake of war. Ebersberg, through which they drove, had been gutted by fire, the street was full of corpses, hideously burned, and, at one point, his carriage had to pass over them.

On May 13 he finally arrived in Vienna. During his first days in the city he felt perfect contentment. Martial Daru was appointed intendant and asked his brother if Beyle might work for him. Pierre Daru agreed, and a delighted Beyle faced the prospect of a long stay in Vienna. His only cause of anxiety was the number of pretty women.[4] On June 15 he told Pauline: "Still not a moment to write. Horses, women, and heavenly music the rest of the time."[5] Among the music was the requiem which he attended that day, to mark the recent death of Haydn.

At times Napoleon's campaigns seemed to pass him by. Since he had several bouts of fever in Vienna, he missed the Battle of Wagram on July 6. It was, so he explained to Pauline,

> . . . a spectacle ever to be regretted. Five hundred thousand men fought for fifty hours, Martial was there: I should have followed him, but I

was stretched out on a chaise longue, overcome by a headache and by impatience; from Vienna you could hear every cannon-shot. . . .

As for this perfect happiness I seek, I have not yet encountered it. I should need a woman who had a great soul, and they are all like novels: interesting until the end, and, two days later, one is astonished that one could have been interested by such common things.[6]

In his constant search for happiness, *la chasse au bonheur,* Beyle was more than once led astray. Sometimes the women whom he loved hardly existed, except in his intense imagination; sometimes they proved to be far from deities. In Vienna he became involved in a violent love affair with a woman known in *Vie de Henry Brulard* as Babet. He was not the first of her lovers, nor was he her only admirer. He was brought to the point of a duel with a French officer who also aspired for her favours.

He was soon concerned with a more practical enterprise. He had reason to believe that he might be made an *auditeur* at the next promotion; the chief obstacle to his advancement seemed to him to be lack of money. He urged Dr. Gagnon to write three letters on his behalf. He asked Pauline to speak to Chérubin. "Tell our father that I promise to ask him only for 2,400 francs a year, as long as I am an *auditeur* in Paris. . . . Be my advocate and plead for me warmly."[7] Throughout November and December, he repeatedly reminded his sister of his eager wish for promotion, of the letters to be written, of the tone to be taken, of the diplomatic lies that might need to be told to achieve his end.

On October 21 Mme. Daru arrived in Vienna. The news of her sudden arrival much disturbed him. "I felt myself changing colour every moment," he noted in his journal. "At half past four I decided to go in. I found her with Jacqueminot. Her first greeting was exactly what it would have been for anyone else. She rose so that I might kiss her. I didn't dare (want of practice) and all I did was feebly take her hand."[8] Their familiarity deepened during their drives and excursions, but when she left on November 20, Beyle remained the aspirant he had been. "If I had been bolder, if I had taken the tone of gallantry from the beginning, . . . I think I'd have come very near to being happy."[9] Later, when he reread his journal, he felt the need to play to the gallery. He added that she had become his mistress and that she had remained so for a year. The statement was outrageously false; the later pages of the journal and the notes of the *Consultation pour Banti* prove that he was never her lover.

On January 2 he wrote to the Minister of the Administration of the War; he intimated that he might deserve promotion to commissary of wars, and he asked to be sent to Spain. On January 3—no doubt with official sanction—he went to Paris to be at the minister's disposal. He stayed at 28, rue du Colombier (today the rue Jacob), and from there, on January 20, he wrote to Pauline, urging her to ensure that the necessary appeals were made for his promotion. On reflection, he was not so anxious to be a commissary of wars in the depths of Spain. He would prefer to be an *auditeur*.

While he waited for a new appointment, he visited the opera, practised his horsemanship, called on Mme. Daru and saw *Le Mariage de Figaro,* in which Mlle. Mars, as Suzanne, was "more divine than ever." He could not see her often enough. On February 26 he noted: *"Beauty.* This evening . . . I had the strongest sensation of beauty that I can remember: Mlle. Mars as Suzanne in the *Figaro.* I was so charmed that I felt on the verge of love. If I had known less about the difference between conduct and appearance, I should have died." Two days later: "I have come out of the *Figaro.* . . . Mlle. Mars makes me rediscover my heart, which I thought was dead."[10]

On March 14 he watched the emperor's artist, the neoclassical Louis David, painting the portrait of Mme. Daru. As four o'clock struck that afternoon, David signed his canvas. Beyle's eyes met those of the sitter, and he persuaded himself that his love for her was returned. Yet did he love her? Or did he merely indulge in reverie? Perhaps, unconsciously, he needed a maternal figure. Mme. Daru was the same age as himself; but David portrayed a full-bosomed bourgeoise, a fussily dressed *mère de famille.* It is hard to see how she could have seemed desirable. Yet for a few days after he had met her gaze, Henri kept his journal in Italian: perhaps to protect his intimate thoughts. He was less timid now, and he could almost see the day when he would no longer be timid with Mme. Daru—or, as he sometimes called her, Mme. Maria.

On May 10 at least for the moment, the question of Mme. Daru was set aside. He was ordered to join the nineteenth military division, at Lyons, as a commissary of wars.

I shall be wonderfully depressed [so he told Pauline]. My days here are filled by a woman. I am not in love with her, but I think about her continually. Since I have seen my departure approaching, I can't read anymore, I think about her so much. I think that I only need a little absence from it all to fall into the most ridiculous melancholy. What makes me afraid of it is that I don't have her. I'll tell you all about that and you'll have a good laugh at me. I'm behaving like a respectable schoolboy.[11]

He still hoped to avoid being posted to Lyons. In his journal he still lost himself in emotional speculation and analysis. Pauline and her husband had another subject of concern: the coming marriage of Victorine Mounier.[12] They clearly wondered if Henri were missing his chance of lifelong happiness through misunderstanding and diffidence. They even seemed to wonder if Victorine had accepted M. Achard, receiver general of taxes, out of disappointment rather than love. They wondered if she would in fact prefer to marry Henri, if her engagement might even now be broken. Pauline had intimated that, if necessary, she would make delicate enquiries. Henri had rejected her suggestion. Late in May François Périer-Lagrange ventured to write to him on the same topic.

I shall never forget the mark of affection you give me [Henri answered], but the sacrifice is made. . . . One must never enter a family where one is not adopted with pleasure. Unfortunately pride has become such a strong habit with me that I couldn't promise not to send all the relatives packing, even the most powerful, the moment they claimed not to be on a perfect equality. That would put this delightful girl into a very embarrassing position. Besides, I haven't got a sou, and there is some difference between being the wife of a receiver general and the wife of a poor devil of an *auditeur*, at 5,000 francs a year: another comparison which would make me unhappy the moment I suspected my wife of making it. . . .

There, my dear friend, is the whole of my soul. So don't say anything to [———] that may make her suspect a project which I have *finally uprooted*. . . . [words emphasised are in English in the diary].

I am not mature enough, or rich enough, to get married. Have children, then, whom I may love as much as I love you.[13]

He had determined, at least for the present, to remain a bachelor; he was attempting to form a philosophy of happiness. On June 4, from Paris (he had not, after all, been sent to Lyons), he wrote to Pauline: "One may find happiness in ones stomach, or in love, or in ones head; with a little understanding, one may take a little of each of these happinesses and make oneself a pleasant destiny."[14]

He himself had a pleasant destiny, an engaging way of life. He enjoyed a visit to the porcelain factory at Sèvres, a glass of excellent malaga at Versailles, a tour of the Trianon and an ascent of the new Colonne Vendôme, on which he assessed the emperor's statue, "clinging to one of his thighs, at a hundred and sixty feet from the ground." In his journal he noted his mild flirtations, but "it is," he wrote, "the knowledge of what is most hidden in the depths of the heart and head that I want to acquire." He continued, above all, to be concerned with Mme. Daru. On June 8 he confessed that being with her set all his other thoughts at rest.[15]

It was with her, two days later, that he attended the fête de la Ville, held to celebrate the emperor's marriage to the Archduchess Marie-Louise of Austria. He escorted her in an elegant barouche, with coats of arms emblazoned on its doors. He felt disdain for the populace who were gaping at the finery. He played the aristocratic part which he felt befitted the occasion, and he enjoyed it, "almost as if I were really a man with five plumes and two stars. That," he wrote, "is so true that the enjoyment of some or other state . . . makes me tired of it, instead of making me delight in the pleasure that I have imagined." It was a characteristic observation. Now, as he moved, a provincial bourgeois, among the dignitaries of the Empire, he coolly assessed "the different degrees of nullity and merit."[16]

He protested his contempt for the social round, but his ambitions remained. He recorded the budget which he would allow himself as soon as he was appointed *auditeur*. It included sums for two servants and the upkeep of horses and carriages. He assessed himself as carefully as he planned his future. He needed—so he decided—to circulate more in society. He needed a sophisticated mistress of twenty-five, who would teach him the art of intrigue. He must make friends to advance his interests.[17] On July 30, earnest as ever, he worked "on the classification of the passions, states and habits of the soul, the means of passion, from half past seven till half past three."[18]

On August 3, "jour remarquable *in my life*," he was handed an official letter, telling him that he had been appointed *auditeur au Conseil d'état*. "I opened this good letter at twenty-two minutes past eleven at night," he noted. "I am twenty-seven years, six months and twenty days old."[19] He was tempted to believe the proverb that one happiness always brings another. The next day Pierre Daru announced that he had recommended him for the post of Inspecteur du Mobilier. "My victory is complete," wrote Henri to Pauline, on August 5. "Success has come in time; I had reached the end, not of my patience, but of my means. . . . Use all your activity in getting me 3, and, if possible, 4,000 francs. I owe 1,800, and I shall be obliged to spend at least 1,000. Good-bye, it's the final problem in my career."[20] Two days later he added: "How have I won this victory? By making the conquest of M. [Daru]. How did I do that? By ensuring that everyone praised me to him, and by doing him honour in every sense of the word. For four years I have worked consistently; I have spent only for this. I have not done anything, for a quarter of an hour, since a certain Monday morning in his room, when he flatly refused to make me what I am—I have not done anything, for a quarter of an hour, without thinking of the goal I must attain."[21]

It was inevitable that he now found his achievement incomplete.

> At the moment when I taste the fruit of four years of pains, my soul sighs for a different kind of happiness. I wish I could love a rather lovable woman and go and spend a fortnight in the country with her. That is my dream, but it will remain a dream for me. My liaisons are so arranged that this refreshment of the soul, this happiness of boundless confidence is precisely the one happiness which is beyond my reach. And when I had grasped it, my thirst for it would be diminished.[22]

For a moment he regretted the warmth of Mélanie. "With a heart like Mélanie's," he wrote next day, "I should have been perfectly happy. I have precisely what was wanting when love made me happy at Marseilles, but, by a just compensation, I no longer have what I had then."[23]

Nine

On August 16 Mme. Daru left for Amsterdam. He suddenly felt weary of Paris. He was irritated by daily life, by the constant interruptions which "inflamed his irascible nature." He was anxious to work at his play *Letellier*. He passionately wanted to be in love.

He thought he might find happiness in a change of surroundings. He found it at Plancy-sur-Aube, with his friend from schooldays Louis Crozet. Crozet was now an engineer. He had a gift for administration. He was perhaps a trifle inclined to hear himself speaking, but he was gentle and wise and understanding enough to help with the play. At Plancy, Beyle enjoyed not only Crozet's company, but his old pleasure, shooting. In the first three days of his visit he shot thirteen swallows and a partridge; on the fourth day he shot twelve swallows. On the seventh or eighth day a letter arrived announcing that he was *inspecteur-général du mobilier de la couronne* and that he had been summoned for an interview.

He left next day for Paris, where—so he considered—he passed his examination with distinction. His new post made him responsible for the maintenance of the furniture in the palace of Fontainebleau. He was also to supervise the making of the inventory of the Louvre Museum. He had no special knowledge of art or interior decoration, but once again, nepotism had played its part.

He set up an office in Paris; he paid two official visits to Versailles. He dreamed of a splendid future: 11,400 francs and a barony. But money and uniform were not enough. "I need," he repeated, "to love and to be loved. If I cannot attain this supreme happiness, I must work at things on which I set self-esteem."[1] On October 9, writing, as usual, to Pauline, he turned from questions of money and social status to the continuing and empty dream of his marriage to Victorine Mounier. It had never been more than a nebulous dream, and yet it had come to have substance in his mind.

> I am [he confessed] a little troubled by the image of solid happiness that I thought I should find with Victorine. I miss loving and being loved. I do what I can to love Mme. Palfy [Mme. Daru], but she lacks *the understanding soul,* she does not understand all the subtleties which make the happiness or unhappiness of those who can perceive them. She sets unnecessary store on all these stupidities of ambition, which cease to mean anything once you achieve them. Don't laugh too much at all these little weaknesses of the heart; not a soul in the world suspects them but you. I shall do everything I can to go to Italy in 1811.[2]

Mme. Daru was not his only weakness of the heart. On December 8 one of his colleagues, Amédée Pastoret, mentioned that he had seen Victorine. Henri's emotions were instantly aroused. He discovered that Pastoret was in fact taking her to the Variétés that evening. He hurried home, changed and rushed to the theatre. There were no seats left except in the fourth gallery, and here, among the footmen and lackeys, he gazed through his lorgnette, trying desperately to find her. Through the goodwill of three *ouvreuses,* he made his way down to the *premières loges,* where he was offered a seat a few paces from her. He did not dare take it. He went up again to the *secondes loges,* where he quizzed her through the screen of a box. It was impossible to make her out.[3]

He continued to be in extraordinary and painful conflict with himself. He refused to allow his family to approach Victorine. He was not prepared to discover whether or not she loved him. Did he genuinely wish to remain a bachelor, this man who strove to hide his tender nature, who feared that he might lose the power to love? In his journal he recorded his physical awareness of women, sometimes with bitterness and cynicism. Five days after he had searched for a sight of

Victorine, he wrote: "I think I should easily lose the habit of women. I've hardly any talent at all for having easy women, otherwise I should have got into conversation a hundred times with Mme. Boucher (I believe) of *Buffa,* and I should have had her after six days."[4] As for Mme. Daru, she was now heavily pregnant and, one surmises, happily married. She was back in Paris, but she had no time for his calculated coldness, Byronic gloom or ardent admiration. After months of deliberation, their relationship remained only a fantasy in his mind, a motive for recurrent speculation. Perhaps that was all that he needed from her.

On December 31, with a toy clown in one hand and a large toy sheep in the other, he paid his New Year call on the Darus. The children revelled in their toys, but he did not see their mother. She had given birth to another child the previous day. "Ambition and finance may be congratulated on the changes which have occurred this year," so Henri recorded in his journal. "But the minister of love has behaved badly; if he goes on behaving like this, he might well become useless."[5]

The minister was soon to show more benevolence. Before the month was out, Beyle had a mistress: Angelina Béreyter, a twenty-four-year-old singer in opera buffa. It had been a curious epistolary courtship. "I had written several letters, at several months' interval, to the lovable and sweet Béreyter. She finally agreed that I might pay my homage to her in person. . . . I kissed her tenderly the first day, I possessed her in my apartment on the second day (January 29, 1811)."[6]

Angelina-Marie Béreyter had been born in Lyons, the daughter of a printer. She was one of the company at the Odéon. She had first appeared there in 1809, in the modest place that she would always keep, playing *seconda e terza donna.* And this, in a sense, was the place she would always keep for Henri Beyle. Years afterwards, in the dust near Lake Albano, he traced with his cane the initials of the women who summarised his life. Among them was Angelina Béreyter, "whom I never loved." The epitaph, recorded in *Vie de Henry Brulard,* was not, it would appear, entirely true. He may not have felt for her the admiration he felt for noble, Cornelian women, the physical attraction he had felt for Mélanie, the overwhelming love which he was to feel for Métilde Dembowski. But his liaison with Angelina lasted for three years. He kept her longer than any other mistress. It took this little actress from opera buffa, the only woman with whom he ever lived, to reveal an unknown Beyle to posterity: a Beyle who was domestic, bourgeois, almost conjugal.

At the beginning of their affair they were tormented by anonymous letters. Beyle suspected that they were sent by a doctor whom she had refused to marry—"a gallant personage with the complexion of a quadroon and some forty-five years to his credit." The letters had alarmed Angelina and drawn her all the closer to her new lover. He was flattered by her need and by her devotion; he was gratified to talk about music with her. She taught him songs from Mozart and Cimarosa, and she spent every night with him.[7]

It was a felicitous life for a man of twenty-eight. For the moment his career faded into the background. Louis Crozet was now in Paris, and when Beyle could steal time from his office, the two of them read Burke on the sublime. It seemed that every prospect pleased. Their study of sublimity was interrupted only by Mme. Daru. She told Beyle that he was to be sent to Italy. Crozet said, immediately, that he would go with him.[8] On March 9, in his curious mixture of French and would-be English, Beyle confessed: "I am in love with my journey, that is to say I have hardly any feeling left for the opera buffa, *and the amiable girl with whom I lay every night.*" His moods were, as usual, variable. He was in bed with his mistress when, on March 20, the gunfire echoed across Paris to announce that the empress had had a child. Twenty-one salvoes meant a daughter. At the twenty-second, he and Angelina heard cheering in the street. The King of Rome was born. "It is," wrote Beyle, "a great and happy event."

On April 19, when Beyle's trunks were packed, his mission to Italy was cancelled. It was a disappointment, but the minister of love continued to be kind. "Everything is going very well with *Maria* [Mme. Daru]. I continue *to lay every night with Angelina.*"[9]

Beyle's emotional life remained complex. He was engaged in a physically demanding love affair, and yet he continued to meditate about Mme. Daru. He was indebted to Pierre Daru for much of his career, but he felt no obligation to show simple friendship for his wife. He felt no overwhelming love for Maria (as he sometimes called her), and yet he noted, still, what he considered the delicate innuendoes of her gestures. He was also prepared—and here he was less delicate—to discuss the relationship with Crozet, who had helped him to break his love affair with Mélanie. On April 3, with the help of Crozet, Beyle wrote his *Consultation pour Banti*. In this document he thought aloud about Mme. Daru and about the conduct which was expected of him. He concluded that he should declare his love.

While he waited for the appropriate moment to do so, he took a few days' holiday (his official duties did not seem to trouble him unduly). He and Faure and Crozet travelled to Rouen. "I have seen the sea again. The smell of the tar reminded me sharply of Marseilles and Mélanie. Is it quite impossible, then, that I shall ever fall in love again?"[10] Beyle asked himself the question on April 30. It could only have been rhetorical, but it is strange to find him asking it.

It is all the more strange since, when he returned to Paris on May 3, he was thinking of marriage. Soon afterwards he told Pauline: *"I will perhaps marry, but the heart is for nothing in this affair*. I despair of finding again the character I imagined in Victorine. *I marry a* nullity."[11] On May 18, in his journal, again in a mixture of English and French, he was more explicit:

Matrimony.
  Félix [Faure] gave Mme. H——— a letter that I had written him, in which I express the desire to obtain *the hand of her daughter*. Perhaps she is thinking of re-marrying. She has already been asked for *her daughter,* she will have a considerable fortune of thirty to forty.
  Félix gives me the very wise advice to talk about this to Mme. Z. [Mm. Daru]. . . .
  I shall tell Marie: "It suits me financially to get married, but my heart is not involved at all.". . . It is M. Leschenault's daughter.[12]

This episode in Beyle's life still remains a mystery. It has been suggested that the girl, Jenny H. or Jenny Leschenault, was only a myth which he invented to rouse the jealousy of Mme. Daru. And yet the tone is disturbingly clear. In his correspondence with Pauline there are only a few vague allusions. But as early as May 23, 1810, Beyle had discussed this Jenny with Faure, who seems to have instigated the whole affair.[13]

Meanwhile, on May 25, Jenny's suitor set out for Bècheville, near Meulan, on the Seine. He intended to declare his love for Mme. Daru.

He was always afraid of seeming ridiculous, and as he reached the Darus' château, he felt understandably timid. He was welcomed, warmly, and stayed for a week. "That time was an island of happiness. I was agreeable, and Mme. de Palfy was infinitely agreeable to me."[14] On May 30, after everyone else had gone to bed, he walked alone in the park.

> There were heavy clouds passing in front of the moon, I was watching their movement and thinking of the tender mythology of Ossian to distract myself from the discontent I felt. . . . Five or six clear reasons proved the advantage and necessity of fighting, but at the sight of the enemy all courage disappeared. One degree more, and I should have blown my brains out rather than tell a woman, who loves me, perhaps, that I love her. And I am twenty-eight, and I've knocked about the world, and I have some character! . . .
>
> My moments of remorse were terrible. The night of the 28th to 29th was particularly horrible. I saw that wherever I might go, the thought that I had allowed such a fine occasion to escape me would make me wretched. The following night I did not dare to think of my cowardice, I cast the idea aside, and thought simply of distraction. . . .[15]

His self-contempt, his pain, remorse and anger were recorded in his journal. Years later, he recalled them again in *Le Rouge et le Noir*. When Julien determined to seduce Mme. de Rênal, his troubled days and nights at Vergy were to echo Beyle's own troubled days and nights at Bècheville.

Eventually Beyle summoned up his courage. He told Mme. Daru about his projected marriage. He felt that she was restraining her tears. He considered these tears a proof of her love for him, and he was tortured by the thought that he had no pretext, now, for timidity. At last, on May 31, after dinner, as they walked together round the garden, he made his declaration of love. "She replied that I must not think of that, that I must only think of her as a cousin who was fond of me."

She had no intention of making him her lover. She was contentedly married, and she was conscious of her position as the wife of Pierre Daru, as a *mère de famille*. Perhaps she also questioned the depth of Beyle's feeling. She recognised his need for an Egeria, one might almost say his need for a mistress of social standing. "You marry for ambition or love," so she had told him. She knew that men took mistresses for the same reasons.

He drove back to Paris. It was, he wrote, "quarter past eleven when I woke up Angelina."[16]

On his return from Bècheville, it might have appeared that his personal life was simplified. In fact, the complications continued. In Paris he still wondered if Mme. Daru's heightened colour might be caused by "the presence of *her lover*"; he pressed her hand repeatedly and wondered why she did not return the pressure or why she did not take her hand away. Sometimes he was natural; sometimes he was purposely cold. He was jealous—stupidly, he knew—of her cousin, who had spent the day with her. They were all, he recognised, microscopic events, but he still saw fit to record them. He paid court, no doubt to vex her, to her children's governess, Mlle. de Camelin.[17]

By June 25 he admitted that Mme. Daru could not love him; his pride was hurt at paying court without any response. She was now afraid to be left alone with him. When he went to dinner, she was formal; he took his revenge by looking ostentatiously at the clock.

On June 26, in a letter to Pauline, he discussed his emotional life:

> I don't believe there exists a second woman such as I imagined Victorine to be. I shall never again find that exquisite sensibility, that soundness of judgment, that nobility of soul. . . .
>
> What can I do except marry a sweet and pleasant nonentity? She is a nice, well-built girl, very well brought up, religious, with a little wit and good sense, in the blond style. . . . Mlle. Jenny is my height, which is tall for a woman. The man of the family will not sign [the contract] unless she is a countess. The mother will not sign unless she is Mme. de Beyle. My father's delays confuse me. . . . I shouldn't be surprised if Mlle. J's family thought that I was the son of some little merchant or out-of-work lawyer, living on a third floor. . . . These low and disgusting ideas spoil everything. But what can I do? . . .
>
> You see that my father is doing me the most cruel turn. If I had enough to live on, I shouldn't marry for six years and I should look for a character like my own. But if, in a year, I am not married or a prefect (an absurd thing to suggest), I shall be forced to leave Paris and to become a *sous-préfet* in a town of 5,000 souls. You know me. You can imagine my despair. But what can I do? That's what it is to

have a good father. Go to Claix, and try to make him decide. I shall sign everything to stay here.[18]

June and July passed by. He still considered marriage; he still analysed the behaviour of Mme. Daru. On July 18, after another visit to Bècheville, he noted that a more cunning man "would not have behaved as I did yesterday, with Marie. But would he have had the pleasure that her looks and her slightest actions gave me? For characters like that, women soon become what *le petit Ange* is to me now. And so I should not envy them at all."[19] *Le petit Ange* was Angelina Béreyter. He was bored by her emptiness and sated by her love.

And so the complex situation was perpetuated. Angelina was used and tolerated; Mme. Daru announced that she would give a handsome necklace as a wedding present to Henri's wife. Henri flirted mildly with other women and observed that "novelty is a great source of pleasure."

The chain of events had to be broken, and he needed change. "My life is happy, but it bores me a little; I need some movement, I am longing to travel." On August 17 he told Pauline that Pierre Daru had given him a short leave.[20] Twelve days later he left, inevitably, for Italy.

Angelina and Faure accompanied him to the diligence. "Angelina adores me," he observed, complacently. "Her tears on the Pont des Arts the day before yesterday. The tears made the boards wet."[21] On September 7 he reached Milan. He could have wept for joy.[22]

Ten

ELEVEN YEARS AND three months ago, in the wake of the reserve army, he had come to Milan as a young supernumerary from the Ministry of War. Milan had plunged him into enchantment. He had fallen in love with Angela Pietragrua, but he had not declared his passion. He was too timid, too aware of his inferior and ill-defined position. But for eleven years, despite his passing love affairs, she had inspired the melancholy reverie which was one of his deepest and most abiding pleasures. Now, on September 8, 1811, he recognised at once that he had not changed. Milan dissolved his Parisian veneer of cynicism, of hardness; he was no longer bitter, calculating and ambitious. Milan had made him, once again, his vulnerable and romantic self.

> As I was then, so I find myself again today! No feeling of ambition enters into this reflection. I bring everything back to Mme. Pietragrua. . . . In the millions of castles in Spain which I built for her, I imagined myself coming back one day as a colonel, or with some other promotion, . . . and then embracing her and bursting into tears.
>
> Admittedly the plan was not complicated, but it had what makes that sort of plan succeed, it was full of feeling, I couldn't even think about it without shedding tears.

90

This plan came into my head again yesterday. I saw myself, after *eleven years,* in the position which I had so longed for.

What a phrase, *eleven years!* My memories were no less strong; they have been given life by my extreme love. I cannot take a step in Milan without recognising something, and, eleven years ago, I loved that something because it belonged to the city in which she lived.[1]

All his feelings for Italy were concentrated in Milan, for in Milan were all his dreams of love. Beside such dreams, his courtship of Mme. Daru was only an exercise in emotion. Angela Pietragrua was, to him, a proud and turbulent figure: the woman with a soul for whom he sought. It does not matter whether she was really the kind of woman he imagined. It is enough that for him she had the necessary grandeur. The memory of her still endowed Milan with enchantment; the prospect of seeing her could still enthral him.

Yesterday evening I felt that emotion [he wrote on September 8]. It is too strong and too tender, and now it pains me because of the certainty, I think, that it will not be shared. I planned to go and see Mme. Pietragrua today, but I was afraid I should burst into tears when I embraced her and be once again ridiculous in her eyes; because I imagined that my unfortunate passion had made me seem ridiculous before. As a certain pride enters into love, this idea made me feel my emotion painfully. I should have shed delicious tears if, with Angelica's ring, I could have entered her salon and been invisible to her.[2]

That day he went to see her, and she did not disappoint him.

I saw a stately and superb woman. She is still grandiose because of the way in which her eyes, her brow and nose are set. I found more majesty and less of that full, voluptuous grace. In my time she was majestic only by the power of beauty, today she was also majestic because of her features. She did not recognise me. That pleased me. I recalled myself by explaining that I was Beyle, the friend of Joinville. "It's the Chinaman, *quegli è il Cinese,*" she said to her father, who was there.

My great passion had not made me ridiculous at all; it happened that she remembered me as someone very gay.

I joked about my love.—"Why didn't you tell me then?" she said to me, twice. . . . There was a little embarrassment between us. . . .

The current lover soon arrived: a Venetian nobleman, attached to the viceroy here with some honorary appointment. I was attentively polite to him.[3]

Mme. Pietragrua invited him to her box at the theatre that evening. This was already a sign of favour. "The box is sacred," Lady Morgan was to write, in her book on Italy. "None can intrude there but the intimate friends of the lady or her husband."[4] The atmosphere at La Scala was conducive to love. The women were *"posées,* graceful, indolent" and remarkably handsome. During the intervals they sipped their ices or, by shaded lamplight, played *tarok;* their thoughts were rarely on music and more often on social graces. The next day Beyle called on Mme. Pietragrua from two till five. On September 10 he hired a carriage, partly from convenience and partly to impress her. "The influence of small things is very great."[5]

He set out, now, with cool deliberation, to seduce her. They went together to the Brera picture gallery, and there he "looked at her twice, with extreme tenderness. Whenever our hands touched," he recorded, "they clasped one another; we often took one another's arm. I paid her some brief and tender compliments."[6] Suddenly he felt less certain of his calculations, recognised that he had lost control. Inevitably, he had fallen in love.

From that moment [so he wrote], a thousand little details which interested me in Milan grew pale. Bells, arts, music, etc., they all charm an empty heart, but they become dull and lose their force when the heart is full of passion.

At six o'clock, I found I loved Mme. Pietragrua; timidity was born. From that moment dreadful gloom filled my soul.

I was *gloomy* largely because a thousand little sources of happiness in memory, little sources which made a river, were instantly dried up.

My carriage bored me, since I no longer compared my present state to that of an employee of M. l'Inspecteur aux revues Daru. La Scala no longer gave me the pleasures which I had found in the memory of the tender, melancholy feelings which I had once felt there. . . .

I had tenderness and melancholy at first hand, I had only to look at the second box in the second row on the right.

I think that a good deal of vanity enters into my behaviour. I don't promise myself great pleasure in being in Mme. Pietragrua's arms. Really, Angelina has sated me with the sight of naked thighs and breasts.[7]

In his journal he noted "the sound that everything makes, when it strikes my soul." He analysed Mme. Pietragrua. In the past few years, she had grown disillusioned; she was bored by the monotony of Milan. Perhaps an intense and unexpected love affair with him might give her pleasure. If he wanted to attract her, so he decided, he must not let her be too sure that she had pleased him.[8]

On September 12 he thought he might make his declaration of love and find out whether or not he should leave Milan. Nothing kept him there, now, except her presence. He called on her; she used the familiar form of address, and she showed increasing tenderness when he reminded her of his old passion.

> She wept, and we kissed one another. . . . We discussed the question of my departure. She repeated several times, with much emotion: "Go, go! I feel that you must go for my peace of mind; tomorrow, perhaps, I shall no longer have the courage to tell you so."
>
> As I told her that I should be too unhappy on my journey, she said: "But you will have the certainty that you are loved.". . .
>
> I want to try to make her really in love, if she is not. I made a fine gesture this morning: I broke the glass of my watch, after I had made her read: *Angelina loves you every minute.*

Angelina Béreyter was dramatically discarded. The gesture seemed to him to be irresistible.[9]

On September 21, at half past eleven, he "won the victory so long desired."[10]

His victory did not, of course, completely satisfy him. "Nothing is lacking from my happiness except . . . that it is not a victory. It seems to me that perfectly pure pleasure can only come with intimacy; *the first time,* it's a victory; *in the three following,* one acquires intimacy. Then comes perfect happiness, if it is an intelligent woman, a woman of noble nature, whom one loves."[11] His happiness was yet to come, and even his victory revealed him to have been less than wholeheart-ed. Beyle could lose himself entirely in his imagination, yet he could not lose himself in love. He remained analytical, even at the moment of passion. His castles in Spain had, it seems, been more absorbing than the moment when he had persuaded Angela to surrender. He had, he said, "played misery and almost despair." It is disconcerting, but he always watched himself play a part.

He was not so enamoured of Angela that he had to stay in Milan. The day after his victory, he left for Bologna. On his arrival he went, almost at once, to the opera. His physical and emotional needs were, for the moment, satisfied, and he studied architecture and painting. On September 26 he arrived, exhausted, in Florence. After two hours' rest at his inn, he took a bath and set out again, in a carriage. At Santa Croce he saw the tombs of Michelangelo, Alfieri, Machiavelli and Galileo. Two pictures in the church made the strongest impression that painting had ever made on him. He was ravished by a picture of the four sibyls; but a painting of purgatory moved him almost to tears.

The effect of Florence was spoiled for him by Adèle Rebuffel, now Mme. Alexandre Petiet. Her husband was intendant of the crown estate in Tuscany, and they were living in Florence. Beyle thought of her, now, and of what (so he claimed) she had made him suffer. Even his triumph with Angela could not efface it. Yet—presumably out of curiosity—he chose to call on her.

> If something could confirm my view of French hearts, it is that visit. Politeness, judgment and coldness. Not even the interest that I should call simple humanity. . . .
>
> And people don't want me to love my dear Italians! They want me not to prefer fifteen minutes' conversation with Mme. Pietragrua to everything that Mme. Adèle can give me![12]

He travelled on to Rome, where he was presented to the Duchesse Lante. She showed him exquisite politeness and invited him to choose the programme for her Thursday concert (and what, asked Beyle, could be further from French customs than a duchess singing with her friends for pleasure?). He felt more Italian than ever. His feelings were intensified when he visited Canova.[13] With Napoleon and Byron, he was one of the men whom Beyle most admired. In Rome he continued to feel with an intensity which he did not experience in Paris. The only architectural monument which had ever moved him was the Coliseum, and standing alone in its ruins, hearing the song of the birds which had nested in the grass on the arcades, he could not restrain his tears.[14]

From Rome he set out for Naples. He passed the long journey in reverie and found, so he confessed, that he thought affectionately about five women, that a meeting with one of them would give him "tender pleasure." These five women were Angela Pietragrua, Mme. Daru, Mélanie, Livia Bialowiska and Angelina. "I think I am in love with the first. . . . I catch myself, seven or eight times a day, thinking about her with tenderness."[15] He arrived in Naples on October 5. During his stay, he visited Pompeii and the theatre at Herculaneum, admired the Teatro San Carlo and marvelled not to see hell fire in the crater of Vesuvius. On October 11 he left again for Rome, "sacrificing to duty the eruption which was expected the following day. It is," he wrote, "the greatest sacrifice that I could make, and I was a fool to make it."[16] From Rome he went to Ancona, where he flirted with one of his five women: his acquaintance from Brunswick, Livia Bialowiska. He could, he thought, have made her his mistress, but he had no desire for her. "What I want is to see my Angela again."

At nightfall on October 22, after more than a month of travelling, he returned to Milan. "For me," he wrote, "it often lessens happiness to describe it."[17]

Next day, transported with love, he set out for Varese, where Angela was on holiday with her husband. He found a room at a local inn and set out in search of her. He saw her at last and begged her to hasten back to Milan. Soon afterwards she announced her return. She was now, it seems, in love with him. She spoke of following him to France. She told him that she detested Italy. She wrote that she loved him more than life itself.

> Without any doubt the most beautiful woman I have had, and perhaps have seen, is Angela as she appeared to me this evening [November 2], as I walked with her in the streets, in the glow of the lighted shops. . . . She was animated this evening. *Yesterday and today, she has had pleasure.* She had just had coffee with me in a deserted back shop; her eyes were shining; her half-lit face had a suave harmony, and yet it was terrible with supernatural beauty. She seemed like a superior being who had put on beauty because this was the disguise that suited her best, and she seemed, with penetrating eyes, to read the depths of your soul. This face would have made a sublime sibyl.[18]

The "little leave" which Daru had granted him had lasted for more than two months. On November 13 he left Milan. A fortnight later he returned to his fourth-floor room in the rue Neuve-du-Luxembourg in Paris. He had hoped to find Angelina Béreyter waiting, with eager love, beside his fire. But his self-esteem was wounded: she had been away a long while, and she was not returning till mid-December.

Eleven

HENRI BEYLE HAD devised his own system of happiness. It must, he decided, be based on independence. But no happiness could depend entirely on self-sufficiency, and he was the least self-sufficient of men. He missed Italy, and above all, he missed Angela Pietragrua. His more or less real intrigue continued with the mysterious Jenny —whom he had once expressed a wish to marry. In his familiar mixture of French and so-called English, he recorded: "On 27 February, *I have been jealous.* Jenny paid as much attention to P. as to me. . . . [I think] that she wanted to make me jealous, and make me *speak (upon the matrimony).*"[1] No doubt she did. She had been approached, months earlier, as a possible wife for Henri Beyle. She was tired of waiting for letters from Grenoble, for his return from Italy, for some indication that he was in earnest. Perhaps she was trying to precipitate a declaration; perhaps she had never been concerned about him and was now concerned with someone else. Such behaviour was what he deserved.

He had become aware, since his return from Italy, that his love for Mme. Daru was over. He did not regret the end of this ill-conceived flirtation. Moreover, Angelina had returned to him. "I still have Angelina, who makes good music for me," he told Pauline. "But love

is like a fever which comes to two people at the same time; the first one
to be cured is diabolically bored by the other."[2] He continued to use
Angelina—the only mistress who never made him suffer.

He also continued his research on Italian art. One fruit of his
Italian visit was to be his *Histoire de la peinture en Italie.* He had drafted
a press announcement of it while he was in Milan, and now he was
working on it. He corresponded repeatedly with Van Praet, the
keeper of the Bibliothèque impériale; he borrowed books in English
and Italian. As *inspecteur du mobilier et des bâtiments de la couronne,* he also
supervised the maintenance of the furniture at Fontainebleau. He
approved the eleven volumes of the inventory. The Duc de Cadore
had succeeded Pierre Daru as *intendant-général de la couronne;* on a visit
to Fontainebleau he had found irregularities in the records. Beyle
checked them. He also reported that several pieces of furniture were
in poor condition. The imperial chairs in the chapel were not pro-
tected from the damp by linen cloth, and they might deteriorate. The
curator of Fontainebleau blamed his subordinates for the unsatisfactory state of the furniture; indeed the palace suffered from the
misunderstanding among the staff. Beyle asked the duc to issue
explicit instructions for each functionary.

One suspects that his activity did not wholly satisfy him. Determined to ensure promotion, he had asked to rejoin the Corps of
Commissaries of Wars. The emperor was now engaged in his Russian
campaign. On July 14 Henri announced to Pauline: "I shall leave
Paris for Wilna a week next Thursday. . . . If I can do so, on my return, I shall see my dear Italy again. It is my true country, . . . in
harmony with my nature."[3]

On July 23, with bourgeois satisfaction, he wrote to his brother-
in-law, Périer-Lagrange, from the palace of Saint-Cloud:

> I am leaving at seven o'clock this evening for the banks of the
> Dvina; I have come to take the orders of her Majesty the Empress.
> This princess has just honoured me with a conversation of several
> minutes on the route that I should take, the length of the journey, etc.,
> etc. When I left her Majesty, I went to his Majesty the King of Rome;
> but he was asleep, and Mme. la Comtesse de Montesquiou has just
> told me that it was impossible to see him before three o'clock; I have
> therefore two hours to wait. It isn't convenient, in full-dress uniform
> and lace. Happily I remembered that my position as inspector might
> perhaps give me some credit in the palace. I presented myself, and
> they opened a room for me.[4]

In his tranquil, imperial setting, while he waited to see the infant King of Rome, Beyle also wrote to Périer-Lagrange:

> I shall have great need of your splendid health. I am going to be twenty days and twenty nights without stopping. I have two enormous portfolios and fifty private packets. Among them is a letter which H. M. the Empress has just handed to me with the command to take it quickly to the emperor. . . .
>
> Farewell; love me although I'm far away, and plant an infinity of trees on your pretty hill at Thuellin. . . . I shall criticise that on my return from Russia.[5]

He set out that evening. He took with him the manuscript of *Histoire de la peinture,* in case he should have time to work on it. On August 14 he joined the emperor's headquarters at Boyardowiscoma. Here, presumably, he delivered the imperial letter—though he left no record of the occasion. Ten days later, from Smolensk, eighty leagues from Moscow, he assured his former schoolfriend, the magistrate Félix Faure:

> The thirst for seeing which I once possessed is entirely gone. Since I have seen Milan and Italy, everything repels me by its grossness. . . . In this ocean of barbarity, not a sound that responds to my soul! . . . Ambition has no hold on me, now. The finest broad ribbon would not compensate me for the mud I'm stuck in. I dream of the heights that my soul inhabits, like the high hills; far from those hills, in the plain, there are fetid marshes: I am plunged in them.[6]

He suffered from physical hardship; he felt—at twenty-nine—that he was growing old. He found no pleasure in work. He wanted to ask for the *sous-préfecture* in Rome. He would not hesitate, he said, if he were sure of dying at forty.[7]

In this romantic, melancholy mood he took part in the Russian campaign. He felt no patriotism, no martial elation. He observed history as an outsider, and he watched the burning of Moscow with the eyes of an aesthete.

> We went out of the city, which was lit up by the finest fire in the world. It formed a vast pyramid which was like the prayers of the faithful, the base was on earth and the summit in heaven. The moon appeared, I believe, above the fire. It was a great spectacle, but one

should have been alone to see it, or surrounded by people of intelligence. That is the sad condition that has spoiled the Russian
campaign for me: it is having done it with people who would have
diminished the Coliseum and the sea at Naples.[8]

Late in September, he found himself in unexpected solitude.
Physical exhaustion and dubious food brought on a bilious fever
which kept him in bed for a week. The fever subsided; it was followed
by violent toothache. After a week of toothache, he set out for
Smolensk, to organize reserves of provisions for the troops. He found
himself concerned with the purchase of 100,000 quintals of flour, with
the buying of hay and cattle. He was also concerned, unexpectedly,
with the whereabouts and the safety of Mélanie. He had last seen her
at Brunswick, on her way to Russia. She was now Mme. Barcoff, the
wife of a Russian general. On the day the French army reached
Moscow, he had gone in search of her; he learned that she had left for
St. Petersburg and that her departure had broken her marriage.
She was said to be pregnant and to have just enough money to travel
to France. On October 15 he instructed his solicitor's clerk that if she
reached Paris, she might live in his apartment.

His life was, as usual, strangely complicated. That day he wrote to
Pauline, to announce his imminent mission to Smolensk. He had a
fine title: director general of reserve provisions. The same day (dating
his letter, whimsically, from Hamburg), he wrote to Angelina
Béreyter: "I still hope to see you again in February, if not in Paris, at
least in Milan. Farewell, cruel woman, you see whether or not I love
you."[9] The next day, still from Moscow, he wrote to Mme. Daru
(whom, he insisted, he no longer loved): "May God get me out of this
soon and bring me back to the rue Neuve-du-Luxembourg where I
am only three and a half hours from Bècheville."[10]

On October 16 he left for Smolensk. He later said that this journey
alone had been worth his coming to Russia. He set out with a convoy
of 1,500 wounded, escorted by 200 or 300 men. There was a multitude
of small carriages; there were constant oaths and disputes as carriages
overturned in the mud or snow. Every evening they pitched camp
and slept in the freezing cold. On October 24, as they lit their fires,
they were surrounded by grey-coated Russian troops, who began to
shoot at them. They repelled the enemy, but they spent the night
on the alert. Next day, at dawn, they planned to form a square

round the wounded and attempt to break through the Russian lines. They drank the little wine that remained and marched forward, beside their carriages, "armed with pistols from head to foot," through a fog so dense that they could not see four feet ahead. "We constantly stopped," Beyle reported to Mme. Daru. "I had a volume of Mme. du Deffand which I read almost from beginning to end. The enemy did not consider us worthy of their anger, we were only attacked in the evening by a few Cossacks who stabbed fifteen or twenty wounded with their lances.... During these ridiculous alarms, his Majesty was pushing back the Russians from the Kaluga road and fighting splendid battles, the eternal glory of our army."[11]

The experience had been enough to rouse Beyle to sudden life. He arrived in Smolensk on November 2. He was now too alert, too excited, too busy to be introspective; he felt uncommonly well, he was probably going to Minsk to buy reserve provisions. "Eighty leagues nearer you," he wrote to Angelina in Paris. "When shall I be eighty steps away? It will be the sweetest moment in my life."[12] It was pleasant to flirt with a mistress who was almost a continent away. But writing the same day to Faure, who had recently married, Beyle assured him: "I am not polluted by the slightest speck of jealousy."[13]

The excitement and elation passed, and depression followed. He felt oppressed, once again, by his colleagues. On November 10 he assured Mme. Daru that "we look like our lackeys.... We are a long way from Parisian elegance." That day he also wrote to Chérubin Beyle; he took advantage of his position to press his familiar claim: "If his Majesty makes me a baron, I shan't have stolen the title."[14]

On December 7, from Wilna, as he retreated with the Grande Armée, he showed that he had had a change of heart. "I am very well, my dear [so he told his sister]. I have very often thought of you on the long journey from Moscow, which has lasted fifty days. I have lost everything and I have only the clothes that I am wearing.... I have had many physical hardships, no mental pleasure; but all is forgotten, and I am ready to begin again in the service of his Majesty."[15]

It was a grandiose statement, but it was true. Beyle's experience of war was to have a marked effect on his work and on his romantic nature.

Twelve

On the last day of January, 1813, he returned to Paris. He felt physically and mentally exhausted. "I am very tired, but not ill," he told Pauline on February 4. "I am cold inside. I drink two or three bottles of excellent wine. I take punch, and coffee; nothing makes any difference; I am still hungry and cold."[1]

That day he began a new volume of his journal:

> I think I am extremely sensitive, that is my most striking feature. This sensitivity is carried to excess. . . .
>
> This faculty produces enchanting thoughts, but they vanish like lightning. I have still been unable to contract the habit of writing them on the wing, although I have several times bought notebooks to do so. . . . What ideas did I not have in my barouche during my eighteen days' campaign between Moscow and Smolensk! I wrote down a few in a volume of Chesterfield which I had pillaged from Rostopchin's country house; it was lost with everything else.
>
> I had more good ideas from Berlin here, I haven't written them down.
>
> I am at present in a state of perfect coldness, I have lost all my passions.[2]

One of the passions he had lost, not surprisingly, was his passion for writing *Histoire de la peinture*. "Will it come back? I have no idea. At the moment I feel dead; an old man of sixty is not perhaps more cold."[3] He recognised, sadly: "I am not worth anything without love."[4] Even the women he knew in Paris now no longer moved him. Mme. Daru seemed to lack soul and wit (perhaps because she was rather haughty to him).

> That is a very dead passion [he wrote]. But what remains to me among women? Really there's nothing. The thirst I had for Angelina was quenched in three days; it isn't anything now except a commodity, but a very important commodity for me. . . .
> Prettechestinneka [Mme. Barcoff] appears on the horizon unexpectedly. But one does not rekindle the ashes. . . .
> All the same, I am offended by men; I need a bourgeois home where I can put my feet up on the fender. . . .
> I am afraid of engaging myself and then going bankrupt, which would be dishonest to Tinneka [Mme. Barcoff] just when she is establishing her emotional life in this country. My position, where she is concerned, is to do nothing and see how the wind blows.[5]

On February 18 he spent part of the morning with her at the Jardin des Plantes. As he recognised, there was nothing bourgeoise about her, and he could talk to her with a certain pleasure. Yet, on March 13, as he surveyed his *carte du tendre,* his map of love, it seemed to him flat and dull.

> Last Sunday . . . I went to Marie's [Mme. Daru's]. Her old feeling for me seemed to revive. . . . As for me, my passion is *entirely dead by the sea's sounding shore.* It is the same with Italy and Mme. Pietragrua. I feel nothing for them, now, but a taste for reminiscence. Mme. Pietragrua wrote me . . . two letters which I feel reluctant to answer. . . .
> What is the quickest way to shake off this premature old age?[6]

He continued to see Mélanie. Writing to Pauline in March, he told her that he and Mélanie had sat up, discussing her, until midnight. In the same letter, he told Pauline that fourteen new prefects were to be appointed. He would be embarrassed if he were chosen, because he would rather stay in Paris than be tied to a provincial town. He was still anxious for a barony. In his journal he added that he would be humiliated not to be rewarded for his services; on the other hand, if he were not a prefect in one of the fourteen Italian departments, it would go against his dearest inclinations.[7]

He continued to consider the promotion or honours he would choose. On March 18, much to his surprise, he began to feel a little of his old interest in Mme. Daru. "Really," he decided, "it would be better for me to remain exactly as I am. The cross [of the Légion-d'honneur] is the only favour which cannot become harmful to my freedom."[8]

He did not receive the Légion-d'honneur, let alone a prefecture, and Chérubin Beyle still prevented him from having a barony: he refused to send an official statement that Henri had the necessary financial security. "I don't care a damn," Henri professed, somewhat unconvincingly, "and I amuse myself by asking for girls in marriage so that my friends can marry them. . . . I am more determined than ever to keep *my beloved liberty.*"[9]

He remained emotionally free, but he was not to enjoy his freedom in Paris for much longer. France was now at war with Prussia. On April 19, much against his will, and once again attached to Pierre Daru, he left for Mayence, to take part in the German campaign.

On April 26, from Erfurt, he announced to his old acquaintance Baron de Strombeck: "The enemy is retreating as if the devil were after it. I am happy as a patriot, but very sad as a man. It is only seven days since I left Paris, and I am already sick at heart with the campaign. I hadn't yet had time to rest after the Moscow excursion. Write to me, my dear friend, and make my stay with the army bearable to me."[10]

Three days later he found it more bearable than he had expected. "It is less unpleasant than I'd thought," he confessed to Pauline. ". . . I count on this campaign earning me the intendance at Florence, which is worth 20,000 francs."[11]

May found him in Dresden; on May 19 he set off for Bautzen. Settled comfortably in a carriage, he travelled "in the midst of all the complicated movements of an army of a hundred and fifty thousand men pushing another army of a hundred and sixty thousand men, with an accompaniment of Cossacks behind them." But Russia had

sated him for life with such occasions; his experience of the Grande
Armée, on the retreat from Moscow, had disgusted him with soldiery
forever. At seven o'clock on May 19 they reached their bivouac near
Bautzen. The next day he and his colleagues observed

> . . . a great movement of cavalry, and His Majesty behind us, to the
> left. . . . We went back; all the preparations were being made for
> battle: the troops were filing to the left, following the emperor, and to
> the right, towards the wooded hills. I had all the trouble in the world
> to persuade these petty souls to come and see the battle. We could see
> Bautzen perfectly from the top of the slope. . . . From noon till three,
> we saw perfectly well all one can see of a battle, in other words
> nothing. The pleasure consists in the fact that one is a little moved by
> the certainty that something is happening there which one knows is
> terrible. The majestic sound of the cannon has a great deal to do with
> it. . . .
>
> [This battle] was the crossing of a river, the Spree. . . . I think that
> it cost two thousand five hundred dead and four thousand five
> hundred wounded. We had a particularly clear view of the action
> between the town and the hills, where Marshals Macdonald and
> Oudinot had the Russians in front of them, putting up an extremely
> stubborn resistance.[12]

So Napoleon defeated the Prussians and the Russians at Bautzen.

On June 6 Beyle was appointed intendant of the province of
Sagan in Silesia, on the borders of Prussia and Poland. Three days
later he was on his way to his domain. He enjoyed his newfound
freedom; his powers of observation were beginning to grow sharp
again. On June 15, in a letter, he announced: "I am reigning, my
dear Pauline, but, like all kings, I am yawning a little." Four days
later he wrote to Pierre Daru, reminding him that a post of intendant in Italy would give him the greatest pleasure.

In the meanwhile, at Sagan, he worked from nine till five,
regardless of the summer sunshine, the promenades and even his
Sunday rest. He was sad to have no mistress, but he consoled himself
by installing a piano in his bedroom and inviting a piano teacher to
play Mozart to him.

Early in July, he developed what seemed to be gastric fever.
Perhaps it was a recurrence of his venereal disease. He became
delirious; he suffered from violent headaches; he "thought he would

have the honour of being buried at Sagan." On July 26 he was feeling what he hoped would be the last effects of his "diabolical fever. . . . They promise me that I am free of it now," he assured Pauline. "I am too weak to write more to you. I can hardly go from the sofa to the window. . . . *Secret.* If I can, when I leave this country, I shall go and convalesce for a fortnight in Milan."[13]

He was authorized to leave Sagan. On August 20 he reached Paris. He was still liable to attacks of fever, and he consulted the celebrated Dr. Gall, who reduced them to bouts of four hours. But his ill health had done him a certain service. On September 1 he reported to Pauline: "His Excellency the Duc de Cadore, enchanted by my appearance, has given me permission to spread myself out in the south, and to get a little warm. So I am going to Milan. . . . This is exactly what I was doing two years and two days ago."[14]

Thirteen

AT TEN O'CLOCK on the morning of September 7 he caught sight of
Milan on the horizon. Two days later Angela summoned him to
Monza, ten miles away, where she was staying. He arrived that
afternoon, stayed overnight in a local inn, and next day he spent
eight hours with her, "eight hours which sped past in sweet conversation." He left that evening for Milan, where a slight recurrence of
fever did not prevent him from going to the opera.

> 11 September.
> *Sono felice.* I go to No. 909. At three o'clock she hasn't yet arrived. I
> change my room at Marchant's. I read the bulletins of the battles of
> Dresden. . . . The Comtesse Simonetta talks to me a good deal about
> the Monbelli family; I hope to be able to see them with her. I think
> that M. Fossati is jealous: she talks too much to me, and about me;
> but what noble failings![1]

The Comtesse Simonetta was his pseudonym for Angela. No doubt
he took the name from the famous echo of *la Simonetta*, two miles
from Milan. It echoed a pistol shot thirty times. One day he was to
visit it with Byron.[2]

15 September [1813]

I haven't written for four days, because happiness is diminished when you describe it. I must however tell the truth, and say that I do not feel the intoxication of 1811. My health—which is now improving—has been too poor, and then the novelty and ten years of absence are lacking. But it seems to me that I have reached that second period of love where there is more intimacy, trust and naturalness.

This evening, having to go four days without seeing her, I saw that all that was lacking from my happiness was a little work.

I hastened to look for work. I haven't got the green notebooks, so I can't work at the *Histoire de la peinture*. . . . I must beware of the pretexts I find for not putting my hand to the trowel. I am like those soothsayers who had to be forced to ascend the tripod. However, I think I'm right this time. This winter, in Paris, I hope to work; but it seems difficult here. . . . I can only work when I am far away from the emotion.[3]

Angela Pietragrua extended her stay at Monza, and he felt that to leave Milan simply to go to Monza would arouse her husband's suspicion. It seemed more natural to spend a few days at Como and visit Monza on his return, "for as long as prudence or rather love allows." On September 16 he hired a carriage and set out. On September 21 he noted: "Anniversary, at almost the same time. . . . Her tears in the cemetery, going round Pellegrini's little temple. She has everything." Two days later, he added: "I have rediscovered all my soul."[4]

He had left Angela at Monza, on the evening of September 21. He had returned to Milan, where, after all, he was working on *Histoire de la peinture*. On Sunday, September 26, wandering round the city, he was overwhelmed by its associations.

I cannot bear the absence of the Comtesse Simonetta. On the way back I called at her house; I learned that her husband left only yesterday to join her and probably won't return to Milan till Wednesday.

Why hasn't she written to me from Wednesday till Saturday? Has she another lover?

I should leave at once for Venice. I should have the pleasure of taking my revenge, whether or not she loves me. But, in either case, I lessen her trust. . . .

Last Sunday, I was at La Framezzina; the other Sunday, with her in her garden. What can I do?

Milan is unbearable to me. . . .

I am leaving this evening for Venice.[5]

"I am very happy with Venice," he told Pauline on October 8, "but my weakness makes me want to be *home* again, that is to say in Milan."[6] No doubt his sister read between the lines of his letter. He had once asked her to look after Mélanie's daughter; now he warned her that Antonio Pietragrua, a boy of fifteen, might be coming to France. "If ever he should write to you, do everything in the world to give him pleasure."[7]

On his return to Milan, he received a letter from Pauline. Dr. Gagnon had died on September 20. He was nearly eighty-five, and he had been ill for some time; but his death weighed on Henri for days. "He had formed my character, to be honest, thinking that he was making me a scholar; but he had given me every care, and I owe him no less gratitude. . . . Since our poor grandfather's death [this to Pauline], you are the only one in the family who loves me."[8]

On his return to Milan, Henri had also received a letter from Angela. She was in Milan again. He found her more beautiful than ever. But she was afraid for his safety. The political situation was tense. In mid-October, Napoleon had suffered a disastrous defeat at the Battle of Leipzig. He retreated across Germany to France. All Germany had risen against the French, and when, on November 2, the Grande Armée crossed the Rhine at Mainz, it had been reduced to 80,000 men. In fifteen months Napoleon had lost two armies. Germany was liberated, and its dispossessed princes had recovered their lands. In southwest France, Wellington was advancing from the Spanish border. In Holland the people were rising against the French officials, and in Italy, Murat—a brother-in-law of Napoleon—tried to save his throne by making an alliance with the Austrians.

It was dangerous for Beyle to stay in Milan. He himself was also aware that he must return to Paris if he were to further his career. On November 10 he noted in his journal: "Charming hours, sweet tenderness, perhaps the most charming hours of this visit." Four days later he left for France.

Fourteen

ON HIS RETURN to Paris, at the end of November, he set about
organizing his future. Since Germany was now liberated, his post at
Sagan no longer existed. He had no wish to return to the army. He
understood that *auditeurs* at the Conseil d'Etat were to be exempted
from conscription, and on December 17 he drafted a letter to the
Duc de Cadore, intendant general of the crown, asking if he might
be exempted on this ground. But the Empire was cracking, now, on
every side. On December 22 the Allied armies began to cross the
Rhine into France. With the Austrian forces advancing through
Switzerland and with Wellington's army in the southwest, they had
more than 500,000 men. Napoleon could muster fewer than 100,000
soldiers to meet the massive Allied offensive. On December 26 Henri
Beyle was appointed assistant to the Comte de Saint-Vallier, to
organize the defence of the Dauphiné. This appointment meant,
ironically, that he would be stationed at Grenoble. He determined
to gain some advantage from such a tedious post. Next day he
wrote to the Minister of the Interior, listing his claims to recognition.
"If," he wrote, "I acquit myself to your satisfaction of the task with
which you have entrusted me, you may present me to his Majesty as
worthy of some distinction."[1]

On January 5 he arrived in Grenoble. Mediocrity always filled him with "invincible disgust," and Grenoble seemed as mediocre as ever. "How can I describe, without reviving my apathy and boredom, the fifty-two days that I spent in this headquarters of pettiness?" He drafted official letters about the movement of French troops, the provision of armaments, food supplies, military pay and political feeling in the district. Saint-Vallier was pleased by his assiduity, but he was concerned about his health. Beyle's "nervous fever" had recurred.[2] On February 27 they left Grenoble; Saint-Vallier was taking up residence at Chambéry. Here Beyle reported to the Minister of Police on citizens with questionable loyalties. He was also sent on a mission to General Comte Marchand, who was attacking Geneva. On March 12 he told Pauline:

> On Monday 14, *le patron* is going to Grenoble, and I am going to La Tour-du-Pin and, from there, to Thuellin. . . .
> I have had great difficulty in getting permission to go. This excellent *patron* is determined to keep me. He really is a good man.
> I shall stay with you for six or seven days, and wait for the capture of Geneva; if the proud ramparts of Jericho do not fall, I shall try to slip to Paris through the Cossacks.[3]

As usual, he showed an erratic concern about his official duties. Considering the gravity of the moment, he showed a deplorable lack of patriotism and responsibility. On March 14 he left Chambéry; on March 27 he returned to Paris. "I am very well and enjoying myself very much, my dear Pauline," he reported, two days later. "The enemy is short of gunpowder. His Majesty is at Langres. Troyes is evacuated." On April 1: "The day before yesterday there was a splendid battle at Pantin and at Montmartre. . . . Everyone behaved well, there was not the least disorder. The marshals did wonders." The wonders were not enough to save the Napoleonic Empire. Henri Beyle was present when the Allied troops entered Paris. On April 6 the emperor abdicated unconditionally.

The next day Beyle assured General Comte Dupont de l'Etang—who was soon to be Minister of War: "M. Henri de Beyle, assistant *auditeur* to the Commissaries of Wars, readily conforms to the acts passed by the Senate since 1 April 1814." He felt no absolute loyalty to the Bonapartes. Like many of his colleagues, he acknowledged the Bourbon Restoration. "I have seen a great spectacle at close quarters," he told Pauline. "It has all gone off with the utmost simplicity. Great and small have followed their own interests without thinking of *what people would say.* . . . I think that your brother will lose his salary. . . . Write and ask the poor devil's father to make him over some property which will bring in a net income of 2,400 francs."[4]

His future was all the more uncertain since the corps of *auditeurs* was probably to be abolished. A few days later he told Pauline, with brotherly candour, that she must lend him 1,200 francs a year so that he could live on a fourth floor in Rome, where his vanity would not suffer; she must also persuade Chérubin to give him an allowance. He hoped that friends would obtain him a small position in Italy, where living was cheaper than it was in France. He could not live in half poverty in Paris. He had 37,000 francs' worth of debts. He was selling his furniture and his cabriolet; the sale would pay for his journey and a few months in Italy.

On May 3, after a quarter century of exile, Louis XVIII (a younger brother of Louis XVI) made his triumphant entry into Paris. There was a rush to seek favours of the new sovereign. On May 23 Henri Beyle asked the Comte de Blacas, the Minister of the King's Household, for the title of *inspecteur honoraire du mobilier:* "It is all the reward I want for fourteen years of service. When I retire to my province, I should not wish to look as if I had been dismissed on the arrival of our king."[5]

It was now, in his last weeks in Paris, at a time of general and personal unrest, that he found himself, once again, capable of intense emotion. On May 26 he recorded:

> I see with pleasure that I am still susceptible to passion. I have just left the Théâtre-Français where I saw *Le Barbier de Séville,* played by Mlle. Mars. I was next to a young Russian officer, aide-de-camp to General Waïssikoff (or something like that). His general is the son of a famous favourite of Paul I. If I had been a woman, this lovable officer would have inspired me with the most violent passion, a love à la Hermione. I felt the first movements stirring within me; I was already timid. I didn't dare to look as much as I wanted. If I had been a woman, I'd have followed him to the end of the world. . . .
>
> If a woman had made an impression on me like that, I'd have spent all night finding out where she lived. Alas! Even the Comtesse Simonetta has only occasionally made an impression on me like this. I think that the uncertainty of my future is increasing my sensibility.[6]

Uncertainty may well have increased Henri Beyle's awareness, but this *coup de foudre,* this sudden, violent love for a man, makes one reconsider his sexuality. Claude Boncompain and François Vermale have seen in him "a clear Freudian fixation on the memory of his mother, which makes him timid. . . . Note his effeminacy, . . : his narcissism, and even his makeup, his wig. He is tempted by homosexuality like Amiel by little girls."[7] Yet this passion for the Russian officer is the only incident recorded in his journal or his letters which suggests that there might have been a homosexual element in his nature. He is not known to have had the slightest physical relationship with a man, nor is he known to have had emotional friendships with men. But no man could have been so susceptible to the nuances of emotion, so appreciative of feeling as Beyle, unless he had had a feminine sensibility.

No doubt the new regime was especially sensitive to criticism; it was afraid of liberal opinion, and it was aware of those whose sympathies might remain with the past. Beyle was viewed, as so often, with suspicion, and his life, in these last weeks in Paris, was carefully observed.

> He very rarely goes to the *salons* [went a police report on May 31] . . .
> He often goes to the theatre and he is always living with some or other actress. When he isn't on a mission, he works four or five hours a day on historical extracts and notes on his travels. . . .
> He lived for a long time with an actress from the opera buffa, but he has apparently broken with her. He never misses a performance at the opera buffa. He spends all his evenings there or at the Théâtre-Français.
> He always has lunch at the Café de Foy, and dines at the [Trois] Frères Provençaux. He is buying a great many books. He goes home at midnight every evening.[8]

He had hoped, in vain, to be given the consulate in Naples; he tried, in vain, to ensure that he was given the consulate in Rome. "I am tired of Paris, not at all angry (I say this for the Beyle of 1820). I was very sick of the job of *auditeur* and of the insolent stupidity of the mighty. Rome, Rome, that is my country. I am burning to go."[9]

The man who had felt sudden passion for a Russian officer had also returned to an earlier love. Angelina Béreyter was forgotten.[10] Now, in the summer of 1814, Beyle had briefly resumed his affair with Mélanie. In his journal, with his usual enigmatic prudence, he recorded: "I have been sleeping for *eight days with the old passion;* as Miss D. is nearer nature, she pleases me more than anything I am leaving behind here."[11]

His friends were content to live in France under the Bourbon Restoration; they accepted the established order. Beyle had always felt profound distaste for the absolutism of the Bourbons; he was an impenitent liberal, and he was still concerned with the triumph of the individual. On July 20—perhaps with the proceeds from his sale—he left for Milan.

PART III

La Chasse au Bonheur
1814–1822

Fifteen

HE REACHED MILAN on August 10. His return was not so triumphant as he wished. The city was full of Sardinian noblemen who were in disgrace with Victor Emmanuel I because they had served Napoleon. Feeling against the French was intense. Twelve days after his arrival, Henri told Pauline: "The Frenchman's presence has excited so much jealousy among Mme. Simonetta's friends that I must go and spend two months in Genoa so as not to compromise her. Write to me there."[1]

One suspects that Mme. Simonetta—Angela Pietragrua—took advantage of politics. As he recognised, she was *un catin sublime;* she organized her love affairs, and no doubt his sudden arrival was inconvenient. However, when he accused her of being unfaithful to him, she wept and created a scene. He capitulated and left Milan.

In Genoa he stayed with the Marchesa Pallavicini. She was the mother of his friend Fabio Pallavicini, *auditeur au Conseil d'Etat.* Her villa, reported Beyle, was 1,200 feet above the sea, and you could see the mice scampering on the ships down below. Mme. Pallavicini invited all the pretty women she knew to entertain him; but he was antisocial, and he remained dissatisfied.

From Genoa he sailed to Leghorn. From Leghorn he went to Pisa, where, in driving rain, he admired the Leaning Tower, the baptistery, the cathedral and the Campo Santo. "I am delighting in my solitude [September 22]. My departure from Genoa lifted an enormous and overwhelming weight from my shoulders. . . . How bored I was with social obligations! And how little I am made for marriage!"[2] When he had settled down for six months and digested the city in which he lived, he would be able to study the human soul.

> Until then, it's impossible. From what I see of work, I should be almost vexed [he slipped into his curious English] *of having been appointed a consul.* I absolutely need all my time and my freedom, fourth secretary at the Embassy in Rome at most. Until then, *I will work with a great pleasure to Peinture.* . . .
>
> At Leghorn, this morning, as I walked along the seawall, I once again felt that inner fire, that aptitude for great things that boredom so completely extinguishes in me, that fire I could not feel at Genoa.[3]

On September 23 he reached Florence, gay and well. He found the city astir with celebrations to mark the return of the Grand Duke Ferdinand III. He dined every day in a cookshop for 35 sous; such economies enabled him to travel. "I have never," he told Pauline, "been so sensitive to the arts, to fine landscapes and all forms of beauty as I have since I've been on short commons." He also became acutely aware of his emotional needs. In the same letter, on October 6, he confessed: "I expected to leave for Rome. But just as I was concluding the deal with the driver, I felt a stab in my heart. As this viscus is very useful in life, I didn't want to push it to extremes. So I'm leaving for Milan in an hour."[4]

Back in Milan, he wrote to Angela. She replied with a formal note, asking him to meet her in a church. On October 16 they met and walked about the city for two hours.

> She told me that since I went fifteen days at Genoa without writing to her, it is all over between us. She told me that the illusion was destroyed; she also told me other things that she would say if she wanted nothing more to do with me. Is it all real? I only doubt it now that I am writing this, an hour after the event. . . .
>
> I have a rendezvous for tomorrow at noon in a room I am to hire. . . .
>
> She was very pretty under her black veil. She told me at the end

that she did not tell me this without regret. That is what gives me a little hope, now I come to think about it. She may have told me that because she saw that I took the break as final. Besides, if she wants to break, why give me a rendezvous tomorrow?

I've thought of ending things, like a fool, with a pistol shot. . . .

Mme. Simonetta told me that I was ambitious, that I was what she loved most, but that I couldn't be in love, that I did nothing to make myself loved. . . .[5]

The next day he confided to Pauline: "I am very troubled and very unhappy. If I break with the Comtesse Simonetta, I shall be grief-stricken. I can't see anything but intensive work to get me through these straits of unhappiness."[6]

He fortified himself by reading Destutt de Tracy. "I see that our misfortunes and our disappointments nearly always spring from contradictory ideas. By reasoning properly, according to Tracy, I am hunting down the contradictions that may still be in my heart."[7] He stayed on at 1175, contrada Belgiojoso. He was constantly disturbed by quarrels and reconciliations. Angela's inconstancy made him more than ever devoted to his sister. "I hope," he wrote, "that our affairs will so arrange themselves that we shall be able to spend our old age together, if we live that long."[8] On January 4, 1815, he added a postscript: "Happy, a thousand times happy, the man who has no passions." A year and more later, he confessed that he had been so unhappy in love, and so disturbed, at this time, by what he considered his father's meanness that he had considered suicide.

> Beaten by the storms of an ardent passion, I was on the point of saying good-night to the world, from 22 December 1814 to 6 January 1815; having the misfortune to be irritated by the Jesuitism of the Bastard, I found myself in no state to be reasonable, let alone lighthearted. So I worked for four to six hours a day, and in two years of illness and passion, I have written two volumes. It is true that I formed my style, and that a great part of the time I spent listening to music at La Scala was employed in harmonising Fénelon and Montesquieu, who share my heart between them.[9]

The volumes in question were the two volumes of *Histoire de la peinture en Italie*.

As the new year opened, Angela once again imposed an exile on

him. "Mme. Simonetta told me that I must be absent for a while. . . .
[She] said that this would spare us a separation once we were
established in Venice. I wanted to plead, but it was useless."[10] In
January, obediently, he went to Turin. He was far from happy, and
his unhappiness became acute when he learned, abruptly, from a
paper, that Mme. Daru had died in childbirth. She left seven
children. She was thirty-seven. "Oh, my dear," he wrote to Pauline,
"what terrible news! . . . She was, after you, the best friend I had in
the world."[11]

On January 28 the *Bibliographie de la France* had announced his first
book: *Lettres écrites de Vienne en Autriche sur le célèbre compositeur Haydn,
suivies d'une vie de Mozart et de Considérations sur Métastase.* The
book—which had been put together in 1814—was published under
the pseudonym of Louis-Alexandre-César Bombet.

Beyle later described his book as "a tap of tepid water." Three-
quarters of the life of Haydn had in fact been taken, shamelessly, from
a recent book by Giuseppe Carpani; it was little more than a translation. The most significant part of the work was the life of Mozart.
Beyle ardently proclaimed his faith in Mozart's genius at a time when
this genius was still not fully recognised. Like Raphael, so he maintained, Mozart had embraced the whole breadth of his art; his name
would last as long as there were men of sensibility. Yet it is clear that
Beyle himself was only moved by Mozart's melancholy. His opinions
were eager, but they were uneducated; as always, he appreciated
music simply as a means of creating mood, of creating that tender
reverie which was one of his own deepest pleasures. It is an illiterate
but Romantic attitude. And Beyle himself is reflected, once again, in
his comparison of musical life in France and in Italy, a comparison
which, as we might expect, is not to the advantage of France. French
music, he observed, existed only in Paris; Italian music flourished in a
number of cities. Any man with a soul must be aware that Italy was
the land of every kind of beauty.

Beyle took little pleasure in the appearance of his book. He was
indifferent to his writing and to politics. On March 5 he learned of
Napoleon's escape from Elba, and his landing in the Golfe-Juan. He
was not tempted to return to France: to fight for the emperor in the
Hundred Days or, on June 18, at Waterloo. He remained in Milan.

"Why should *le Chinois* go back to the rue du Luxembourg?" he asked Pauline in April. "With a father like his, he would have to create more debts, and more difficulties. I shouldn't come back unless the Bastard gave me an allowance; he won't do that, nor shall I ask him to. So here I stay. The death of Mme. Daru takes away all my regret."[12] He continued to ponder the question. "I shall probably stay," he added three days later. "I haven't many regrets about it. The avarice of this tender father will prevent my getting married and wearing the uniform of a *préfet.*"[13]

He was frustrated not only in love and ambition, but in his intellectual life. The censorship cut him off from the literary world.

> I am weary of being without books [he told Pauline]. Write *secondhand books* on the parcel, in several places, and *libri usati*, so that the censor doesn't get hold of mine.
>
> Nothing gets by: letters or papers. I live in utter ignorance. Forgive this scrawl. I'm writing in bed, where I've been kept for a long while by an inflammation of the chest. I have been much weakened by numerous bloodlettings; this will continue, and I want to have books for my convalescence.[14]

On May 30 his younger sister, Caroline, was married to Alexandre-Charles Mallein. "He is a good man," was Henri's comment. "He may help to save us from the ruin into which we are led by the too familiar union of a bad heart and a bad head."[15] His own affair of the heart remained sadly uncertain. On July 11: "Lady Simonetta is determined to make me believe that she is making a sacrifice for me by going to Venice. I was wrong to give her the three thousand francs for this journey all at once." The statement was significant. It was not the first proof in his journal that Angela set a price on her favours. In 1814—enriched, no doubt, by the proceeds of his sale in Paris—he had thought of giving her an annual sum.

On July 12, by way of Verona, he set out for Venice.

> I was [he wrote] a little uncertain about my health, and about the disposition in which I should find the Comtesse Simonetta. . . .
>
> I slept at Verona. Next day by carriage to Padua. . . .
>
> Lady Simonetta had absolutely forbidden me to go to the same hotel. That is exactly what I should have done.[16]

No doubt he should. One can only surmise that Angela had found some casual but tempting lover, for she chose to remain in Padua while Henri went on to Venice. He reached it on July 22. While he waited for her to join him, he sat, one day, at the Café Florian, and there he learned from the newspapers of "the misfortunes and the degradation of France, I mean to say the entrance of the king and his first acts. . . . I shall not," he wrote, "return for a long while to a country without freedom and without glory." He had acknowledged the Restoration for the sake of expediency, but he still detested the absolutism of the dynasty. Long ago, as a child, he had rejoiced in the execution of Louis XVI; now he lamented the restoration of Louis XVIII—a Bourbon imposed on France by the victorious Allies. "It seems clear to me," Beyle added now, "that Venice is the place which suits me best. . . . For the first time in my life I really feel a love for my native land. I don't like the mean Frenchmen of today, but I regret what they might have been fifty years hence."[17] His opinion of his compatriots was, to say the least, erratic. "How fortunate that we lost the Battle of Waterloo!" So he was to write later. "If Napoleon had won, we should still be imbeciles, dazzled by military glory, as we were in 1812."[18]

He was not so happy, now, in Venice as he professed to be. Angela appeared in no haste to join him. On July 25 he returned to Padua. She chose to greet him with "a great fund of tenderness. . . . The Comtesse Simonetta," he noted, "will come to Venice on Sunday. She told me that since she had seen by my letter that Venice suited me better than Padua, she hadn't thought of Padua anymore. What is most remarkable is that this seems to be true. If there were to be such frankness between us, I should have nothing more to desire."[19]

He asked only to believe what he hoped was true. But Angela was no longer the deity for whom he had built his castles in Spain. He was now playing the part for which he had handsomely paid her. On July 27 he wrote coldly:

> I have had her, but she talked a little about our arrangements. There was no longer the illusion of yesterday morning. I had no pleasure in it. Politics kill desire in me. . . .
>
> I am leaving again for Venice this evening. . . . Mme. Gina is coming to Venice on Monday morning (that will give me some pleasant company).[20]

They were in Venice for about ten days. When they left, he was ill; he suffered from constant sweats and from sharp pains in his side. His old illness had recurred. The doctors wondered if he had been recontaminated.[21] No doubt the suggestion caused further quarrels with Angela. On November 1 he told Pauline that he was still under medical care, but he felt small concern about the result. It had taken him a long time to see that he was only a toy in Angela's hands. In November, it seems, her maid informed him "that there was a different lover for every day that he spent in exile." Mérimée, who recorded this, added that Beyle had hidden in a cupboard and seen, through the keyhole, the ultimate proof that Angela was unfaithful.[22]

December brought the inevitable end of his love affair. On December 1 she wrote to him: "You behave in such a way that I no longer feel love or friendship for you. . . . Henceforward we are dead for one another."[23]

For another week or two the arguments continued, but on December 22 she threatened to denounce him to the police —presumably for political activities. He could do nothing, now, but leave her.[24] It was some five years since he had become her lover and some sixteen years since she had first inhabited his dreams.

Sixteen

THE DEITY HAD revealed herself to be made of clay. She had destroyed a part of the mythology by which he lived. And yet, on January 4, looking at the pictures at Brera—where, long ago, he had courted her—Henri already found comfort in philosophy. "I had a veritable transport . . . in recognising the truth of my principles about ideal beauty, and, above all, in rejoicing in my great soul."[1] The favours of women were the only pleasures for men who were not aware of the sublime. Angela's common delights were not for him.

It was, apparently, in July that his ideas took a new, decisive turn. He was introduced to Monsignor Ludovico di Breme, the leader of the Italian Romantic movement. He often spent an evening in Breme's box at La Scala, where literary society assembled. Presumably it was Breme who introduced him to some distinguished English visitors. Aristocratic and civilised, they made him aware of trends of thought in England: of liberal politics and of the brilliant and many-faceted Romantic movement. On September 28, Henri announced to Louis Crozet:

By one of the happiest chances in the world I have just made the
acquaintance of four or five *Englishmen of the first rank and understanding.*
They have illuminated me, and the day when they gave me the
means to read *The Edinburgh Review* will be a great epoch in the
history of my mind. At the same time it is an epoch which is very
discouraging. Just imagine that nearly all the good ideas in *Histoire de
la peinture en Italie* are consequences of general and loftier ideas, set out
in this wretched book.[2]

As André Strauss observes, in *La Fortune de Stendhal en Angleterre,*
England was liberal at a time when France had returned to reactionary ideas. The only periodicals which were recognised to be of
real and general interest were the British reviews. Beyle was drawn
to England by this liberalism, by this determination to develop
individuality. As he read *The Edinburgh Review,* he was tinged with
English radicalism. When he later came to write novels, some of his
characters even seemed to have an English nature.[3]

On September 30, 1816, writing again to Crozet, he was afire with
intellectual and literary plans. He now wanted to write original work.
He thought of returning to *Letellier,*

and trying to write a score of comedies between the ages of thirty-four
and fifty-four. Then I shall be able to finish the *Peinture*. . . . When I
am older, I shall describe my campaigns or write my psychological
and military memoirs. There will be about fifty good characters in
that.

At the Jesuit's death, if I can, I will go in England for 4,000 francs, and
to Greece for the same amount of money, after which I shall try Paris,
but I think that I shall come and end my days in *the land of beauty*. If, at
45, I find a widow of 30 who wants to take a little glory, cash down,
and who also has two-thirds of my income, we shall spend the evening
of life together. If glory is lacking, I shall remain a bachelor.

That's all that I'm doing with my future life. The difficult thing is
not to get indignant with the Bastard and to live with 1,600 francs.[4]

The next day he sent Crozet a note on English Romanticism.

The logical superiority of the English, produced by the discussion
of cherished interests, puts them miles above those poor ninnies of
Germans, who believe anything. The romantic system, spoiled by the

mystic Schlegel, triumphs as it is explained in the twenty-five volumes of *The Edinburgh Review* and as it is practised by Lord Ba-ï-ronne (Lord Byron). *The Corsair* (three cantos) is such a poem for the expression of the strong and tender passions that the author is placed in this genre immediately after Shakespeare. The style is as fine as Racine. *Giaour* and *The Bride of Abydos* have confirmed the reputation of Lord Byron, who is generally execrated as the original of Lovelace. . . . When he enters a drawing room, all the women leave it. This farce was performed several times at Coppet. . . .

He travels accompanied by an excellent pimp, an Italian doctor. He is expected here at any moment, and I shall be presented to him.[5]

On October 13, accompanied by Dr. Polidori, Byron arrived in Milan. Three days later, Beyle was introduced to him. On October 17 John Cam Hobhouse recorded in his diary:

Went to the Casa Roma to dine with Mons. de Breme, who lives in that large palace with his brother, the Marquis. . . .

There was a M. de Beyle, one of Napoleon's secretaries. Unfortunately, I had hardly had a word with him. . . .

It was a very noble dinner in the true style, Byron and I on each side of Breme.[6]

"I have dined with a handsome and charming young man, with a face eighteen years old, although he is twenty-eight, the profile of an angel, the sweetest expression." So Beyle announced to Crozet. "He is the greatest living poet, Lord Byron."[7]

On October 23, in Breme's box at La Scala, Hobhouse met Beyle again—or, rather:

M. de Beyle, one of the *intendants de la mobilière de la couronne,* and secretary of Napoleon's Cabinet, who told us several extraordinary stories. . . .

Beyle was in waiting on Napoleon on the Russian expedition. After the affair of Maristudovitch, and when the cavalry was dismounted, Napoleon quite lost himself. He actually signed 8 or 10 decrees of advancements, or some such things, "Pompey"; and when Beyle took the occasion afterwards to say, "Your Majesty has made a slip of the pen here," he looked with a horrid grimace, and said, "Oh yes," and tore the decree and signed another. . . .

During the retreat he was always dejected; his horse not being able to stand on account of the ice, he was obliged to get off and walk with a white staff. . . . M. de Beyle walked close to him for three hours then; he never spoke a word. . . .

I have every reason to think that Beyle is a trustworthy person—he is so reported by Breme. However, he has a cruel way of talking, and looks, and is, a sensualist.[8]

One wonders if Beyle had in fact been truthful in conversation. He did not commit these recollections to paper; they escaped his letters and his journal, his *Vie de Henry Brulard* and his two works on the emperor. In the dazzling presence of Byron, he was conscious of his bourgeois status. He needed to give himself some distinction. Byron admired Napoleon; it was only natural that Beyle should claim a close acquaintance with the emperor and invent some history to impress "the Lord Bard." He had a store of Napoleonic memories, invented or not. On October 28, Hobhouse continued:

De Beyle told us that the finest day of Napoleon's life was the battle of Borodino. . . . When Napoleon heard that Ney and his corps were saved after having been lost for four days in the Russian campaigns, he jumped up higher, de Beyle says, than he ever saw a man before, with joy; but still, he did not make Ney a prince till he got to Paris, when he told someone: *"Dites à Ney qu'il est prince."*

De Beyle told us that Napoleon, for the latter years of his reign, signed and generally read at an average eighty-five decrees a day. He made the calculation in order to get two more secretaries named, which Napoleon . . . assented to with satisfaction.

Nov. 3. Left Milan with Byron.[9]

Beyle, still in Milan, worked at *Letellier* and sent Crozet instructions for the proofs of *Histoire de la peinture en Italie*. He planned to travel, to study Italian art and Italian music, and he asked a Milanese acquaintance for introductions to art lovers in Rome and Naples. On December 13, by way of Florence, he arrived in Rome, where he was to spend the rest of the year.

He remained unsettled. "Nothing more sublime than the *objets d'art,*" he told Crozet. "Nothing more disheartening than my moral state. I am walking continually from eight o'clock in the morning till four in the afternoon, I go on foot, and with reason. I am so harassed that I sleep from six till eight next morning. For the rest, no nervous attacks in the past eleven days. . . ."[10] His health was uncertain. One wonders if his syphilis again affected him. His financial prospects were gloomy: Chérubin Beyle had lost considerable sums of money in agricultural ventures, and in 1816 Furonières had been sold.

Early in 1817, the question of economy became still more acute. On January 6 Beyle learned of the death of François Périer-Lagrange. He was only forty. Beyle had been fond of his brother-in-law. But he showed a strange lack of sympathy for Pauline. He did not understand the strength of marital love; he did not try to imagine the desolation of sudden and premature widowhood. His thoughts were practical, and they were selfish. "My sister is more overwhelmed than I should have thought," he wrote to Crozet. "She doesn't even tell me if there is a will. Périer had made one which left everything to her, on condition that she paid 90,000 francs to the nephews. That would give her 120,000 or 100,000 francs in an estate two leagues from La Tour-du-Pin, in picturesque woods. With this income of 4,000 francs and Dominique's 4 or 5,000 [Beyle often referred to himself as Dominique], they might make shift to live together in some or other corner. Where will this corner be? In Paris or Milan?"[11]

He continued to make notes on Michelangelo's paintings in the Sistine Chapel, for he still had to write the last chapters of his *Histoire de la peinture en Italie.* On January 13 he sent Crozet "the *Sistine* copied from nature. Stitch that in where it belongs." He was still considering a future with Pauline. He was so enamoured of Italian music that he doubted whether he could ever live in Paris, but this problem would now arise. He was morally obliged to visit Grenoble. "I shall," he wrote, "lose two months without pleasure or profit. What will become of *the good sister?* I shall religiously leave her free, but I think she will see that at thirty-one it suits her to live with Dominique. Their two small lamps together will be able to shed an honest light."[12]

On January 26 he left Rome. Two days later he reached Naples. It was in Naples that he met George Alexander Otis, a sophisticated American from Boston. Otis told him that there would soon be a printing works in the southern United States for the benefit of European liberals. It was a dream for a writer so concerned with censorship.

On March 4, by way of Rome, Beyle reached Milan. He was all too aware of the benefits of a printer in America. Next day, writing to Pierre Didot, the Paris printer, he agreed: "If I absolutely must, I declare that I am the author of the two volumes which you have printed under the title of *Histoire de la peinture en Italie*. I do ask you to see that my name is known as little as possible. I hope, Monsieur, that, according to the existing laws, you are perfectly covered by the preceding information. . . . Having established this, I should like you to put on the title-page of the work: 'By M. Jules-Onuphre Lani (of Nice), printed in Edinburgh.' " Beyle attached a list of those who were to receive his book. They included Destutt de Tracy, Mme. de Staël, Talma, Benjamin Constant and Mlle. Mars; five copies were to go to the editors of *The Edinburgh Review,* one to Hobhouse and one, of course, to Byron. Didot was then to send 600 copies to a bookseller in Geneva, Neufchâtel or Brussels, who might sell them or store them. "I should like to save six hundred copies by sending them out of the kingdom," Beyle explained. "For family reasons I do not want my name to reach the papers. . . . I have no wish at all for a *succès de scandale.*" He was well aware that his book would be politically contentious. Thinking of his contemplated journey to America, he also asked Didot to send two copies to the American ambassador in Paris, one for the former President, Thomas Jefferson, the other for James Monroe, now President of the United States.[13]

George Otis, now in Milan, helped perhaps give him his ideas about English politics. Less than two years after Waterloo, Beyle was not inclined to be an Anglophile, and politically he remained antagonistic. He had not set foot in England, but reading the papers in Milan, he decided:

> Revolution seems to me to be imminent in England. The ministers are behaving as stupidly as a king; instead of yielding *a little* to the very general wish for reform they are increasingly despotic. . . . I believed that America would confute England for us. But they like money too much and they reason too coldly to make war in anger.
>
> England will perish through the stupidity and the egoism of her ministers.[14]

Doris Gunnell claims that Beyle was well informed about English politics; he was, she says, an assiduous reader of English newspapers and periodicals, and he read a good number of the brochures, travel books and memoirs which appeared on England.[15] If this is so, it is all the more strange that he contented himself with the platitudes of his compatriots. He showed little genuine curiosity about the English way of life, English history or the English character. "The Englishman is entirely devoid of all the graces of the mind. He only shines by reason, good sense and logic."[16] Such comments are curious when one reflects how Beyle enthused about English literature and *The Edinburgh Review*. He was delighted to meet Byron and Hobhouse; he referred to Shelley as his friend; he claimed to have met "Monk" Lewis and his sister, Lady Lushington. It was no doubt in Breme's box at La Scala that he encountered Henry Brougham, the brilliant barrister, one day to be the unconvinced defender of Queen Caroline at the hearing of the Bill of Pains and Penalties. In Rome he gladly attended the receptions of Lady Jersey and the Duchess of Devonshire.[17] He had some social glimpses of England, some knowledge of its literature, but he was far from being an informed or an understanding observer.

He spent the second half of April, 1817, in Grenoble. On May 1 he left for Paris. He stayed at the hôtel d'Italie, place des Italiens, and here, from apartment no. 20, he negotiated with the printer of *Histoire de la peinture*. On August 2 the two volumes were announced in the *Bibliographie de la France*. The author was given as "M.B.A.A.": M. Beyle, Ancien Auditeur.

The next day, for the first time, the *ancien auditeur* found himself in London. In his *Souvenirs d'égotisme*, he was to confuse this visit with the visit he made in 1821. But there remains an account by Baron Schmidt, who was one of his companions, and Beyle himself seems to have had a hand in it. The travellers admired the exterior of St. Paul's, strolled happily down Oxford Street and Bond Street and sat in the Green Park to record their impressions. They went down the Thames towards Whitechapel and dined off steak and potatoes and cheese for three shillings and sixpence. They visited several theatres and drank wine with Dessurne, the French bookseller, and for 24 sous, they saw the panorama of Waterloo. Schmidt admired Waterloo Place, and thinking of John Nash's plans for Regent Street, he decided that no town in the world would have anything to compare with it.

Beyle remained in London until August 14.[18] On August 16 he was again in Paris, where he stayed until the end of September. Late in August, from Troyes, Crozet wrote to him in alarm about his forthcoming book. He was as well aware as Beyle of the dangers of censorship, and even in his letter, he did not mention Beyle by name. He prudently referred to him as Dominique (it was the pseudonym which Beyle himself often used). "I have," wrote Crozet, "many things I must say to you about our friend Dominique. He is mad and more subject to illusions than any man in France. I am deeply convinced that *his book shall be denounced.*"[19] On September 13, in spite of Crozet's fears, *Histoire de la peinture en Italie* was published.

Seventeen

Histoire de la peinture en Italie, like Beyle's book on Haydn and Mozart, consisted largely of unacknowledged extracts from other authors, interspersed with original critical comments,[1] and rarely, it must be confessed, was a book on painting put together by a man with so subjective an approach to the visual arts. In his *Portraits historiques et littéraires,* Mérimée wrote later: "The dramatic side of the arts is what we French best understand, and this is probably why Beyle explained beauty by passion.... He seemed to me much less sensitive to sculpture than to painting.... He had small consideration for colourists.... He had profound contempt for Rubens and his school.... He paid very little attention to architecture."[2] Just as Beyle judged music by its ability to inspire his dreams, so he sought in painting only a means of exaltation, and the work of art in which he most clearly recognised the moving image of his secret soul, his memories, his desires and his dreams, always seemed to him the most sublime. As a critic he asked only for an invitation to reverie.

Yet *Histoire de la peinture en Italie* had its significance, for if Beyle said little about art itself, he was among the first to maintain the theory of the social origins of painting. He presented the principles of a *relative taste*—a taste, that is, which was relative to society, to the period and even to the climate in which it had evolved. The theory was not his own invention. In *Réflexions sur la poésie et la peinture,* the Abbé Dubos had set down certain essential ideas which were to mature in Beyle's mind. Dubos maintained that the artist must concern himself, above all, with expression and that colour was a quality of secondary importance. It was a theory which led the critic to turn psychologist. Dubos maintained that despite morality, the artist must have an ardent temperament and that he must understand the passions. Most significant of all, Dubos had discussed the influence of climate, "which makes the Italians . . . more apt to succeed in painting" than the northern peoples; he explained that climates created differences of temperament and that a good artist should discern these differences, not only in the nature of the earth and of the air, but in the social conditions of the nations.[3] This was the theory which Beyle developed not only in his study of the arts, but in *De l'Amour,* in his study of human passions; it was the theory which Taine was to make his own. In 1863, in his introduction to *Histoire de la littérature anglaise,* Taine was to emphasise the importance of physical and psychological factors in cultural and social development. Taine's theory of *la race, le milieu, le moment* helped to establish him as the theorist of Naturalism.

What is most clearly lacking in this ill-organised miscellany, *Histoire de la peinture en Italie,* is some genuine Beyle. Arbelet says that the part of the book which most belongs to him is the lengthy passage on ideal beauty.[4] One also hears the voice of Beyle in the aggressive liberalism which he makes a point of expressing. This history of Italian art is a vehicle for Beyle's own passionate political views. "I should say to the princes of today: 'As king, you are nothing. . . . Recognise that all men are weak when they are tempted by absolute power.' "[5] Painting will be reborn "when fifteen million Italians, united under a liberal constitution, esteem what they do not know, and scorn what they adore."[6] And again: "The brushes are silent [*sic*], but monarchical government . . . opposes masterpieces . . . by destroying the souls of the artists."[7] Beyle attacks not merely the Austrian Empire over Italy, but the government of the Vatican: "All the court know only too well, in Rome, that everyone's first interest is that religion should continue. The Pope behaves well as Pope; but you know that, as sovereign, his only aim is to promote his family. He is a poor old man surrounded by avid people whose one hope lies in his death."[8] Beyle also finds occasion to criticise his compatriots: "The reason for bad taste among the French is infatuation. This is explained by a more serious circumstance, utter lack of character."[9]

Histoire de la peinture en Italie taught its readers little about painting; but it left its mark on criticism, and it was, not unexpectedly, to have its political repercussions.

It was followed, almost immediately, by *Rome, Naples et Florence en 1817,* and here, for the first time, Beyle used the most famous of all his pseudonyms: "M. de Stendhal, officier de cavalerie."

He had been haunted by the police state of the Napoleonic Empire; he had lived in the shadow of Joseph Fouché. Hence the precautions he had taken in his journal, the enigmas in his writing, the prolific use of Italian and so-called English phrases. His friends had many aliases, and he had countless noms de plume—more than 260 in his correspondence—to put unwanted readers off the scent. He took his latest name from a little town in Brandenburg, which lies across the road that goes from Hanover to Berlin. It has been suggested that Stendal struck him because it was the native town of Johann Joachim Winckelmann, the historian of ancient art. But perhaps he simply remembered the name of a place which was a centre of communications. He wrote *Stendhal* as he heard the name pronounced.[10]

Despite its title, *Rome, Naples et Florence* is largely devoted to Milan and Bologna. Once again, Beyle is aggressive: gratuitously pugnacious. In this travel book he cannot escape irrelevant political views. "I find more new ideas in an English page than I do in a French volume in octavo. Nothing can equal my love for English literature, except my repugnance towards Englishmen."[11] And again: "In France, one finds the most remarkable collection of men in the galleys. They have the great quality which is lacking in their fellow countrymen, *strength of character.*"[12] Beyle is both audacious and permanently afraid of the police state, in Italy as in France. "Thinking is dangerous here," observes a Milanese in his book, "and writing is the height of imprudence."[13]

Nonetheless, Milan remains, to Henri Beyle, the intellectual capital of Italy. And it is here, he writes, "that the great art of being happy is practised with this additional charm: that these good people do not know that it is an art, and the most difficult art of them all."[14] And again: "All one can do, in this fine country, is to make *love*. . . . *Love* is delectable here, and elsewhere you *merely find the copy.*"[15]

Years later the final version of *Rome, Naples et Florence* was to give a reflection of Beyle's great love, Métilde Dembowski, "a beautiful version of the charming *Hérodiade* of Leonardo da Vinci." It was she, "with her perfect feeling for the fine arts," who advised him to look at the Duomo in moonlight,[16] and even with his distaste for the Gothic, Beyle admired it. Milan also brought a vignette of Ludovico di Breme, "a tall, very thin young man, dressed in black, . . . sometime almoner of Napoleon, King of Italy, and son of his Minister of the Interior." In Bologna, on December 29, 1816, Beyle records that he was introduced to the Abbé Mezzofante by "M. Bysshe-Shelley, that great poet, that most extraordinary man, so good and so maligned."[17] Unfortunately, Shelley left no record of this occasion or of Beyle.

For all its moments of defiance and pugnacity, *Rome, Naples et Florence* suggests the more endearing qualities of its author. In this book, Beyle abandons himself to the charm of existence, the art of living as he understands it. *Rome, Naples et Florence* reflects not only the Italy of 1817, but a way of seeing and feeling; it reflects what Beyle himself calls "a sensitive soul." In this book the man of feeling and the wit unite. Beyle responds to the naturalness in the Italian character, to the warmth and energy which he did not find in his own countrymen. He writes with an unconcealed love of Italy and of the Italian way of life. Landscape, architecture, social customs, historical anecdotes: he records them with enthusiasm. He does so with much less pedantry, much more coherence than he was to show in *Promenades dans Rome*.

Many years later an Italian angrily observed: "Stendhal loved everything that we detest about our country, he represents everything that displeases us in our past. Italy, the inn of the world, the land of dilettanti, . . . a courtesan Italy for whom we should blush if she had really existed, an antique shop, the bric-a-brac of the Quattrocento and the Roman Empire! No, a thousand times no!"[18]

But if the Italians of the future were to disapprove of Beyle's attitude and of his vision, some of his contemporaries showed a lively appreciation of his new book. One of the most interesting judgments on *Rome, Naples et Florence en 1817* was that of Goethe. On March 8, 1818, writing to his friend Zeller, he sent him two long passages on the composer Jean-Simon Mayer and on music in Italy.

These details [he wrote] are taken from a rare book which you absolutely must obtain. The name is assumed; the traveller is a Frenchman, full of vivacity, passionate about music, ballet and the theatre. These two samples show you his free, audacious manner. He attracts, repels and interests, and in the end one cannot leave him. I always reread this book with fresh delight, and I should like to learn certain passages by heart. He seems to be one of those gifted men who, as officer, functionary or spy, perhaps all three together, have been swept hither and thither by the broom of the war. He has seen a great deal for himself; he also knows very well how to use what he is given, and *above all, he knows very well how to appropriate foreign writing*. He translates passages from my *Voyage en Italie* and maintains that he heard the anecdote from a *marchesina*. In short, it's a book that one mustn't just read. One must possess it.[19]

Eighteen

In October, 1817, Beyle stayed in Grenoble. He disliked provincial life as much as ever. He was aware of the political discontent, the violence, the informers, the mediocrity of authority. But his widowed sister was engaged in a lawsuit, and he was obliged to stay in France.

On November 21, with Pauline, he arrived in Milan. He found her an apartment, introduced her to his acquaintances, and within a fortnight she had three good friends. For the next few months she remained in Milan, losing a little of her sorrow in her comfortable way of life. But here, again, reality did not match the dreams of Henri Beyle. He had professed devotion to his sister, as long as she was safely independent. While she was under her father's roof or married to Périer-Lagrange, he had speculated on setting up house together. He had imagined her, years ago, living with him and Mélanie in Paris; he had imagined her, in widowhood, giving him comfort in his restless bachelor existence. He had, one suspects, considered such arrangements from a largely selfish point of view. He wanted her constant admiration, her financial assistance. But Pauline was to be left far from rich on her husband's death; for the rest of her days she was to depend on her brother or her sister. And

Henri was now set in hs ways; he wanted independence. Mme. Périer, he wrote, harshly, "had all the virtues and she was pleasant and sensible enough. I was obliged to break with her in order to shake off this annoying oyster which was stuck to the keel of my ship."[1] It is not clear whether this break (if it actually occurred) took place after Pauline's first visit to Milan, in the spring or early summer of 1818, or after her second visit, in 1821. In *Le Coeur de Stendhal*, Henri Martineau suggests that it was in 1821, after Beyle's return to Paris, that she suggested coming to live with him, and he categorically refused.[2] He did not finally quarrel with her, and all his wills were made in her favour; but his comment on her reveals, all too clearly, his violent and inexorable egotism. Years later, after Beyle had died, his cousin Romain Colomb wrote sadly: "Friendship has its rights and its obligations. . . . Beyle was especially aware of the rights. . . . Beyle did very few services compared with the number which he received." [3]

In the meanwhile, in November, 1817, he settled down delightedly to his familiar Milanese routine. He read till two o'clock, walked till four, and dined at five. At seven he paid a visit or two; at eight he appeared in his sister's box. Some of his friends would join him there, and he would make his little tours of La Scala until midnight; then he would come home and read in bed until one o'clock in the morning.[4] He was not only reading, but working on another book. It was no doubt his distaste for the France of Louis XVIII which crystallised his feeling for the emperor and led him to begin his *Vie de Napoléon*.

"We have shown Napoleon with the features that seem to emerge from the most faithful accounts; we ourselves lived for several years at his court." So he wrote in the last chapter of his work. But for this final statement, one would hardly surmise that the author had held any official position under the emperor. The most striking feature of *Vie de Napoléon* is indeed its objectivity. Beyle records Napoleon's life from his birth until the Hundred Days—with a brief reference to Waterloo. He presents him as a hero—and yet no account of a hero could be more dispassionate. He discusses Napoleon's massacre of his prisoners at Jaffa, his poisoning of the sick and wounded at Saint-Jean-d'Acre, and his execution of the Duc d'Enghien. He criticises his despotism. His political errors might, wrote Beyle, be easily explained: he was always afraid of the people and he never had a plan. He had a ridiculous craving for the imperial crown and for the panoply of a court. On the other hand, he recognised the nature of the French people. "The French are indifferent to liberty," Napoleon had said. "They do not understand it or love it. Vanity is their only passion; and political equality, which allows every one of them the hope of attaining every position, is the only political right which concerns them." Never, thought Beyle, had a truer observation been made about the French nation.

Vie de Napoléon adds nothing to Beyle's literary reputation. It is a draft which he clearly intended to enlarge and revise when the political climate allowed. In the event, like so much of his writing, it remained unfinished.[5]

The beginning of 1818 found him, as usual, absorbed by Italian opera and by musical and theatrical gossip. He was also ardently keeping pace with literary progress. "I am burning to receive by post No. 56 of *The Edinburgh Review*," he told Mareste on January 25. ". . . If every month I had three conversations with you and an *Edinburgh Review*, I should be happy."[6]

One element was clearly lacking in his life: the element of love. He was soon to find it. Angela Pietragrua was now a stranger to him; but he enjoyed rewarding friendships with Luigia Cassera and with Elena Vigano, and no doubt, it depended only on him to make them more intimate. Elena was the daughter of Salvatore Vigano, the choreographer. She was twenty-four, she sang delightfully, and in February he formed the habit of going to her *salon* to hear her sing. She had already had an unhappy and dramatic past; all the women of Milan detested her because—so he explained—she could assemble fifteen men every evening and forty men on Fridays. He himself was clearly charmed by her, until he first set eyes on Matilde Dembowski.

Nineteen

MATILDE WAS TWENTY-EIGHT, the daughter of Carlo Viscontini, a Milanese of old bourgeois family.[1] At the age of seventeen she had married Jean-Baptiste Dembowski, a Polish army officer—naturalised Italian—who was twenty years older than herself. He was General Baron Theodore Lechi's chief of staff at Naples. On his return from service in Spain in 1810, he had been promoted general of brigade. In 1814, the year before his retirement, he had become commander of the garrison at Milan. He had brought his military glamour to the marriage; Matilde had brought 150,000 francs and a noble nature which, perhaps, was of less concern to him. Dembowski had given her two sons, Carlo and Ercole; but in 1814 she had fled from a husband who beat her and was frequently unfaithful, and she had taken refuge in Switzerland with her younger son. There she had met another exile, the poet Ugo Foscolo. Dembowski accused her of being Foscolo's mistress. Paul Arbelet, who read her letters to Foscolo, surmised that their relationship had been platonic, but the letters revealed her pride and her anguish. She had stayed more than a year in Berne. In June, 1816, she had returned to Milan on condition that she lived apart from her husband. She found that he was determined to take Ercole from her, and she want back to Switzerland.

Henceforward, "to feed her ardent soul, and perhaps to escape the brutal love of men, ... Matilde dreamed only of liberating her country."[2] It needed liberation from Austrian domination. Lady Morgan, visiting Milan in 1820, noted Austrian sentinels outside government offices and Austrian officers smoking cigars outside coffeehouses. The audience at La Scala was sprinkled with Austrian uniforms, and "every door was doubly guarded by foreign soldiers." Italy seemed "little more than a great prison, guarded at all its barriers by Austrian armies, headed by Austrian chiefs."[3]

Early in 1818, Matilde Dembowski had settled in the piazza della Galline, in Milan. Then she moved to the piazza Belgiojoso. It was there that Beyle came to know her.

Her face revealed a Lombard beauty: exquisitely oval, lit by two dark, timid, melancholy eyes. She had the majesty, the strength of character, the fire that he had sought unceasingly. When they first met, on March 4, 1818, he fell overwhelmingly in love with her. His relationships with Elena Vigano and Luigia Cassera were sacrificed in order to deserve that she should love him. "The lover would rather dream of the woman he loves than receive from an ordinary woman all that she can give."[4] Henri Beyle's love for Matilde—Métilde, as he called her—was the great love of his life.

From the first moment, Métilde kept him severely at a distance. She recognised the feelings of this obese and balding suitor, and she was not drawn to him. "Even now," he wrote long afterwards, "after an interval of so many years, I can still only guess the motives for her behaviour. She was openly dishonoured, and yet she had had only one lover [*sic*], but the women of good society in Milan took their revenge for her superiority. Poor Métilde could never outmanoeuvre this enemy, nor could she disdain it."[5] But the truth was all too plain, and it was bitter. Métilde did not love him. And there were other reasons, too, for her cold politeness. She was, one surmises, too disillusioned by men to take a lover. Besides, this inexplicable French expatriate had been a government official under Napoleon. She knew that he was politically suspect, and involved as she was in politics, she could not afford to show him more than civility. She did not intend to make herself a subject for gossip. She was, so Beyle himself believed, encouraged in her views by her cousin Francesca Traversi. This seems very probable. Signor Traversi was violently anti-French; in 1814 he had helped to instigate the Milan Revolution, in which the minister

Count Giuseppe Prina had been murdered. Francesca had actively supported her husband's politics. She was not likely to welcome a Frenchman. Beyle himself had refused to meet her because of her political views, but he had committed a worse error. She was renowned for her easy virtue and for her malice, and he had not merely ignored her as a woman, he had chosen to visit Luigia Cassera and Elena Vigano. Francesca took her revenge by telling Métilde that he went with prostitutes.[6]

"We who have the inappreciable fortune to be passionate must try to uproot the passions we shall probably be unable to satisfy."[7] So he had written, once, to Pauline. He must have known, from the beginning, that he could not satisfy this passion. It was, as Henriot observed in his *Stendhaliana,* "a great and useless love."[8] But Beyle loved too much to be wise. His passion thrived on Métilde's severity, in his melancholy reverie. It eclipsed all other feeling.

He continued to work as much as he could on his *Vie de Napoléon* and on a second edition of *Rome, Naples et Florence.* He was also anxious to take part in the debate on Romanticism which now absorbed intellectuals in Milan.

The young Italian writers were campaigning fiercely for the principles which had been maintained by Mme. de Staël. It happened that their theories were precisely those which Beyle had set down in his books, the theories that he had rediscovered, much developed, in *The Edinburgh Review.* He was in complete agreement with the Italian Romanticists; he frequented them and joined in their discussions. It was a way of showing that he had become Italian.

In the spring of 1818, the Romantic conflict was raging in Milan; it was to grow still more intense in the autumn and winter that followed. Early in 1819 Beyle was to note that "the word 'romanticism' has even reached those classes of society which know nothing about literature."[9] Romanticism, in Italy, was already more than a literary creed; it was a sort of modernism, tinged with liberal ideas. Rossini was declared to be ultra-Romantic. "We do not know the music of the Greeks," wrote Beyle, "and at La Scala we shouldn't listen for a moment to the music which delighted our fathers in 1719."[10] In the first months of 1819 he was to write several fragments on aspects of Romanticism. When, a few years later, he published *Racine et Shakespeare,* his Romanticism had remained Italian.

On April 2, 1818, he was once again in Grenoble, where Pauline's case against her husband's creditors was being judged. Repeatedly he wrote to Mareste. Writing took the place of conversation, and the recollection of Milan kept him, for a time, from the provincial reality of Grenoble. "I spend an hour or two," he wrote, "in the box of M. Louis Arborio de Breme, son of the Breme who has an income of 200,000 livres. He is a friend of Mme. de Staël, of M. Brougham, a witty man, the leader of the Italian Romantics. By the way, the war of the Romantics and the Classics is raging furiously in Milan; they are the *greens* and the *blues.* Every week, some lively brochure appears. I am a wild Romantic, that is to say, I am for Shakespeare against Racine, and for Lord Byron against Boileau."[11] He grew increasingly concerned with the English Romantics. On May 1 he asked a Parisian bookseller to post him all the novels reprinted in English by Firmin Didot. "Let's try with four volumes of Walter Scott, in English, by post each month." The same day he asked Mareste to arrange for the complete *Edinburgh Review*—more than fifty volumes—to be sent to him.

On May 4, still from Grenoble, he told Mareste that Pauline had lost her case and that they were appealing to the Court of Cassation. He added: "At last I am leaving tomorrow, the 5th. I am getting out of this country *hating* and breathing in *assassination.* . . . The English books have arrived in Milan and in my library. The opera is pleasing. I believe it's Weigl's *Il Rivale di se stesso.* I shall enjoy it on May 12 unless Mont-Cenis swallows me up."[12]

On May 11 he returned to Milan. He delighted in Vigano's ballet *La Vestale* at La Scala. The moment when the heroine was buried alive was, he said, as powerful as Shakespeare. He welcomed the English books which Mareste was sending him. "Your English opuscules were the delight of *the happy few,"* he told him in a letter on July 15. "Good-bye. Think a little about my poor finances and about my *curiosity."* His financial worries remained acute: in August he wrote twice to the Minister of War, asking for half pay or a pension.

On August 25, with his friend Giuseppe Vismara, a Milanese advocate, he set out for the mountains of the Brianza. They travelled to Asso, where "the tortuous little streets, with their steep and slippery surfaces, reminded me," wrote Beyle, "of la Madone del Monte in 1811, when I was so mad about La Gina."[13]

The journal makes it plain that he was far from well. He had pain in his arm, his thigh and his left leg. He was in a highly nervous state. He was sufficiently concerned about his health to tell Mareste: "When I don't have *nerves,* that is to say, four times a week, I am happy."[14] Perhaps his nervous condition owed something to his painful and growing love for Métilde.

The expedition to the Brianza ended on August 31. It had been a brief escape from anxiety. Now the anxieties only grew. His father still refused to send him money, and the Minister of War refused him half pay or a pension. On September 3 he told Mareste that if there were a political change in France, he might try to obtain a post in Paris. "It is a hard decision, but you know the wolf comes out of the forest."[15]

His financial straits made him think of preparing another edition of *Rome, Naples et Florence en 1817.* It would no doubt have soothed him to know that his books already reached a select but appreciative English public. This September, staying with Lord and Lady Lansdowne at Bowood, Maria Edgeworth, the Irish novelist, reported that "the book sur la peinture by Mr. Beyle alias Count de Stendhal diverts Lord Lansdowne every evening delightfully. It is so conceited—so absurd and yet such sparkling mica of talent."[16] The Count de Stendhal had already earned Miss Edgeworth's benevolence by sending her a copy, and she returned the compliment by despatching her two-volume novel *Leonora.*[17]

On October 5 Beyle left Milan for La Tremezzina. He was, by now, obsessed with love for Métilde. The day before his departure, he drafted a letter to her.

> I am very unhappy, I seem to love you more every day and you no longer feel for me the simple friendship which you used to show.
> There is a very striking proof of my love, and that is my awkwardness when I am with you. It makes me angry with myself, and I

cannot overcome it. I am brave until I reach your salon, and the moment I catch sight of you, I tremble. I assure you that no other woman has inspired me with this feeling for a long while. It makes me so unhappy that I should like to be compelled not to see you any more. . . .

I am leaving tomorrow, I am going to try to forget you if I can, but I'm setting about it badly, because I couldn't resist the urge to see you again this evening.

My great occupation all today has been to seek the means of seeing you without being imprudent.

I love you much more when I am far away from you than I do when I am in your presence. When I am far away, I see you indulgent and good to me; your presence destroys these sweet illusions.[18]

At La Tremezzina he had a room overlooking Lake Como. In the evening there was a gay social life, very *musicante,* he reported. During the day, in his letters to Mareste, the literary arguments continued. The correspondence went on from Varese, where he found himself on November 14. To Mareste, an old and trusted friend, he did not mention Métilde. Two days later he wrote to her. His letter reveals his increasingly desperate attempts to forget her and to find emotional stability.

Madame,

I should like to write you a rather entertaining letter, but I spend my life with good bourgeois who concern themselves all day with the price of wheat, the health of their horses, their mistress and their money. Their vulgar happiness and their easy contentment make me envious. . . .

The liveliest pleasure I have had today is that of dating this letter; I hope, in a month, to have the pleasure of seeing you. But what shall I do for these thirty days? I hope that they will pass like the nine long days which have just gone by. Every time an entertainment or expedition is over, I fall back again on myself and I find a frightening void. I have criticised a thousand times, I have given myself the pleasure of hearing another thousand times the slightest things that you said on the last days that I had the happiness of seeing you. My weary imagination is beginning to reject those images which, henceforward, are too bound to the terrible idea of your absence, and I feel that my heart is growing more sombre every day.

I have found a little consolation in the church of the Madonna del

Monte; I remembered the heavenly music that I heard there once before. I am going to Milan, one of these days, in search of a letter from you, for I count enough on your humanity to believe that you won't have refused me a few lines, so indifferent for you to trace, so precious and consoling for a heart in despair. . . . I know myself. I love you for the rest of my life. Nothing that you do will change in the least the idea that struck my soul, the idea that I have formed of the happiness of being loved by you, and the scorn that this has given me for all other happiness. In fact I need, I thirst to see you. I think that I should give the rest of my life to speak to you for a quarter of an hour about the most trivial things.

Farewell, I leave you to be more with you, to dare to speak to you with all the abandon, all the energy of the passion that devours me.

HENRI[19]

As the new year, 1819, opened, as spring turned to summer, his passion continued to bring him desolation. On May 12 Métilde left Milan to visit her sons at San Michele college, in the little Etruscan town of Volterra. Her departure overwhelmed him. His emotional life was centred in her, in the sound of her voice, even in the brusque disdain, the unconcealed dislike which she accorded him. She had forbidden him to follow her to Volterra, but he needed her physical presence, the expectation, the recollection of her; he needed her in his imagination. Now, for a month and more, she would be gone. On the afternoon of her departure he wrote to her. His letter had the formal beginning which she would accept and the warmth of feeling which he could not restrain. It had to be drafted and carefully corrected; it reflected all his uncertainty and humility.

Madame,

Oh! how heavily time weighs on me since you have gone! And it is only half past five! What am I going to do for these forty mortal days? Should I abandon all hope, and leave, and throw myself into public affairs? I'm afraid I might not be brave enough to pass Mont-Cenis. No, I shall never consent to put the mountains between you and me. Can I hope, by force of love, to revive a heart which may perhaps be dead to this passion? But perhaps I am ridiculous in your eyes, my timidity and silence have annoyed you, and you considered my visits a calamity. I hate myself; if I were not the last of men, should I not have had a decisive explanation yesterday, before you left, and seen clearly what I must expect?

When you said, with the accent of a truth profoundly felt: *"Oh! thank goodness it's midnight!"*, was I not to understand that you were pleased to be delivered from my importunities? Should I not have sworn to myself, on my honour, that I would never see you again? But I am only brave when you are far away. In your presence, I am timid as a child, the words die on my lips, I can only watch you and admire you. Must I find myself so dull, so inferior to what I am?[20]

Beyle believed in behaving naturally; he believed that only spontaneous conduct could touch the heart. He knew that a man could best succeed if he were himself. In his passion for Métilde, he ignored all that wisdom had taught him, all that common sense and instinct dictated. In his writing, he showed himself sensitive to the slightest tremors of feeling, the most subtle nuances of emotion; in his behaviour to Métilde he was self-conscious, clumsy and unnatural. He watched himself break every rule that he had recognised. He despised himself, and he was helpless.·

On May 24, twelve days after her departure, he left Milan. He did not plan—so he later told her—to visit Volterra; he was not bold enough to risk her displeasure. He found that Leghorn was near Volterra; he learned that from Pisa he could see the walls of the town. It was unwise to venture so near, but he had no time for wisdom. As he sailed southwards down the coast, his passion, predictably, overcame him. Beyle, the analyst of love, the gifted theorist of passion, was driven to behave like an adolescent. He decided that if he changed his clothes and wore green-tinted spectacles, he could well spend two or three days at Volterra. He would go out only at night, and Métilde would not recognise him.

On June 3 he arrived at Volterra. She was the first person he saw. It was one o'clock; she had no doubt just left the college and she was going back to her house to dine. She did not see him. At quarter past eight that evening, when it was dark, he took off his spectacles, so as not to seem eccentric. As he took them off, she passed, and his plans were ruined.

I thought at once [he explained to her]: if I approach Mme. Dembowski, she will say something harsh to me, and at that moment I loved you too much, a harsh word would have killed me. If I approach her as her friend from Milan, everyone in this little town will say that I am her lover. And so I shall show my respect for her much better if I remain unknown. All this reasoning took place in the twinkling of an eye; and this was what guided me all through Friday 4 [June]. I can swear to you that I did not know that the Giorgi garden belonged to your house.[21]

Métilde had in fact forbidden him to follow her to Volterra. She was understandably angered by his disregard of her wishes, by his invasion of her privacy, by this compromising visit from an unwanted suitor. No doubt she felt even more contempt for him since he followed her so furtively and in so ridiculous a disguise. She should have dismissed him months ago; she should have dismissed him now. Perhaps it still suited her to have a desperate admirer at her feet. As it was, his mistaken visit was made more complicated by misfortune and by his own tortuous reasoning. On the night of June 4 he lay awake considering his next move; he thought he would present himself as her oldest friend.

I was very proud of this idea [so he later told her]. . . . [I decided]: I shall go and write her two letters so that, if she wants, she can explain my arrival to her friends here, and receive me. If she doesn't want to, she will answer *no*, and it will all be over. . . .

I confess, Madame, and perhaps I risk displeasing you by my confession, that so far I see no want of delicacy.

You wrote to me in a very harsh manner; you believed, in particular, that I wanted to force your door, which hardly seems to be in my character. I went to meditate about it all outside the town gate at Selci. . . . I wanted peace and quiet to devote myself to my thoughts. And so it was that I was led to the field where you later came. I leant against the parapet and there I stayed two hours, looking at the sea which had brought me close to you, and in which I should have done better to end my destiny.

You will observe, madame, that I was completely unaware that this field was your customary walk. Who could have told me that it was? . . . I saw you arrive; I immediately began a conversation with a young man who was there and I was going off with him to see the sea on the other side of the town, when M. Giorgi approached me. . . .

I was very happy but, at the same time, very timid. Had it not been for the resource of talking to the children, I should certainly have compromised myself. It was much worse when we went into the college: I was going to find myself face to face with you and see you perfectly—in a word enjoy the happiness which had kept me alive for a fortnight, the happiness which I dared not even hope. I was on the point of refusing it at the door of the college. I did not feel strong enough to bear it. As I went up the stairs, I could hardly endure it. . . . I saw you at last; and from that moment until the moment I left you my ideas are confused. . . . Such is the unhappy destiny of loving souls; one remembers sorrows in their smallest details, and the moments of happiness sweep the soul so completely out of itself that they escape the memory.

The following evening I saw clearly, when I approached you, that I had displeased you. Could it be possible, I thought, that she is in love with M. Giorgi? You gave me the letter which began *Monsieur*. I could hardly read anything else in the letter, at the college, except that fatal word, and I was in the depths of despair in the place where, the previous evening, I had been wild with joy.[22]

On Monday, June 7, he answered her letter.

Madame,
You cast me into despair. You accuse me several times of lacking in delicacy, as if, from your lips, this accusation was unimportant. . . .

Oh, madame, it is so easy for the man without a passion always to behave with circumspection and prudence. . . . A force more powerful than all my resolutions drew me to the place where you were. I see it too clearly, this passion has become henceforth the great affair of my life. All interests and all considerations have paled before it. This unhappy need I have of seeing you impels me, dominates me and transports me. There are moments, on long solitary evenings, when I should be a murderer, if I had to murder to see you. . . .

Love me if you will, divine Métilde, but, in the name of God, do not despise me. This torment is more than I can bear.[23]

Métilde continued her ruthless coquetry. On the evening of June 7, as they left the San Michele college, she leant ostentatiously against Giorgi. Beyle was overcome by consternation and grief.

I thought that there was nothing left to do but go. I thought I would simply make a formal call on you, on the evening before my departure, when the chambermaid ran after me in the garden, where I already was with M. Giorgi, and cried: "Madame says that she will see you at the college this evening." It was for that reason alone that

I went there. I thought that you were indeed mistress to love whom you chose; I had asked you for an interview so that I could express my regrets for being importunate, and also perhaps to see you at my ease and to hear the sound of that delightful voice, which always echoes in my heart, whatever the meaning of the words it utters.[24]

It seems that Métilde, ruthless as ever, finally persuaded him to go, by promising to see him in Florence. No sensible man would have trusted her promise, but on June 10 Beyle left Volterra. The next day, from Florence, he begged her forgiveness for his "lack of delicacy and respect. . . . My repentance is sincere; since I have displeased you, I wish I had never gone to Volterra. I should have expressed this profound regret to you yesterday, when you deigned to admit me to your presence; but, allow me to say so, you have not accustomed me to indulgence."[25]

She was not to show him indulgence now. It was ten days before she answered. He remained in Florence, in the torrid heat of June and July, reading Scott. On July 20 he wrote, bitterly:

Madame,
   Perhaps, in my position of disgrace, it may seem very unbecoming that I should dare to write to you. If I have become so odious to you, I want at least to try not to deserve my misfortune any longer, and I beg you to tear up my letter without going further.
   If, on the contrary, you want to treat me as an unhappy friend, if you deign to send me your news, would you write to me at Bologna, where I am obliged to go: *Al signor Beyle, nella locanda dell'Aquila Nera.* I am really worried about your health. Would you be so cruel, if you were ill, as not to send me a word? . . . I am very unhappy.
                                                      HENRI[26]

Two days later he reached Bologna, to find unhappiness of a different kind. There were letters waiting for him, to tell him that Chérubin Beyle had died on June 20. One of the letters contained a copy of his will: "a kind of manifesto against poor Henri." The manifesto was hardly surprising: Henri had never concealed his antipathy to *le bâtard.* But he had constantly dreamed of the day when his father would die and he would become his heir.

By August 10 he was in Grenoble. His visit there was lightened by a letter from Métilde—presumably a letter of condolence. To him it was a fine day in the heart of a fetid desert, and utterly harsh as you are to me [he answered], I still owe you the only moments of happiness which I have found since Bologna. I think unceasingly of that happy city where you must have been since the 10th. My spirit wanders through a portico that I have often passed, on the right as you go out of the gate. I see unceasingly those fine hills crowned with palaces which form the view from the garden where you walk. Bologna, where I have received no harsh treatment from you, is sacred to me.[27]

To Métilde, who for a moment, seemed less harsh to him, he wrote—a strange tale—of his father's hatred for him. Chérubin had made him his heir, but he had left little but debts. Henri's dreams of handsome horses and of distant travels would not now be fulfilled, and "I should have been bitterly disappointed," so he told Métilde,

if all these tastes . . . had not long since disappeared to give place to an unhappy passion. I deplore this passion today simply because it has led me, in its madness, to displease what I love, and what I respect more than anything in the world. Everything else on earth has become completely indifferent to me. . . .

Farewell, madame, be happy. I believe you cannot be happy unless you love. Be happy, even in loving someone other than myself.[28]

The intransigence of Métilde and the death of his father had brought him to a watershed in his life. It was clear that he might need to change his mode of existence, perhaps to find a sinecure in Paris. It was, perhaps, with this in mind that on August 30 he wrote to Pierre Daru, announcing Chérubin's death. "My father has left enormous debts," so he explained. "If I am left with an income of 4,000 francs *en terre,* I shall go back and live in Milan; if I am not, I shall go to Paris for the humble task of soliciting."

He was, in fact, finally left with 3,900 francs.[29] On September 18 he arrived in Paris. He was tempted to stay there and solicit some or other position. But the thought of Métilde was too strong. "As long as you are yourself," he wrote to her, "I shall live only for you."[30] On October 14 he set off, once again, for Milan.

He reached it on October 22, and the next day he called on her. She rebuked him fiercely for the letters he had dared to send her—no doubt from Volterra and Grenoble. Del Litto has suggested, convinc-

ingly, that these letters had not been merely expressions of love:
Beyle might have slipped in some observations which would have
compromised her in the eyes of a censor. Métilde, after all, was in
league with the patriots who were conspiring against the "paternal"
Austrian government.[31] She was disturbed by the curious ways of this
Frenchman who pursued her, who prowled at night beneath her
windows, hoping to see her raise the curtain, so that he could follow
her with his eyes. She also found his passion politically dangerous.
She did not dismiss him, because his absence would have caused
speculation, but she limited his visits to one a fortnight. He begged to
be allowed to visit her once a week, but she refused.

Since she forbade the slightest allusion to his love, he did not know
where to turn for relief. Early in November, he decided to present
their respective situations and his own emotions in a novel—a novel
written for her alone, to be read by her alone. Since a passionate letter
would be returned, this seemed the only means of moving her which
now remained to him. He worked at it for a morning; then he rightly
abandoned it as ineffectual.[32]

On December 27 he found himself in a salon where they happened
to be discussing love. The conversation inspired some ideas, and he
jotted them down on a concert programme. On December 29—his
"day of genius"—he thought of making a book of his reflections. He
threw himself into a task which constantly brought him back to
Métilde.

Some might be surprised by his acceptance of unrewarded vas-
salage, but, as La Rochefoucauld had said, "one knows more happiness in the passion one feels than in the passion which one inspires."
More than once Beyle affirmed this belief as his own. So it is that all
resentment and bitterness have vanished from De l'Amour. Beyle
delights in the depths of his despair. It is a surprising phenomenon,
but it is characteristic of his sensibility. Beyle always draws a purer
and more vital poetry from his griefs than he does from his happiness.
De l'Amour was a confessional, inspired by the most profound,
unhappy and significant love of his life. His disappointments in love,
it is said, are as beautiful as operas by Mozart, for he enriched them
with all his imagination.[33]

Twenty

BEYLE'S RETURN TO Milan in the autumn of 1819 had made him more aware than ever of differences in the intellectual climate. Writing to Mareste on December 21, he assured him that the French style which they knew was unintelligible in Italy. He was particularly concerned with the Romantic movement which—though felt in Italy and long triumphant in England—had not yet been fully appreciated in France.

He spent his evenings in Milan with Vincenzo Monti, the elderly epic and dramatic poet, and with Rossini, whom he steadfastly admired. "All things considered," he told Mareste, "I prefer extraordinary men to ordinary ones." He delighted, as always, in the music of Cimarosa and Mozart, and no doubt made restless by the cruelty of Métilde, he dreamed of travel. "I shall go to Paris in September," he informed Mareste on March 3, 1820. "I shall certainly have some money, but not much; perhaps I shall wait until 1821 to go as far as Edinburgh or even New York. . . . I should spend six months there and then come back. One can do it . . . quite cheaply." The ambition persisted. On March 21: "I often dream of going to spend six months in Edinburgh or in Philadelphia. An inhabitant of that city [presumably George Otis] has shown me that you can lead a nice little philosophic life there for a hundred dollars (500 francs) a month."[1]

In one of his fragments on Romanticism, Beyle had observed that "the great geniuses in America turn straight to the *useful.* That is the character of the nation."[2] The observation was fair, and yet, he thought, it would be pleasant to be known there. It occurred to him that his *Histoire de la peinture* might be translated into English, as his book on Haydn had been. On March 21, from Bologna, where he was spending a few days, he urged Mareste to have new title pages printed for the book, giving the name of Beyle and the rank of *auditeur;* thirty of these title pages must be sent to Dessurne, the French bookseller in London, to be attached to copies which he had yet to sell.

Beyle was happy in Bologna, for Métilde had been there, and it was still hallowed by her memory. "Bologna pleases me very much," so he told Mareste. "I shall be in my ordinary lodgings on 1 April. . . . If you haven't sent the epistle to Thomas Moore, discard the old one, here is a new one."[3] This "new epistle" was perhaps the covering note which was addressed to Moore with three copies of Beyle's book. "The friends of the charming author of *Lalla Rookh,*" wrote Beyle, "must be aware of the arts. No doubt they are among that *happy few* for whom alone I have written, very vexed that the rest of the human rabble should read my dreams. I beg you, sir, to present these three copies to your friends."[4] Beyle was increasingly anxious about his reputation in England. On March 25 he also wrote to Dessurne:

> I have some idea of spending several months in the singular country where you live. In order to have an adjective to add to my name, I consent to be the author of *Histoire de la peinture,* which No. 64 of *The Edinburgh Review* treats all too kindly.
>
> If, by chance, this work were accorded the same honour as the others, I should be pleased to see my name on the title page of the translation. That would open the artists' studios to me, and I particularly hope to be concerned with them in England. . . . I am sending you new title pages for the copies which may remain; I should be glad if you would attach them.
>
> You can give free copies, done up like this, to Murray, Colburn, Longmann [*sic*]. Give them in fact to the publishers whom your firsthand knowledge of London tells you might be interested in a translation.
>
> But the respect I owe myself forbids me to do anything whatever to

instigate this translation, and I only think of putting my name to it so that I can be received by MM. Say, Lawrence, and other artists who are men of talent.[5]

The next day Beyle explained to Mareste: "If I can collect 4,000 francs, I shall not go to Paris, but I shall go to England in 1821; and there, with an adjective to my name, I may overcome the pride of some of those aristocrats and see the fine things that they hide away in their *country seats.*"

On March 26 he arrived in Mantua and reported on his Bolognese visit. He had, he said, been promptly introduced to society in Bologna. If he had been ten years younger (he was two months past his thirty-seventh birthday), he would have done marvels. "The women measure up a man for you in three minutes, and they do well, and our Paris prudes are very stupid, as I am getting ready to prove in my learned dissertation called *De l'Amour.* If one does not have the happiness to feel *l'amour-passion,* [one must] at least have physical pleasure, and, if one deprives oneself of this for two years, one loses ones skill at it."[6]

He had not denied himself such pleasure. On February 8 he reported to the same correspondent that he was in love with a woman who had given him blennorrhagia.[7] On March 21 it was still troubling him. But though he seems to have satisfied his passing physical needs he remained enthralled by Métilde, and he continued to work on *De l'Amour.* Back in Milan he continued to revise it. On June 12 he promised that Mareste would have the two volumes immediately. He authorised him to correct and print them. The printing was a complex affair: there were to be 150 copies of the complete manuscript. Then seven or eight passages must be suppressed. They were, explained Beyle, "the life of one of my friends who has just died of love here, and they would make people recognise me." One hundred and fifty copies of the revised version were to be printed, and only these were to be sold. The unrevised edition was to be carefully kept for four or five years, when the facts would no longer be remembered. It might then be put on sale. Beyle added the list of those who were to receive the revised edition. They included Destutt de Tracy, Moore, Talma, Chateaubriand "and two or three Englishmen of distinction." The chapter on fiascos was to be cut out of certain copies, and these expurgated copies were to be sent to Mlle.

Mars, the Duchesse de Duras, and various other "fashionable women of easy virtue." Beyle's instructions presented a curious mixture of cynicism and indifference, of delicacy and concern. The letter was not sent to Mareste for two months. On August 8 he finally despatched it with the postscript: "I have been ill, and then calumnied, that is what has delayed my correspondence."[8]

On May 21 he had gone to see the gardens at Belgiojoso; he had developed inflammation of the lungs. His illness was not serious; but it was protracted, and it left him weak. He was more vulnerable than usual to anxiety, and now he had good cause to be disturbed. On July 12, in his would-be English, he ended a long letter to Mareste: *"I am worried because the consul of Milan has said that I am a periculous liberal* and it is known that Dominique had made the [*Histoire de la*] *Peinture."*[9] On July 23 he added, in profound anxiety:

> I have just had the greatest misfortune which could befall me.
>
> Some jealous people (for who does not know them?) have circulated the rumour that I was here as the agent of the French government.
>
> This has been circulating for six months. . . . What a terrible blow! For what in fact is this Frenchman doing in Milan? The Milanese will never be able to understand my philosophic life, and accept that I live better here with 5,000 francs than I do in Paris with 12,000. . . .
>
> I am too disturbed to write about anything else.[10]

Beyle's situation in Milan grew increasingly delicate. Revolution had broken out in Piedmont, and the Austrian government was prosecuting Italian liberals. Silvio Pellico was imprisoned by the Milanese police. It was indeed hard to explain why a Frenchman who had been in government service should choose to lead the life of a dilettante in Milan. It is easy to see that this apparent *farniente* might have seemed a cover for political activity. At a time of tension and suspicion, liberalism was dangerous, and liberals included all those who maintained democratic rights under the Austrian occupation: all those who wanted to change the established order for expressed unorthodox and radical views. Milan was not the place for an aggressive liberal like Beyle, who liked to publicise his opinions.

Claude Boncompain and François Vermale suspect that he belonged to the secret service of the Duc de Decazes, who was then the French ambassador in London. He had, they suggested, informed the duc about Queen Caroline, the estranged wife of George IV, who was living her scandalous life on the shores of Lake Como. "He is a secret agent, whom M. Decazes kept in Milan, who kept watch on the Queen," we read in a police report of July 2, 1820.[11] The suggestion seems far-fetched, but it gained some credence when George IV had his Milan Commission at work, gathering evidence of his wife's infidelity.

It seems more probable that Beyle's imprudent letters and his controversial *Histoire de la peinture* had made him suspect to his friends and to Métilde. But, whatever the truth, the suspicions remained. His letters to Mareste were intercepted. The liberals considered that he must be a French spy; the Austrian police believed that he was an informer and a carbonaro. "The harm is done," wrote Crozet to Mareste, "and I don't see what we can do to put it right. . . . Once a suspicion like this has been expressed, it cannot be entirely uprooted. His status, his money and his way of life were certain to arouse suspicion, and it would also be a skilful move by the Austrian police to discredit him among the liberals whom he certainly frequented more than anyone else."[12]

It was no wonder that Beyle had aroused suspicion. He was far from open. He was still afraid of censorship, still driven by his love of mystery. He continued to sign his letters with whatever pseudonym came to mind, to date them from wherever caught his fancy. On October 20 he told Mareste that he was in Lucerne and had just been reading Byron on the lakes. In fact, he remained in Milan. He urged Mareste to write to him in a similar guarded manner. "Never name anything in your letters, from time to time the essential word in English, and for the rest write whatever comes into your head." But it was clear, from the same letter, that Beyle was more serene. For the moment, at least, the slander about him had died down. He had also sent Mareste by post, by way of Strasbourg, the manuscript of *De l'Amour*.[13]

On November 4 he made a blunt and touching request: "What is the best way to dye grey hair black or dark brown? This is very important to me." He was afraid of age, and he had not lost his vanity. He also reminded Mareste to send the proofs of *De l'Amour*.[14] Two days later he sent him a few thoughts to add to the second volume. On

November 13 he confessed: "I begin to be anxious about the two red[-bound] volumes which were at Strasbourg on October 7. You should have received them."[15] On December 4, increasingly anxious, he asked a friend in Paris to make enquiries about the mail from Strasbourg. The new year opened. "I am mortally weary of *De l'Amour*," he told Mareste on February 23. "If I have to redo a manuscript from all the indecipherable notes I threw into a bag six months ago, I shall die."[16]

As for Métilde, who had inspired the work, she showed him unrelenting disdain. He had drafted a letter to her marked *"to send the 3 janvier 1821."* It is a pathetic measure of their relationship.

> Madame,
> Would you find it unseemly if I dared to ask permission to see you one evening for a quarter of an hour? I feel overwhelmed by melancholy. . . . You can trust yourself, without danger, to the generosity of your noble soul.—I shall not be indiscreet; I do not claim to say anything to you. I shall be pleasant. I am, with respect,
> DOMINIQUE[17]

"I shall be pleasant." The phrase suggests occasions on which he had been unable to hide his despair. Métilde would have been much kinder to dismiss him long ago; it is surprising that she had allowed him to continue even his regulation visits. But perhaps she took a certain pride in the persistent worship of this man to whom she gave no charity, let alone affection. The longer he continued his visits, the more she despised him, but she was not averse to admitting him, once a fortnight, to her presence to earn the pity of other guests, to find still more cause for unhappiness, to fix her still more clearly, still more firmly in his mind as his ideal. There was no hope that she would ever change.

From his earliest childhood, he had always found it hard to bid farewell; now, on April 1, he told Mareste, in a mixture of French and English that he had decided to return to Paris. *"I have enfin took* la plus pénible résolution *in all my life, that of coming back to Bruxelles's hotel."*[18]

Political pressure, advice from friends, the failure of his love for Métilde had conspired to lead him to this decision. He was finally brought to it by a letter from Grenoble which left him more anxious than ever about his finances. Even now he wondered if he would be strong enough to carry out his resolution. The thought of leaving Milan threw him into a turmoil. Next day he told Mareste:

> *I send to the fire a letter just written to you. I will be with you somewhat toward the middle of May. The hunger brings the wolf out of the forest. . . . I should have only three poor thousand a year.*[19]

On April 14 he wrote again: *"Dominique will be with you in a month. . . . He leaves with the greatest regret to have a try at Lutèce; when he has made the experiment, if he finds nothing he will return gladly to the land he loves."* [20]

On May 18 he wrote to the dilatory lawyer at Grenoble who was winding up his father's estate. He repeated his approval of the projected sale and gave him directions for sending money to Paris. On June 6 he announced to Mareste "that the bitter departure of Dominique from the finest country in the world will take place about 15 June. And you will see him on the 23rd. . . . Let M. Petit know about a room."[21]

Only Métilde could now have kept Beyle in Milan. Next day, June 7, she said good-bye to him without regret. She had known him for three years; she had left a branch in the depths of his imagination which would crystallize for the rest of his life. It would coruscate in *De l'Amour* and irradiate novels yet unwritten.

On June 13, 1821, Beyle left Milan.

Twenty-one

His DEPARTURE HAD something almost clandestine about it. He left so hurriedly that he did not even take his books and papers. Eleven years later, in his *Souvenirs d'Egotisme,* he was to recall how he had left Milan with 3,500 francs; he had believed that his only pleasure would be to shoot himself when this sum was spent.

> I found it very hard to resist the temptation to blow my brains out.... It seems to me that political curiosity prevented me from making an end of it; perhaps, without my suspecting it, it was also the fear of hurting myself.
> I finally took leave of Métilde.
> "When will you come back?" she asked.
> "Never, I hope."
> There followed a final hour of vacillation and vain words, one alone could have changed my life....
> I finally left in a state which may be imagined.... I went from Milan to Como, fearing at every moment and even believing that I should turn back.
> I thought I could not stay in this city without dying; I could not leave it without feeling that my soul was torn away. It seemed to me that I was leaving my life [behind me] there—for, indeed, what was life beside Métilde?[1]

Henri Beyle. From a portrait by Boilly, painted in about 1810.
Grenoble Museum.

Pauline Beyle (Mme. F. Perier-Lagrange), the favorite sister of Henri Beyle. Stendhal Museum in Grenoble.

Photo Piccardy.

Victorine Mounier. Stendhal Museum in Grenoble.

Photo Piccardy.

Photo Piccardy.

Dr. Henri Gagnon (1728–1813). From an oil painting at the Stendhal
Museum in Grenoble.

Henri Beyle at twenty-four from a crayon portrait by Kennedy drawn
in 1807.

Henri Beyle in consular uniform. From the portrait painted by Silvestro
Valeri in Rome, 1835–36.

Photo Piccar

Henri Beyle, August 8, 1841. This pencil drawing by Henri Lehmann
is the last known likeness of him.

Mme. Pierre Daru, portrait by Jacques Louis David (1810).

Detail showing Salome in painting by Luini of Salome receiving the head of John the Baptist. In this "Salome," Beyle saw a striking likeness to Métilde Dembowski.

Uffizi Gallery, Florence.

Clémentine Curial (1788–1840). From a terra-cotta bust in a private collection.

Photo Piccardy.

Giulia Rinieri de' Rocchi (1801–1876). After the portrait by Gaetano Ricasoli, 1831. Private collection.

Photo Piccardy.

"France has always displeased me," he wrote, "especially the environs of Paris, a fact which proves that I am a bad Frenchman." His heart sank as he left the mountains of Switzerland for "the terrible, flat misery of Champagne." Langres reminded him of Volterra, a town which he still loved, "for it had been the scene of one of my boldest exploits in my war against Métilde." It would, he thought, be the worst misfortune if the cold-hearted French were to guess his passion—a passion for a woman whom he had not possessed. This fear was to be the guiding principle of his life for the next ten years. "I arrived in Paris," he recorded, "which I found worse than ugly, insulting to my grief, with a single idea: *not to be guessed.* After a week, observing the political emptiness, I said to myself: Profit from your grief and kill Louis XVIII."[2]

In his *Souvenirs d'Egotisme* Beyle wrote this final phrase in abbreviation: "t. l 18." The idea was astonishing, but Henri Beyle, who had served under Napoleon, had always detested the Bourbons. Beyle, the man of feeling, had suffered many nervous attacks in the past few years, and never in his life, one suspects, had he suffered so violently as he did now. His grief was all the more violent for repression.

He controlled himself and lived the next few months in the hôtel de Bruxelles in the rue de Richelieu. He lived them in a kind of dream. He overwhelmed his Milanese friends with letters to obtain some indirect news of Métilde, but they disapproved of his folly and did not mention her. He was not to see her again. Yet when he thought of her, nothing destroyed the crystallisation inspired in him by "the proudest little head in Milan." Such was his power of self-delusion that he sometimes wondered if perhaps she had loved him.

She died of consumption on May 1, 1825, four years after she had said good-bye to him. When he learned of her death, he wrote in his copy of *De l'Amour,* underneath the date, the words: "Death of the author."

He could later recall very little of the summer and early autumn of 1821. His thoughts remained in the piazza Belgiojoso. He had always lived from day to day, not thinking of the morrow. The progress of time had been marked for him only by Sundays, when, for some unknown reason, he had always been irritable and bored. "In 1821, in Paris, Sundays were really horrible for me. Under the great chestnut

trees of the Tuileries, so majestic at that time of year, I thought of
Métilde, who always spent that day with the opulent Mme. Traversi.
That fatal friend, who hated me, was jealous of her cousin. She had
persuaded her . . . that she would be completely dishonoured if she
took me as her lover."[3]

Beyle had gone to the hôtel de Bruxelles because Mareste lodged
there. Mareste, in his mid-thirties, had the maturity of a man who
was twenty years older. He was still a bachelor, still free to give Beyle
much of his time. He now became his constant companion, and they
saw each other twice a day. Some said that Beyle made him "a kind of
appendix, a supplement to his own person."

In *Souvenirs d'Egotisme* Beyle himself maintained that "if chance, or
a little prudence, had [now] led me to seek the society of women,
despite my age, my ugliness, etc., I should have found success and
perhaps consolation." As it was, love gave him "a very comic virtue:
chastity."[4] His friends attempted to cheer him by arranging an
evening with some women of easy virtue. He was overcome by the
thought of Métilde, and he could not make love. His friends considered that he must have become impotent, and he did not lose this
unfortunate reputation until Mme. Azur described, virtually in
public, the accomplishments of Henri Beyle, her lover.[5] It is clear,
now, why he could not make love to a courtesan, but he always
suffered from his timidity. This timidity was the cause of his fiascos. It
is one of the reasons why he possessed only a few of the women he
desired.

> I have very few memories of those days [he wrote, later]. . . .
> Everything that pleases in Paris filled me with horror. A liberal
> myself, I found the liberals outrageously stupid. . . .
> The gross Louis XVIII, with his ox-eyes, drawn along slowly by his
> six gross horses, whom I constantly encountered, gave me particular
> horror.
> I bought a few plays by Shakespeare, an English edition at 30 sous
> a volume, I read them in the Tuileries and I often set down the book
> to think about Métilde. The interior of my solitary room was dreadful
> to me.[6]

He was mortally weary of Paris; he wanted a sea voyage, and he longed to see a performance of Shakespeare. Shakespeare was now the only author whom he could read, and he needed a cure for melancholy. "I had to put a hill between myself and the sight of the cathedral at Milan, Shakespeare's plays and the actor Kean were this event."[7]

On October 18 he pocketed the little money which remained to him, and he left for London. In the Calais diligence he met an engaging Englishman, Edward Edwards, who had been in Wellington's army of occupation. Beyle recognised his courage and his modesty, and he appreciated his literary conversation on the long and monotonous road to the coast. When they reached Calais, Beyle was already strangely relaxed, "drunk with gaiety, chatter and beer. . . . That was my first infidelity to the memory of Milan."[8]

On October 19 he arrived in London. He stayed at the Tavistock Hotel, Covent Garden, a hotel frequented by well-to-do provincial visitors. London, he wrote, "touched me very much because of the walks beside the Thames towards Little Chelsea. . . . There were little houses there, adorned with rose trees. . . ." During the day he often went to Richmond and admired the view of the Thames. "There is nothing to equal the freshness of green in England, and the beauty of its trees. . . . The view of Richmond, and that of Windsor, reminded me of my dear Lombardy, the mountains of Brianza, Desio, Como, la Cadenabbia, the sanctuary of Varese, the fine landscape in which I spent my fine days." One Sunday, at Windsor, he attended a church service, and he was moved by the singing of the psalms.[9]

One wonders if, on this visit, he called on John Murray, who published the English translation of his *Vies de Haydn et Mozart.* One suspects that he made his appearance in Albemarle Street. As Murray's biographer observed, there was then no Athenaeum. "That institution was only established in 1823. . . . Until then, Murray's drawing-room was the main centre of literary discourse in that quarter of London. Men of distinction from the Continent and America presented their letters of introduction to Mr. Murray, and were hospitably entertained by him."[10] Beyle would not have been averse to meeting the man who published his own work and that of Byron.

Soon after his arrival, he was "infinitely amused" by a performance of *She Stoops to Conquer.* He also saw Edmund Kean in *Richard III.* The prospect had made him "leap for joy." For years he had felt unbounded admiration for Shakespeare. "My passion for him does not grow," he had written in 1810, "simply because it cannot be any greater."[11] He was so angered, now, by the alterations to the text that he sent a ponderous broadside to *The Examiner:* "When a modern pretender resolves to give us his own paltry sentiments instead of the great thoughts of Shakespeare, I detect the last stage of the ridiculous. . . ."[12]

Beyle's outburst was published on November 26. Five days earlier he had left London. He had set Shakespeare between himself and Milan cathedral; he had also set a woman between himself and Métilde. In Westminster Bridge Road, *un quartier perdu,* Miss Appleby had given him "the first real and intimate consolation for the misfortune which poisoned all my moments of solitude."[13]

He arrived in Paris on November 24. Soon after his arrival, he found that another misfortune might be forgotten. He finally retrieved the manuscript of *De l'Amour.* It had been lost in the post for a year.

He was now confident enough not to need the company of Mareste at the hôtel de Bruxelles. At the end of the winter, or early in the spring of 1822, he moved to the hôtel des Etats-Généraux, 36, rue Sainte-Anne. In June or July he moved again: this time to the third floor of the hôtel des Lillois, 63, rue de Richelieu. On another floor lived Giuditta Pasta, the Italian prima donna, and her lover. Mme. Pasta was twenty-five; Beyle found in her the Italian virtues he admired, and they became devoted friends.

The year brought another change in his life. It was in 1822 that he began to contribute to English periodicals. In January he became a contributor to the *Paris Monthly Magazine,* and in November he began to write for *The New Monthly Magazine.* It was then a distinguished publication. Cyrus Redding, in his memoirs, was to look back nostalgically to the time when "M. Beyle, Leigh Hunt, Mr. Turner of the Foreign Office, Himalaya Frazer, Brown of Florence, Wrangham, and Dodd of the Temple, had been of our number."[14] Martineau says that from 1822 to 1828, Beyle earned most of his additional income from English magazines.[15]

He not only intensified his work as a journalist; he also resumed his life as an habitué of the salons. Now that the great emotions of the

Empire had subsided, people felt a need to form into groups, a need to belong. A new society was taking shape, and the salons once again opened their doors. The Restoration saw the renewal of an ancient and respected tradition. Parisian salons reflected a need for social elegance; they mirrored the intellectual, literary and artistic preoccupations of the time. No one needed the stimulus of mixed company and intelligent conversation more than a restless bachelor like Beyle.

He was not always a welcome guest. His friendship with Mme. Pasta (one doubts if it was more) proved to be his undoing with M. de Tracy.

> In the rue d'Anjou, which was really my most respectable society, not even old M. de Tracy, the philosopher, forgave me for my liaison [*sic*] with an actress. . . .
> I was going to give all the friendship in my heart to the Tracy society, when I noticed a white surface frost. From 1821 to 1830, I was only cold and machiavellian there, that is to say, perfectly prudent. I can still see the broken stalks of several friendships which were going to grow again in the rue d'Anjou.[16]

There was another social failure. Claude Fauriel, the critic and historian, introduced him to Mary Clarke and her mother. Mary—who later married Jules Mohl, the Orientalist—had been born in London in 1793; she had inherited Scottish blood from her mother, and Irish from her father. Mrs. Clarke had often gone to France to escape the English climate, and after her husband's death she had settled, with Mary, in Paris. They were installed there by 1814; they finally made their home in the rue du Vieux-Colombier, where Mary's Irish vivacity, her knowledge of English literature, of German and Italian, and her love of France drew many friends. Among them was Prosper Mérimée, who brought Victor Hugo. From the end of 1821 to the end of Beyle's Parisian years, Mérimée was one of his intimates. But some friendships are made impossible by chemical reaction. Mary Clarke reported to Fauriel: "I cannot bear M. Beyle." When she learned that he was writing a book about love, she was "revolted by the idea that his filthy paw should touch such a subject." The dislike was mutual. Beyle expressed himself quite as frankly when he deigned to talk about her.[17]

He found himself much more at home in the rue de Chabanais,

where, every Friday, Emmanuel Viollet-le-Duc, the writer and functionary, gathered his friends together. Among the habitués were Saint-Marc Girardin, the anti-Romantic critic, and Sainte-Beuve, still in his teens, one day to be a warm supporter of the Romantic movement. The conversation was animated: the quarrel between Classic and Romantic had now become quite lively in France, and some of the guests at the rue de Chabanais gathered behind the banner of the iconoclastic Beyle.

> He used to say, then, to anyone who cared to listen to him, "that, like many others, he had long thought that he would enjoy himself by going assiduously to the Théâtre-Français; but that, during a visit he had made to England, the works of Shakespeare had unsealed his eyes and opened his mind, and from that moment Racine had seemed to him an insipid poet." Beyle constantly developed this theme with the most amusing verve and apparent conviction. Even the friends of Viollet-de-Duc who might have been most shocked had grown accustomed to this sophism, and smiled at it as they would have smiled at a spoilt child.[18]

As it happened, Beyle's conviction was not apparent, but real.

He was not only a regular guest at Viollet-le-Duc's; he also knew his brother-in-law, Etienne Delécluze. Delécluze, two years older than Beyle, was an artist in the classical tradition, but while he accepted the narrow inflexible doctrines of the historical painter Jacques-Louis David, he showed himself, in life, to be a man of catholic tastes. Artist, historian, novelist, art critic in *Le Journal des Débats,* he was also an inveterate reader of the classics, an admirer of Dante, Petrarch and Chaucer, a lover of the works of Handel, Gluck and Palestrina.

Salon was perhaps too grand a word for the attic in which, every Sunday, at two o'clock, he received his literary friends. In February, 1822, Beyle first climbed the ninety-five steps to meet the ardent, controversial guests whom Delécluze gathered round him. The attic was adorned with *objets d'art* and dominated by a portrait of Richelieu. The most distinguished visitors shared a red sofa by the fire. Delécluze's friends were constantly recalling the political revolution and hoping to bring about the emancipation of litera-ture; they constantly affirmed the need to encourage the two revolutions together. Delécluze himself watched Beyle with amusement: "The more unreasonable he was, the wittier and the more amusing he became." He revelled in sophistry and paradox, and he was extremely anxious that everyone should talk. This was not surprising. Since he had contracted to write for an English magazine, "he felt the need to frequent some of the houses in Paris where people knew all that was happening and being said. . . . After the *session*, as he went downstairs with his confidant, he would sometimes say: 'I haven't got anything, have you?' Or, when his harvest had been good, he would exclaim with pleasure: 'My article is done!' "[19]

In the summer of 1822, Beyle began to be "a little reborn to the things of this world." He managed, now, not to think of Milan for five or six hours in succession. This was all the more remarkable since on May 1 he had signed a contract with Mongie for the publication of *De l'Amour*. In June and July he was correcting the proofs, and on August 17 the two volumes were put on sale.[20]

Twenty-two

"Love has always been the greatest thing to me—perhaps the only thing." So Beyle once confessed, and he asked that the word *amo* should be engraved on his tomb. It was almost inevitable that he should write a treatise on the passion which brought him sporadic happiness, exquisite agony and countless hours of study, longing and reflection. In *De l'Amour* he set down his cherished thoughts, his personal beliefs, and the whole science of happiness to which he attached such profound importance. He considered it his most important work; perhaps he preferred it to the rest not so much for the theories it contained as for the memories which filled its pages.

Critics have often chosen to see him as a cynical libertine. *De l'Amour*—like his letters to Métilde—proves how faithful he remained even when he knew that he was unloved. Beyle had a hearty appetite for physical love, but he often said that he enjoyed tender reverie more than anything else on earth. Nothing is more delicate, more tender than his reflection: "The greatest happiness that love can give is the first time that the woman you love clasps your hand."[1]

In fact, love gave him a pleasure like that of music, a pleasure which inspired his imagination. He talked of love like a musician; he talked of music like a man in love. *"Ave Maria* in Italy, hours of tenderness, of

the pleasures of the soul and of melancholy: emotion intensified by
the sound of those lovely bells. Hours of pleasure which hold the
senses only by memories."[2] Beyle understood the poetry of the inaccessible. His almost religious exaltation of the privileged moment
owes much to Rousseau. Like the author of *La Nouvelle Héloïse,* he has
a cult of those rare, ineffable, evanescent hours. This legend of
"impossible" love remains at the heart of all his work. In his
mythology of love, it is not physical intimacy that matters; it is inner
tension and desire. In his novels, love was to be the great affair of his
heroes' lives. But this affair was only significant because it involved
the deepest energies of the soul.

In *De l'Amour,* Beyle hardly touched the subject of physical love; the
thought of Métilde prevented his doing so.[3] He did not reduce love to
a mere imaginary feeling, but he still tried to sublimate it as far as the
study of love allowed. This reserve, this loftiness of thought revealed
the Cornelian side of his nature. In *De l'Amour,* with tact and discre-
tion, he analysed the only kind of love which, in his eyes, deserved the
name of *amour-passion.* He gave an exact description of "a sort of
madness which is very rare in France": a kind of love which, so he
claimed, appeared ridiculous to his compatriots. Sainte-Beuve was
later to object to Beyle's denigration of love in France. "One of his
great themes . . . is that love is virtually unknown in France: love that
is worthy of the name, as he understands it, *l'amour-passion.* . . . But
when I see what this *amour-passion* becomes in these narratives from
Beyle's pen, I return to loving and honouring love in the French
way."[4] Sainte-Beuve was indignant, but *De l'Amour* was not French in
spirit; it was, as Beyle observed, a study of the Italian soul.

It has been said that one practises love rather than dissects it. Two
lines in a dictionary will define it; what one adds is theory or
pornography. Beyle had kept his childhood taste for mathematics
and for demonstrations based on sound definitions. And so he chose
to classify four kinds of love. He was clearly not interested here in
physical love, or in *l'amour de vanité* (love for the sake of status), or in
l'amour-goût (an elegant passion in eighteenth-century style). He was
only concerned with *l'amour-passion:* "that of the Portuguese nun, that
of Héloïse for Abelard," and with its seven phases.

First the soul felt admiration; then it thought of the delights of
giving and receiving love. Then followed hope. "One studies the
perfections. It is at this moment that a woman should surrender, for

the greatest possible physical pleasure." Then love was born, and "loving means to enjoy seeing, touching, feeling with every sense, and as close as possible, someone lovable who returns our love." Then began the first crystallisation.

> One delights in adorning with a thousand perfections a woman of whose love one is sure; one catalogues all ones happiness with infinite complacency. . . .
> Let a lover's mind work for twenty-four hours, and this is what you will find:
> In Salzburg they throw a branch of some or other tree, leafless from the winter, into the abandoned depths of the salt mine; two or three months afterwards they take it out again covered with brilliant crystallisations. The tiniest twigs, which are no larger than a tomtit's leg, are adorned with an infinity of diamonds, mobile and dazzling: one cannot recognise the original branch any more.
> What I call crystallisation is the operation of the mind, which draws from everything that appears the discovery that the beloved has new perfections.[5]

This idea was not new when Beyle wrote De l'Amour. It could be found in the moralists, whom he read attentively. It was Chamfort who suggested that love only loves the perfections it supposes. But though the idea was in the air, Beyle made it his own by giving it his own precise and eloquent image.

He rightly placed his theory of crystallisation at the beginning of his book. It helped him to explain all that he had experienced in love. His own memories and observations illustrated the process of crystallisation, just as they would later, in his novels, illuminate the loves of his protagonists. But, so he wrote, this happy, complacent state of crystallisation could not last, and doubt arose. When the lover felt sufficiently encouraged, he wanted more positive assurances of love. He was rebuffed. The moment of intoxication was over. The woman was afraid that she had been immodest. Perhaps she withdrew from prudence or from coquetry. Then the lover came to doubt the happiness he had promised himself. He turned to the other pleasures of life and found that they were destroyed.

> There follows the second crystallisation. . . .
> Every quarter of an hour in the night which follows the birth of his

doubts, ... the lover says to himself: "Yes, she loves me.". ... Then doubt with haggard eyes takes hold of him. ... He cannot breathe; he asks: "But does she love me?" Caught between these harrowing and delightful alternatives, the poor lover feels acutely: "She could give me pleasures that she alone could give."

It is the evidence of this truth ... which makes the second crystallisation so superior to the first.[6]

Beyle goes on to speak of the birth of love in innocence and isolation—a theme which he was to enlarge in his short story "Ernestine." Man, he continues, is bound to do what gives greater pleasure than any other possible action. Love is like fever, it comes and goes independent of human will; this is one of the principal differences between *l'amour-goût* and *l'amour-passion.*

Crystallisation, says Beyle, almost never ends in love; the second crystallisation is much stronger in women than it is in men because their fear is more acute: vanity and honour are compromised, and distractions are more difficult. Women have no demanding tasks to occupy their minds, they tend to abandon themselves to their imagination, and they prefer emotion to reason. Briefly—all too briefly—Beyle indicates the difference in the birth of love in the two sexes. It is different because the hopes are different: one attacks and the other defends; one asks and the other refuses; one is bold, the other is timid. In man, the hope depends on the actions of the woman he loves; nothing is easier to interpret. In woman, hope must be founded on moral considerations which are difficult to appreciate.

Léonore is the name which Beyle gives to Métilde in *De l'Amour.* Time and time again the book reflects his own absorbing passion, and sometimes, suddenly, a cry escapes him: "I make every possible effort to be *cold.* I want to silence my heart, which believes that it has much to say. I am always afraid that I have written only a sigh, when I think that I have noted a truth."[7]

He reflects on the nature of beauty. "But what is beauty? It is a new aptitude to give you pleasure." And since pleasures vary according to the individual, crystallisation must always take the colour of the pleasures of individual men. It would seem (and here, again, he is dreaming of Métilde),

> it would seem that by some strange, bizarre action of the heart, the beloved communicates more charm than she herself possesses. The image of the distant city where one briefly saw her casts a deeper and sweeter dream than her actual presence. . . . Every great poet who has a lively imagination is timid, that is to say, that he is afraid of men because of the interruptions and disturbances they can bring to his delightful dreams. . . . It is by the habit of feeding his soul with touching dreams, and by his horror of vulgarity, that a great artist is so near to love.[8]

Yet love is so intense that when, in the midst of the most violent and most thwarted passion, one suddenly believes that love has ceased, it is like a source of sweet water in the midst of the ocean.

It was not a source from which Beyle chose to drink. A few lines later he noted:

> I have just understood this evening that music, when it is perfect, puts the heart in exactly the same situation in which it finds itself when it rejoices in the presence of the beloved; that is to say, that it gives what seems to be the liveliest happiness that exists on earth. . . .
>
> Now, this evening, I cannot hide from myself that I have the misfortune *of being too great an admirer of milady L[éonore].*[9]

Beyle remained enough of a mathematician to suggest that a man's mistress promised him "a hundred units of happiness"; he remained cool enough to explain how, in love, even ugliness could acquire its beauty. But analyst though he tried to be, he remained an incurable Romantic, and he remained the afflicted suitor of Métilde. "When a man has felt his heart beat at the distant sight of the white satin hat of his beloved, he is quite astonished how cold he feels at the approach of the greatest beauty in the world." And again, a few pages later, he gives a sad self-portrait:

> In one's first conversations with the woman one loves, there escape a multitude of things which have no meaning, or have a meaning contrary to what one feels; or, more poignant still, one exaggerates ones feelings, and they become ridiculous in her eyes. . . . And yet one cannot be silent because of the embarrassment of silence, during

which one could think about her even less. And so one says with great
feeling a mass of things which one does not feel and which one would
be most embarrassed to repeat; one stubbornly refuses her presence so
as to be more with her. . . .

I understand cowardice and how conscripts get out of their fear by
throwing themselves blindly into the battle. The number of stupidi-
ties I have said in the past two years so as not to be silent casts me into
despair when I think of them.[10]

The whole art of love, it seems to him, is to speak according to
ones soul—yet when a man who truly loves hears kind words from
his mistress, he will be incapable of speech. The man in love must be
natural—and yet, in the presence of his beloved, even his physical
habits seem forgotten. "When I gave my arm to Léonore, I always
seemed to be about to fall, and thought of walking properly. All
one can do is never to be deliberately affected." Love, writes Beyle,
lives on doubt. "Always a little doubt to still, that is what creates perpetual thirst."[11]

In the first volume of *De l'Amour* he had explained the inner
workings of *l'amour-passion*. He had shown how love appeared and
evolved in the human heart. In the second volume, he studied the
external conditions which modified *l'amour-passion*. Among them
were climate, government, temperament, sex and marriage. In this
second volume, much less finished, much less coherent than the first,
he discussed—on strangely inadequate evidence—the character of
love in different nations, at different periods in history; he also
pleaded—and here he is remarkably modern—for the education of
women. "What an excellent counsellor a man would find in his wife if
she could think!" And again: "Most men have a moment in their lives
when they can do great things, the moment when nothing seems
impossible to them. The ignorance of women makes the human race
lose this magnificent chance."[12]

Beyle might have said more about the fact that men and women
love in different ways; it would have been a rich vein to explore.
Perhaps his plan might have been more methodically followed. But if
the parts of *De l'Amour* are worth more than the whole, that is because
once again he wanted to see his book appear without delay. He filled
out the end by drawing, casually, on new reading; he threw in the
notes which he had been too impatient to mature or to put in their
logical places.

In 1822 the second book of *De l'Amour* contained a collection of fragments: the jottings which he had made on odd scraps of paper, on 300 or 400 playing cards, on the nature of love. In 1853, eleven years after his death, his cousin Romain Colomb made various additions to the 1822 edition. Among them were three prefaces which Beyle had not published, some pages on fiascos, the anecdote "Le Rameau de Salzbourg" and the short story "Ernestine." They did not substantially alter the value of the book. *De l'Amour* remains a shapeless work, a collection of miscellaneous thoughts. Crystallisation apart, André Billy was to write, "the book is full of exaggerations, and of ideological postulates which Stendhal completely discounted in his novels. It is hardly of interest except in relation to its author."[13] The judgement is severe, but it is largely true.

Twelve days after *De l'Amour* was published, Claude Fauriel told Mary Clarke that Beyle had sent him the work, "and I read a few pages which took away my courage to go on. People assure me, however, that there are many interesting things in it."[14] Hazlitt considered *De l'Amour* a "charming little work."[15] Prosper Duvergier de Hauranne, writing in *Le Globe* in 1829, told his readers that the two volumes were "certainly the most bizarre work that M. de Stendhal has written. If, at the tenth page, you don't throw them down in vexation, you will be surprised, when you come to the end, how much they have stimulated your imagination."[16] In the early years of the twentieth century, Rémy de Gourmont observed that "it had taken twenty years to sell out an edition of the best known essay on love, that of Stendhal."[17]

Posterity was to make amends. In 1903, when the assassins burst into the bedroom of Alexander I of Serbia, they found a copy of *De l'Amour*. It had been annotated by the queen. In 1953 a copy of the first edition was sold in Paris for 125,000 francs.[18]

PART IV

The Ardent Missionary
1822–1830

Twenty-three

In ITALY, THE Romantic movement had been fused with liberalism from the start. In France, on the contrary, the Romantic theme of regeneration was at first attached to the monarchist theme of the Restoration. As an ideologist and a Jacobin, Beyle could not belong to it in a political or literary sense. At first he was only an attentive spectator. In 1822, however, a chance event produced the decisive break between Classics and Romantics and then divisions between the Romantics themselves. Beyle threw himself into the melee.

On July 31 a company of English actors opened a Shakespeare season in Paris. It was only seven years since Waterloo; Parisian youth gave such a hostile reception to "Shakespeare, aide-de-camp de Wellington," that *Othello* did not reach a second performance. The liberal press, especially *Le Constitutionnel*, sided with the demonstrators in the name of patriotism; the ultra press, with *Le Moniteur* and *Le Journal des Débats*, supported the English venture. It has been observed that Beyle fought for Romanticism when he could fight under the English flag; he lost interest in it when it became French. Henri Martineau observes that he kept intellectual independence; it amused him to appear too Anglophile in France, and too chauvinistic across the Channel.[1]

The reception of the English actors had shown him, decisively, that Romanticism was used for political purposes. But the quarrel was not entirely political, for the Shakespeare who was performed in France was, above all, the Shakespeare of *The Edinburgh Review,* the Shakespeare who was presented as a guarantee of the new literary movement. It was a Romantic Shakespeare who was booed by the liberals and defended by the ultras at the Porte-Saint-Martin. As Doris Gunnell observes, in *Stendhal et l'Angleterre,* people "read Shakespeare against Racine."[2] The scandal at the Porte-Saint-Martin led Beyle to write his first *Racine et Shakespeare.* He was working on the pamphlet early in 1823, and it was put on sale on March 1.

Beyle recognised that literature must be separated from politics. The chief grievance against Shakespeare, the literary argument of patriotic bad temper, had been that he transgressed the classical rule of the three unities. Beyle refused to pose the problem of the definition of Romanticism in classical terms. By doing so, he attempted to establish the autonomy of the idea. In the dialogue between the Classic and the Romantic, the Classic is led to admit that a drama consists of long moments of imperfect illusion broken by short moments of perfect illusion. The Romantic then introduces his decisive argument: these moments are more frequent in the Romantic theatre than they are in the Classical theatre, where noble lines and long tirades interrupt the spectator's illusion. The Romantic finally establishes a link between the idea of illusion and the idea of pleasure. Perfect illusion is the true source of pleasure, and the value of a work is measured by the "quantity of pleasure" it procures. Beyle is then led to make his celebrated definition:

> *Romanticism* is the art of presenting nations with the literary works which, in the present state of their customs and their beliefs, are capable of giving them the greatest possible pleasure.
> *Classicism,* on the contrary, offers them the literature which gave the greatest possible pleasure to their great-grandfathers.[3]

The definition might have been extended to include music and the visual arts; but it is a valid definition, insofar as it makes Romanticism the movement of freedom and modernity. And Beyle adds, wisely: "The Romantics do not advise anyone directly to imitate the work of Shakespeare. What we must imitate in that great man is the way of studying the world in which we live, and the art of giving our contemporaries precisely the kind of tragedy they need, but which they are not bold enough to demand, because they are terrified by the reputation of the great Racine."[4]

If Beyle restricted himself to the question of the theatre, it was not only because his tastes led him to do so, but because he knew that a victory in this field would bring with it success in all the others. Theatrical victories have always been decisive in France. But *Racine et Shakespeare* is significant because it goes beyond the question of freedom of expression: it proclaims that Romanticism is contemporary, the natural movement for modern times. Here we see not only the influence of *The Edinburgh Review,* but the influence of Italian Romanticism. As Sainte-Beuve remarked, with his usual wisdom, Beyle opened doors to his compatriots. He was the first French Romantic to go abroad. More than sixty years after *Racine et Shakespeare* was published, Jules Lemaître observed that the Romanticism which Beyle defended was not the same thing for him as it was for the Romantics. This revolution, in his eyes, was "only a natural development of the national genius in the direction of true simplicity and honesty of observation."[5]

In the first months of 1823, the author of *Racine et Shakespeare* was also working on his *Vie de Rossini.* In May he was making arrangements for a publisher, and, not for the first time, he needed help with a book. Once before he had been accused of plagiarism; now he simply asked for a contribution.

> Sir and dear compatriot [this to Mareste],
> You really should do a history of the opéra bouffe in Paris, from 1800 to 1823. That would make a fine chapter in the *Vie de Rossini.* . . .
> If you don't do this chapter, it will be a diabolical problem for me, for since I was absent I have no *memory of the facts.*[6]

Presumably Mareste refused this invitation. The chapter did not appear in *Vie de Rossini.*

Beyle sometimes showed a curious detachment about his writing. He was prepared to let others contribute to a book, and he showed no concern for its architecture or its style. He did not trouble himself unduly about *le mot juste,* about the music of a phrase, the orchestration of a paragraph. He would let others read his proofs. He would plagiarize without shame. When he was accused of doing so in his *Lettres . . . sur Haydn,* he had sent an indignant rejoinder to *Le Constitutionnel.* He had published the book under the pseudonym of Bombet; he had replied as Bombet's brother. He had been amused by the complexity of the deceit; he had been very far from penitent.

And yet, despite this lack of care for the work itself, he cared about his reputation. In January, 1823, he asked for copies of his books to be sent to René de Perdreauville, a headmaster and journalist in New Orleans, so that he might "make these works known to an impatient America." And while he made this particular request tongue in cheek, he was seriously concerned with his reputation among English readers. He drew up the free lists for his books with obvious care. He was always anxious to earn the respect of those whom he called the happy few: the band of brothers who were, like himself, men of sensibility and liberal views. It was not surprising that he gave his works to Gian Pietro Vieusseux and asked him to publicise them. In 1819–20, Vieusseux had founded a celebrated reading room in Florence, and from 1821 he had published his *Antologia.* As a propagator of ideas, he played a part in the formation of Italy; he was one of the apostles of national unity.[7]

Beyle was not averse to Vieusseux's approval. He could only have been delighted, in June, 1823, to receive appreciation from "the Lord Bard."

Genoa, May 29 1823.

Sir,

At present that I know to whom I am indebted for a very flattering mention in the *Rome, Naples and Florence, en 1817,* by M. Stendhal, it is fit that I should return my thanks (however undesired or undesirable) to M. Beyle with whom I had the honour of being acquainted at Milan in 1816. . . .

Of your works I have only seen "Rome, etc.", "the lives of Haydn and Mozart" and the brochure on "Racine and Shakespeare." The "Histoire de la peinture" I have not yet the good fortune to possess. . . .

I beg you to believe with a lively recollection of our brief acquaintance, and the hope of one day renewing it, I am ever your obliged and obedient humble servant,

NOEL BYRON[8]

Paris, 23 June 1823

Milord,

You are very kind to attach some importance to individual opinions; the poems of the author of *Parisina* will live for many centuries after people have forgotten *Rome, Naples et Florence en 1817*, and other brochures like them.

My publisher put *L'Histoire de la peinture en Italie*, and *De l'Amour*, in the post for Genoa yesterday. . . .

It has been a great pleasure for me, milord, to have some personal relations with one of the two or three men who, since the death of the hero I adored, help to break the dull uniformity into which the affectations of high society have thrown our unhappy Europe. . . .

I have the honour to be, milord, your most humble and most obedient servant,

H. BEYLE[9]

At the end of the year, as he waited for the final episode of his Greek saga, the author of *Childe Harold* instructed Charles Barry to sell "all the things left in Genoa or Albaro, excepting my best travelling carriage, and some few books—presents from the authors. . . . Also reserve a copy of the *Caliph Vathek*, and *Rome, Naples et Florence en 1817*."[10]

Had Beyle ever heard of Byron's compliment, he might have worn it as a decoration.

Twenty-four

Late in July, he went to stay at the sixteenth-century château of Monchy-Humières, near Compiègne, with Clémentine Curial. It was some ten years since he had first met her in the salon of her mother, Comtesse Beugnot. He had admired her fine and candid eyes, but she does not seem to have occupied his imagination. He had sent her only formal greetings when he wrote from Russia to her mother. Indeed, he had been concerned with the mother rather than the daughter, and it was to Mme. Beugnot—under the pseudonym of Mme. Doligny—that he had dedicated his *Vies de Haydn, Mozart et Métastase*. He was fond of Mme. Beugnot and not unaware of her husband's growing importance (Comte Beugnot was now Minister of State). It was, perhaps, as a friend of her family that he accepted Clémentine Curial's invitation to Monchy. She had, one suspects, invited him because she was in love with him, and she hoped that proximity might rouse his emotions. She clearly wanted to become his mistress.

Clémentine was thirty-five and the wife of Lieutenant General Comte Philibert Curial, who was fourteen years her senior.[1] She had wanted to marry a Colonel Morland, but her father had opposed the match. The colonel had been killed at Austerlitz, and she had

182

married Curial in 1808. He had been created general, baron and count by the emperor, but he had been quick to rally to Louis XVIII, who had made him a peer of France. Now, in 1823, the Duc d'Angoulême's army had invaded Spain to re-establish the absolute monarchy of Ferdinand VII, and since February 12 Curial had been commanding the Fifth Division of the Pyrenees army corps.

The Curials' marriage had at first been happy; but Philibert had a marked taste for maidservants, and he had also beaten his wife. She had already revenged herself by taking a lover. Philibert's violence and infidelity had not been her only source of grief: in 1821 her youngest daughter, Claire-Charlotte, had died. She found consolation, now, in her surviving children, and Beyle—who more than once revealed great affection for children—took a decided fancy to her nine-year-old daughter Bathilde. She was clearly a remarkable child: tactful and responsive, a lover of books and music. No doubt they talked happily as they fished together on the banks of the Aronde. On August 1, immediately on his return to Paris, he wrote to her, to explain the fading of Rossini's popularity and the composition of the musical public in the capital.

On October 18, two years and four months after his departure from Milan, he set out again for Italy. For the first time in four years, he felt inspired to keep his journal, and in it he recorded his haste to leave "the *ugliness* around Paris." He took the mail coach to Dole, reached Isola Bella on October 26 and, four days later, found himself at Alexandria, in Piedmont, where he went at once to the opera. He kept his old intensity of feeling. "A Frenchman of forty is hardly susceptible any more to love. It is only in Italy that one cannot help loving."[2]

On November 7 he arrived in Florence. On November 15 his two-volume *Vie de Rossini* was published in Paris.

It has rightly been said that if Beyle had a special feeling for Rossini, part admiration, part hostility, part sympathy and part repulsion, that was because Rossini's work was too like his own: Rossini was the Stendhal of music. He too, at least in his early works, showed energy and a certain formlessness, brilliance and lack of discipline. Beyle had been introduced to Rossini in November, 1819. The conversationalist had amused him, but the man himself had been antipathetic. He had been shocked to find a man who carried

Beylism to extremes: who sought for happiness, pursued *la chasse au bonheur,* with the same blind egotism as he did himself. He was also disillusioned to find that Rossini merely wrote operas to earn his living and that, if he assured himself an adequate income, he would abandon music altogether.

Vie de Rossini is far from being conventional biography; the biographical element is small. One suspects that Beyle made his friends produce analyses of the operas, for Rossini's first Neapolitan opera, *Elisabetta, regina d'Inghilterra,* had been performed in 1815, and Beyle gave a vivid account of the first night, which he had not attended. He gave the wrong date for the premiere of *Il Barbiere di Siviglia.* But whatever its borrowings and its inaccuracies, the book is a lively improvisation, and Beyle's personality is clear from beginning to end. *Vie de Rossini* is the journal of Beyle's sensations on a journey through music.

He was not—as his book on Haydn and Mozart had made clear—an enlightened amateur of the art. His knowledge of it was limited to Mozart and Cimarosa, Paesiello and Rossini. He was not concerned with the techniques of music; only the sound it made could move him. "There is nothing real in music," he wrote in his introduction, "except the state in which it leaves the soul." Music, he insisted, must be heard in isolation if its sensations were to be enjoyed. Simple melody that charmed the ear was to him like the sweet fruit that had delighted him in his childhood. One of the most remarkable points about Beyle's criticism of music is that it led him—as it would lead Théophile Gautier—to perceive the *correspondances* between the senses. Long ago, at Marseilles, a château and an avenue of plane trees, with their contrasting moods, had seemed to him like a work by Cimarosa. Now he declared that the sound of the flute reminded him of the ultramarine blue draperies in the paintings of Carlo Dolci.

Vie de Rossini—like many of Beyle's works—is unorganised and full of irrelevancies. It gives him a chance to praise Italy as the home of the arts: "Italy is the land of *beauty* of every kind only because the Italians feel the need of something new in ideal beauty."[3] *Vie de Rossini* also enables its author to discuss the English sensibility to music, and to maintain that this sensibility seemed more marked in Scotland. "When I arrived in Scotland for the first time, I disembarked at Inverness. By chance I was immediately confronted with the sight of the funereal ceremonies of the Highlands. . . . The next day, as I travelled through the villages, I heard the murmur of music on every side."[4] Was this visit to Scotland one of Beyle's inventions? There is no other record that he had made it or that he had made the visit to Liverpool which he described. Beyle combined a strict regard for truth with an irrepressible love of fantasy.

The mediocrity of contemporary music obliged him to recognise the superiority of Rossini. It is not considered, now, that Rossini achieved anything revolutionary in music, but his contemporaries thought otherwise. Indeed, apart from his freshness of style, he must have the credit of having grafted onto *opera seria* many of the conventions of opera buffa. Many of his contemporaries, including Beyle, deplored the passing of the improvisations which had been the singers' prerogative.

Berlioz was to condemn *Vie de Rossini* as pretentious nonsense. Beyle's eagerness to look beyond French frontiers, in all forms of art, did not endear him to his compatriots. When, in Parisian salons, he proclaimed that Shakespeare was superior to Racine, the other guests tolerated what they considered to be an aberration. When he professed his admiration for Rossini, he aroused controversy.

> One might say [wrote Mérimée] that he discovered Rossini and Italian music. . . . In the early years of the Restoration, the memories of our reverses had exasperated the national pride, and people turned every discussion into a question of patriotism. To prefer some foreign music to French music was almost to betray one's country. Very early on, Beyle had set himself above the common prejudices, and perhaps on this point he was sometimes excessive.[5]

But his mania had one good result: it helped to acclimatise Italian music in France.

And since *Vie de Rossini* was published in November, 1823, the month in which the composer arrived in Paris, it enjoyed a topical success. It was translated into German; and it lent apparent authority to its author, who had recently become music critic of *Le Journal de Paris*. He wrote for the paper from September, 1824, until June, 1827.

The author of *Vie de Rossini* had been in Rome for some days when, on December 5, 1823, he wrote to Clémentine Curial:

I was simply longing, madame, to reach a city whose name allowed
me to use your permission, and send you news of what's happening in
the world. High society here appears at M. de Montmorency's [at the
French embassy], and at M. Demidoff's [at the Palazzo Ruspoli]. M
de Montmorency does the honours of his embassy with a truly perfect
grace. . . . There are three or four Roman women of the greatest
beauty. . . . They wear extremely low-cut dresses, one would have to
be very hard to please not to be exceedingly grateful to their *couturière*.
Imagine, madame, the combination of forty women, dressed like this,
and fourteen cardinals, plus a cloud of prelates, abbés, etc. The
expression of the French abbés is enough to make one die of laughter;
they don't know where to look, in the midst of so many charms. . . .

In spite of these women's pretty dresses and the pleasant masterpieces which one sees in the mornings, Rome does not attract me, I
feel too isolated. . . .[6]

He stayed on in Rome, where the oranges glowed on the trees in
the private gardens and the heat was often pitiless. As the new year
opened, he reported to Mareste: "The weather is incredibly beautiful; not a cloud, and half a degree of frost every night. I've made
friends in abundance; I got so tired with two friends today at the
Villa Borghese and the Pincio, in a walk of five and a half hours, that
I'm going to bed instead of attending the rout at the Austrian
ambassador's."[7] He remained in Rome until February 4, exploring it
until he reached exhaustion. Then he spent a fortnight in Florence
and visited Bologna, Parma, Geneva and Lyons, before, in March, he
returned to Paris. He took a room at 118, rue du Faubourg-Saint-
Denis, and began to write his second Romantic pamphlet and to
recast *Rome, Naples et Florence en 1817*.

His work was not enjoying the success he could have wished.
Delacroix had looked through his *Vie de Rossini* and decided:
"Really, this Stendhal is an insolent fellow; he is too haughtily right,
and he sometimes talks nonsense."[8] On April 3 Mongie, the
publisher, told Beyle that he would have liked to announce his profits
from *De l'Amour*, but he had not sold forty copies of the book. "I can,"
he lamented, "say of it, as of the *Poésies sacrées* by Pompignan: sacred
they are, for no one touches them."[9]

De l'Amour remained unsold, but Beyle was at last to console
himself for the prolonged unhappiness which had driven him to write
it. Since his visit to Monchy, his thoughts had turned to Clémentine

Curial. "I don't know if it is a sign of old age," he had written to her from Rome, "but I feel a need of intimacy which, since another is impossible, almost makes me regret the fogs of Paris."[10] Perhaps she recognised his need for love; clearly she herself was in love with him. Beyle later said that she had already loved him for two years. In May she declared her feelings.

> What a sad thing prudence is, or at least how sad it makes me [he wrote to her on May 18]! I was the happiest of men or at least my heart was beating with extreme emotion when I went to see you this morning, and it was a sweet emotion. I have spent the evening, almost the day with you, but with such an appearance of indifference that I have to make an effort to persuade myself that it can be otherwise. For the first time in ten years, I regret that I have forgotten French customs.
>
> How can I see you? When will it be convenient for me to call again at your house? I didn't go there yesterday because, the day before, a servant had seen me ask the doorkeeper if you were there. Are you satisfied with my prudence? Did I look indifferent enough? I am angry with myself. I beg you to tell me, by post, exactly when I can find you alone. I am very far now from avoiding these moments, and I despair of seeing them occur, because of the number of visits you receive.
>
> A little sign at the window of the boudoir where you were this morning, for example, a shutter half closed, or the blind half down would tell me that I could come up.
>
> If I don't see this sign of solitude, I shan't knock at the door, but I'll come back fifteen minutes later.[11]

It seems that the shutter was left half closed at 9, rue des Saussaies, and Beyle went to see her. She asked to see him again before she left Paris. "Tell me, monsieur, how we can see one another before Monday, if only for ten minutes. To leave for the country without hearing 'I love you' seems to me more of a sacrifice than I can bear."[12] On May 22 she became his mistress, his first real mistress for several years. "And only then," he confessed, "only then did the memory of Métilde become less agonising. She became for me a kind of tender ghost, profoundly sad; a ghost which, by its sovereign apparition, disposed me to tender, good, just and indulgent thoughts."[13]

Beyle's letters to Clémentine, dated only by the year 1824, reflect the course of his new and violent passion. He apologises for showing his indignation at a dinner party, when she called him a *littéra-teur*—the term appears to have hurt his self-esteem. He expresses his resentment of her grand way of life, of her social acquaintances; he apologises for his dullness; and, after days of particular delight, he writes to her:

> When I have seen you on three consecutive days, my angel, it always seems to me that I love you more, if that were possible; that is because we are more intimate, that is because what separates us are the prejudices that come from your carriage, and that, after three days of intimacy, neither of us seems to care about prejudice any more, and we only think of loving and being happy.
>
> My God! how happy I was yesterday, Wednesday! I mark that day, for God knows when I shall dare to send this letter. I write to unburden my soul. I love you so much today, I am so devoted, that I need to write it, as I cannot say it to anyone. If we spent a week together and our hearts still beat so ardently, I think that, in the end, we should never part.
>
> I was less happy on Tuesday, the day of the *Frères Provençaux;* I was a little shocked. But yesterday's dinner was perfect for happiness, intimacy, sweetness.[14]

He warned her that he was stormy and that he was sometimes difficult. But he assured her: "Don't be anxious about me in the least. I love you passionately; and this love may not be like the love you have seen in society or in novels. I wish that it was like the tenderest thing you know in the world, so that you would not be anxious."[15]

The letters are loving, yet the few that survive are far from reflecting the continual, urgent passion which we find in the letters to Métilde. It has been suggested, convincingly, that Beyle cannot forgive Menti—as he called her—for having become his mistress so readily.[16] He had had no time to crystallise his love. Only when their liaison ended was her poetic image to take shape. In the meanwhile, he soon showed his remarkable aptitude for tormenting those who loved him. Claude Boncompain has rightly defined Beylist love as "cerebral, . . . musical, cultivated as an art, egotistic even in suffering, a love which sometimes seems like a strange perversion of the heart."[17]

It was in June that Menti set out to take Bathilde to the waters. The child's health was already causing grave concern, and in fact, she was to die some two years later. Surprisingly enough, Beyle showed no interest in Bathilde, no sympathy in Menti's anxiety. He was only afraid that he might be forgotten. "You cannot imagine the sombre thoughts that your silence gives me [June 24]. I thought that yesterday night, when you were packing, you would have found time to write me three lines. . . . Not seeing a letter yesterday, I hoped for one this morning.—When she changed horses at S———, she will, I thought, have asked for a sheet of paper. But no. She is entirely preoccupied with her daughter."[18]

That month they quarrelled violently. Menti had, it seems, admitted that she had loved someone else; Beyle answered that he had had many women, that someone else loved him now and had given him the ultimate proof. It was, he said, Rosine (who has been identified as Mme. Victor de Tracy, and—by François Michel—as Mme. Pasta).[19] Menti was in anguish—an anguish which she had to conceal from her family and her large social circle. She was also desperate with fear that she might be pregnant; she had told Beyle that if she found she was bearing his child, she would kill herself. On July 4, from Monchy, where she was entertaining some forty guests, she sent him a long and hysterical letter.

> It is me again, monsieur. You're going to say you are persecuted, and so indeed you are. After your infamous behaviour I should find enough dignity not to make you enjoy, at least positively, all the grief you cause me. But in the dreadful state to which you have reduced me I don't know what I'm doing, I forget everything and think only of what I am suffering. I want a remedy. If I am to bear my life for another few months, I need to summon every kind of courage. You are the only person, monsieur, who can be useful to me at this moment. Tell me, in friendship, tell me that your conduct was dictated by indifference. Perhaps this idea will cure my heart by breaking it. What could I expect of you? Must I not have been mad to expect anything other than grief? In the six weeks since I was weak enough to confess my feelings, how have you treated me? . . . Yes, Henri, you are bad and you have loved me only physically. It is already much for me to recognise a fault in you. Last month, you were

terrible to me. Why? Because I had admitted a weakness. You, who
have had a hundred mistresses, had you the right to maltreat me as
you did? Fly to Rosine, then, Henri. I hate her. Run into her arms, I
shall be delighted, because I believe that your love is the most terrible
misfortune that can befall a woman. If she has happiness, you will
take it from her, if she has health you will make her lose it, the more
she loves you the harder and more barbaric you will be. When she has
told you I adore you, then will come the system by which you refine
her grief so much that she cannot bear it anymore. . . .

You have pretended to love me, Henri. Where are the proofs, then?
Have you ever tried to see me? You have always escaped me. For two
years you avoided a confession, and when I made it to you, a week
later you dismissed me. Your only pleasure has been to thrust a
dagger continually into my heart. And yet I love you still, I love you.
Don't believe me, I don't love you anymore; at least my reason insists
that this is so; I am sure now to cure myself of this mad passion, I
shan't be able to see you until the first of February. And so the
memory of the harm you have done me and an absence of seven
months will give me satisfaction for my extravagance, or else God will
pity me and take me from this cursed earth. . . .

Henri, I don't ask for anything more. I am writing to you again
because it relieves me a little to talk to you; but now I can see quite
well that you have deceived me, I don't ask you for anything more,
not even to deceive me again. Go and carry your grief where you will,
but don't concern yourself with me anymore. If I am pregnant, you
know my resolution: it is irrevocable and it will not be changed in the
least, whether you love me or abandon me. I don't urge you to keep it
secret, after me it doesn't matter what happens; if I am not pregnant,
then I shall bear the happy life that you have prepared for me,
praying heaven to give me the strength to hate you.[20]

She proved not to be pregnant, and later in the month the love
affair was more passionate than ever.

I should like to spend whole months with you and not to be able to
give you anything [so she wrote to him in July]. Only then should I
believe that I was really loved. As for tours de force of a certain kind,
I take advantage of them, and I swear to you that it seems to me that
it is because you have been too sublime in this way that I have felt
some coldness. It seemed to me that it was too vulgar a way of proving
your tenderness to me.[21]

That month he stayed for three consecutive days, so it is said, concealed in a cellar in her château. She had to set up and remove a ladder every time she saw him, but she provided all his needs.[22] Such reckless behaviour proved that there was much passion on both sides. On August 10 she wrote: "Your little note on Saturday made me quiver like your dear hand does when it wanders over my old hide. You should lavish them upon me more often."[23] Beyle was no doubt thinking of Menti's own impassioned letters when, in *Le Rouge et le Noir*, Julien Sorel received a letter from Mme. de Rênal, "written in haste, bathed in tears, and with no sense of spelling at all."

Sometimes Beyle and Menti met in country inns; constantly they had to devise elaborate stratagems to escape the observation of the household.[24] Not only was Beyle adept at the art of love, but his conversation "had a persuasive charm, and . . . he struck the imagination of women by the curious and changing, never banal nature of his existence."[25] Menti, who was one of the four great loves of his life, was by far his most intelligent mistress.

And so the tempestuous love affair continued. More than once she was to fear that she was pregnant; more than once she decided to kill herself. She died at Montpellier on June 14, 1840, and Romain Colomb maintained that she had in fact taken her own life; Jean Mélia was to endorse the statement.[26] Her great-grandson, the Vicomte Curial, using medical evidence, protested against the tradition of suicide. Whatever the cause of her death, André Billy suggests that her liaison with Beyle aggravated her mental instability.[27] One wonders if she was manic-depressive. Sometimes her passion made her exalted; sometimes she reproached herself for lacking the spirit to kill herself. She often thought that Beyle could not accept the abstinence which was sometimes inevitable; then she allowed him temporary substitutes—and often withdrew permission in the same letter. Sometimes she seemed to be afraid that he had given her venereal disease, she said she would never see him again, and their moments of pleasure were destroyed by savage outbursts and by brutal answers.[28]

Twenty-five

Romanticism had been growing, inevitably, in France, since the Revolution of 1789; it had received new impetus from the saga of Napoleon. Now, in the oppressive days of the Restoration, when censorship was strict, when liberalism was a term of political opprobrium, it was coming into its own. Rousseau, Chateaubriand and Mme. de Staël had already practised Romantic principles in French literature, and, in the life and works of Byron, the historical novels of Scott, French men of letters saw new dimensions of achievement. The Romantic movement in England, the most fertile creative movement since the days of Queen Elizabeth, had virtually spent itself by 1824—the year in which Byron died at Missolonghi. Keats and Shelley were both dead; Wordsworth had passed his peak; Coleridge had written his best work. But in France, Lamartine and Hugo were publishing their early poems, and—strangely, it seems to us, today—the sides were taking up position to determine whether or not the arts should assert themselves in the modern age. The Classics maintained the immutable rules codified by Boileau; they insisted on the perpetual cultivation of the correct and the impersonal. The Romantics believed that *L'Art poétique* was outdated, that art, whatever its form, obeyed no laws. Art existed to express beauty and truth: the beauty of all countries and all ages of history, not simply the great ages of Greece and Rome. Art must embrace all aspiration, mood and experience; it must have freedom of movement and expression. The battle between Classic and Romantic was not merely a contest between two modes of thought; it was a contest between ancient and modern, between retrospection and progress. Such was the natural conservatism in France that the issue was not publicly decided until the *bataille d'Hernani* in 1830.

Meanwhile, on April 24, 1824, at the annual plenary session of the Institut de France, Louis-Simon Auger had violently attacked the Romantic sect. "I should have liked [the manifesto] to be less stupid," Beyle told Mareste, "but, anyway, such as it is, it is repeated in all the papers."[1] He decided to answer it. On April 30 the *Feuilleton littéraire* published a note from Beyle—or, rather, from Stendhal: "If, in his dejection at M. Auger's triumph, no Romantic tries to make himself heard, . . . I shall dare to fight the Académie." This flamboyant challenge was introduced with the editorial comment: "To arms, Classics, to arms! . . . A Teuton chief is advancing."[2] He advanced slowly: his answer to the Classics was not to appear until March, 1825.

On March 19, 1825, the *Bibliographie de la France* announced *Racine et Shakespeare, II.* The second *Racine et Shakespeare* is a charter of independence for literature. It is more constructive and more polemical than the first. It is presented as an answer to Auger's manifesto. Beyle attacks the Academicians, who simply deny that Romanticism is a system of literary composition. He sets out to prove the existence of Romanticism. The second *Racine et Shakespeare* is a pamphlet against a literature which depends on politics for its themes. Its first task is to force literature to come face to face with itself and with modernity.

"By no means an able or powerful defence of the Romantic school, which is, however, . . . making way in France." So wrote Crabb Robinson, the diarist. "Stendhal confines himself merely to a vindication of tragedies in prose and without regard to the unities. But the blending of comedy with tragedy is a more important and essential part of the Shakespearean school. His style is pleasant enough, and I am interested in the turn literature is taking in France."[3] Mérimée told Beyle: "I have read your charming little pamphlet twice over. You have treated the question in a most luminous manner."⁴ Auguste Mignet, the historian, also sent congratulations on a work which he considered "very intelligent and very true." He added: "The arts are lost, and we may say *De Profundis:* our century will understand them, but it will not practise them."⁵ Beyle answered: "It is for want of *courage* that we have no more artists. . . . Every epoch has a branch of human knowledge on which it concentrates all its attention: only there do we find *life*. . . . In our day, alas! politics are robbing literature, which is only a last resource."⁶

Politics and literature were eagerly discussed in the salons of Paris, and here again, in the last years of the Restoration, one may catch a glimpse of Beyle among his livelier contemporaries.

It is clear that he became increasingly difficult. "Beyle enjoyed quizzing those who were present and those who were absent," Louis Spach was to recall. "He enjoyed scratching his questioner's skin, but he took care not to put ointment on the wound. He gave himself the airs of a braggart of vice, he liked to seem more wicked than he was."⁷ He was deliberately outrageous. What excused God, he used to say, was that He did not exist. All great men had had curious tastes: Napoleon himself had had a weakness for one of his aides-de-camp. As for his own democratic opinions, they grew more violent, more aggressively independent, every day. Delécluze rightly judged "from the awkwardness of his movements, and the pretentious clumsiness of his speech, from the often brutal energy of his observations, that high society is not his element."⁸ There was something essentially bourgeois about him.

He spent his life railing against two accidents in his destiny [added Delécluze's biographer]. He was fat and squat, and he would have liked to be delicate and slender; he had been born a commoner, and he could not console himself for not belonging to the nobility, and his poverty always seemed to him to be an injustice of fate. This struggle of dreams and realities perpetually in conflict made Beyle the most incoherent of men. And so it was that with the deepest and least concealed scorn for everything that was bourgeois, he also pursued the aristocracy with the epigrams of radical liberalism, and showed no more mercy to those who had been greatly blessed by fortune. As for his explanation of all these disappointments, it was, so he said, that everything in this world depends on chance. . . . In short, Beyle proclaimed himself to be an atheist, and he said so openly to those who wished to listen.[9]

Sometimes even Delécluze felt impatient with him. Early in January, 1825, after an evening of Viollet-le-Duc's, he confessed: "I hope that Stendhal will get tired of my company. . . . I have an idea that he is beginning to find us stupid, and this delights me. Yesterday he left very early. He had been bored all the evening by a Classicist whom I was very careful not to interrupt."[10]

One habitué of Delécluze' attic was Joseph Aubernon, sometime prefect of Seine-et-Oise. Mme. Aubernon's own salon was a centre of liberal opposition, where Mérimée would rub shoulders with Beyle; Béranger, the patriotic *chansonnier,* would find himself with Adolphe Thiers, the historian and politician, years hence to be President of the Republic. Thiers, who always took an interest in the arts, discussed them with Beyle and the artist Ary Scheffer before he reviewed the salon in *Le Constitutionnel.*

Every week, towards the end of the Restoration, Delécluze and Beyle would meet at the rue Bonaparte. Here, opposite the church of Saint-Germain-des-Prés, lived the artist Baron Gérard. He entertained his friends in a suite of four small rooms, simply furnished, and every Wednesday, at midnight, tea was served, always with the same kind of cakes. But Gérard's salon remained sought after, because it remained exclusive, and if the setting was undistinguished, the guests were remarkable. Among them were such artists as Paul Delaroche, David d'Angers, Horace Vernet and Ingres. And among them, too, was Eugène Delacroix, "whose gentle, subtle conversation had as much grace, restraint and reserve as his artistic genius had energy, fire and inspiration."[11] It was in Gérard's salon that Delacroix met the man whom he would always describe as "poor Beyle." He had, at first, no great appreciation of him, but he later became a friend. Beyle was in fact among the first to recognise and appreciate the genius of Delacroix, whom, as early as 1824, he called "a pupil of Tintoretto."

Mme. Ancelot, recalling Gérard's salon, also remembered how

M. Mérimée and M. Beyle talked together with inimitable originality. Their entirely different minds and characters set off one another by their very contradiction, and roused their exceptional spirits to the highest pitch. Beyle was moved by everything and he felt

a thousand different sensations in a few minutes. Nothing escaped
him and nothing left him cold, but his sadness was hidden under
jokes, and he never seemed so gay as he did when he was feeling
wretched and frustrated. And then what lively wisdom, what wild
nonsense!... No one had livelier sympathies, or indeed more
pronounced dislikes: among these dislikes was Madame Gay, who
came, from time to time, with her daughter Delphine.[12]

When Sophie Gay appeared, he embarked on such outrageous
babble and paradox that she was obliged to move away. When she
left to play cards, and Delphine remained alone with them, the
conversation again became delightful.

In *Les Salons de Paris. Foyers éteints,* Mme. Ancelot gave a shrewd
assessment of Beyle in society: of his wit and humour, his curious
love of fantasy and mystification. One day she invited him to her
salon.

> He accepted, on condition that he would be announced under
> whichever pseudonym suited him that day.
> On the Tuesday morning, he sent me that book of his which
> contains a life of Haydn, written under the name of *César Bombay* [*sic*].
> Early that evening, when I still had only a few guests, M. César
> Bombay was announced; and Beyle came in, more chubby-faced
> than usual, and said: "Madame, I am too early. That is because I am
> a busy man. I get up at five in the morning, I visit the barracks to see
> if my equipment is well made. For, as you know, I equip the army
> with stockings and cotton caps. ...."
> He continued in this style for half an hour, going into the details of
> what he earned on every cap, talking about the rival and envious and
> denigrating caps which wanted to compete with him. Nobody knew
> him except M. Ancelot, who escaped to a neighbouring room, unable
> to restrain his laughter; I certainly wanted to do the same, but I
> bravely kept my self-control.

Occasionally, it is clear, she found his mystification irritating. One
day, from Italy, he sent her a letter signed "Giroflay" and dated
from Smyrna. "Luckily," she wrote, "by that time I knew his
indecipherable writing, and I guessed that it was him."[13]

* * *

During the year 1825, Beyle's private life had gradually been changing. His love for Menti was ardent, still, but it was not cloudless. Already, in the summer of 1824, Philibert Curial had resented Beyle's assiduous interest in his wife. "I must consult you about a *husband,*" Beyle had told Mareste. "I fear I may be obliged to fight a chevalier de Saint-Louis."[14] Now, on October 11, 1825, Menti wrote to assure him of her love, but admitted that she found him strange, indisposed to be pleasant to her. She did not believe in his love for her, she foresaw that he would leave her and she seemed prepared to accept his departure. She reproached him for living among women of easy virtue. "Physically," she added, "I do not need a lover, . . . but I do feel the want, the need to be loved."[15] Their relationship grew still more tense. On November 13 she sent a forbidding note: "I have had a rude lesson. . . . I must dismiss from my private life someone who brings me nothing but trouble and misfortune."[16]

The misfortunes of love were much in Beyle's mind. In 1824 the Duchesse de Duras had published *Ourika.* The novel described the impossible passion of a black woman for a young French nobleman: a curiously modern racial theme. *Edouard,* which the duchesse published in 1825, described the love of a young man for his adopted sister: another socially impossible passion. In *Olivier, ou le secret,* Mme. de Duras took a much more delicate theme: that of sexual impotence. Olivier's secret was his inability to prove his love to Mme. de Nangis. Constantly obliged to elude her or to feign indifference, he finally confessed his passion, a passion that would always be hopeless. Mme. de Nangis, much enamoured of him, could not understand his behaviour or his growing melancholy. Rather than reveal his secret, Olivier killed himself in her presence. He proved his devotion by freeing her. Mme. de Duras did not publish her novel; indeed the manuscript, found in her family archives in 1970, was published only in 1971. But the subject of *Olivier* was discussed in literary circles in Paris in 1825, and late that year, or early the following year, Henri de Latouche stole the subject and the title. Using the same format as Mme. de Duras had done for her two previous novels, he anonymously published an *Olivier* of his own. On January 18, 1826, Beyle sent his review of this *Olivier* to *The New Monthly Magazine.* On January 30 or 31 he himself began to write a novel on the subject. *Armance,* like *Racine et Shakespeare* or the *Vie de Rossini,* was a topical book. On February 8 the first draft was virtually finished. Then, suddenly, he stopped. Perhaps he was deterred by the difficulties of his subject. Perhaps he was distracted by his worsening relationship with Menti.

Early in 1826 Philibert Curial was appointed commandant of the training camp at Saint-Omer. On Easter Day, March 26, Beyle still proved his love for Menti, but their relationship was already threatened. She spent the summer with her husband. "Storm over San-Remo," noted Beyle. The note has been interpreted as the memory of a scene between himself and Menti at Saint-Omer. He was passing through, on his way to England. Doris Gunnell has suggested that he went abroad as a means of breaking the liaison, but this seems extremely unlikely.[17] Everything suggests that Menti wanted to break with him.

On June 27 he landed at Dover. In London, it is said, he received a letter from her which gave him "the most acute unhappiness of his life." No doubt it was a letter of dismissal, but one is tempted to take the arrival of this letter as the momentous but unspecified event which occurred on August 28. "From 28 August 1826 to 12 January 1827: the 134 days," he wrote, later. And, on January 16, 1827: "Appeasement of the grief of the 134 days." As François Michel has observed in an illuminating essay, January 12, 1827, was the day Bathilde Curial died.[18]

In the autumn of 1826, while her parents were at Saint-Omer, her grandfather, Comte Beugnot, became anxious about her health; he took her from her convent to stay with him. No doubt her mother was aware of the child's condition. Perhaps she knew that Bathilde had consumption; perhaps, in one of her violent moments, she told Beyle that her daughter's illness was her own punishment for their liaison. So Mme. de Rênal, in Le Rouge et le Noir, was to pray heaven to forgive her for her adultery and so to save her son. Beyle was to be deeply distressed by the death of Bathilde. He gave her name to Mme. de Chasteller, the heroine of Lucien Leuwen; and when Octave de Malivert, the hero of Armance, visited Père-Lachaise, "he saw the place where the young B——— lies at rest, . . . and shed tears for her."[19]

Meanwhile, in the summer of 1826, Beyle stayed at a hotel in Covent Garden, and for three months, he tried to alleviate his unhappiness. It was the first time that a woman had left him. He still hoped, it seems, that his absence might alter her decision and lead her to take him back.

He was indifferent to his surroundings. He felt little interest in London. He had no taste for Gothic architecture; he was still too much of a man of the eighteenth century to see it as anything but a barbaric form of art. He did not feel the sympathy for the mediaeval which Romantic generations were to know. He remained untouched by Westminster Abbey, although, we are told, he set it, with Salisbury Cathedral, above all the other Gothic buildings in England.[20] (One wonders how many of these—including Salisbury—he had seen.) St. Paul's, he thought, exemplified the alliance of Christianity and beauty, but it could not be compared with the Coliseum in Rome.[21] As for Regent Street,

> it astonishes but it gives no pleasure, and it lacks style. One sees extremely rich barbarians, the first men in the world for the *steam-engine* and the jury, but men who are otherwise only moved by the sombre melancholy of Gothic architecture, or, which comes to the same thing, by Hamlet's monologue, as he holds Yorick's skull in his hand.[22]

It was, so to speak, the classic comment of the French Romantic.

Beyle—one suspects—was paying this third visit to England at the invitation of the young English barrister Sutton Sharpe. The nephew of Samuel Rogers, the poet, Sharpe was devoted to Paris, where he regularly spent his vacations. Liberal, vital, versatile, he earned the affectionate respect of distinguished politicians and men of letters. It was no doubt through the barrister J.-A. Buchon that he had met the Cuviers (and, for a time, thought of marriage with Cuvier's stepdaughter, Sophie Duvaucel). It was through Buchon that he had met Mérimée and Beyle. He had been touched by *De l'Amour* and offered to help to find an English publisher for *L'Essai de l'histoire de la musique en Italie de 1800 à 1823*. He was constantly doing errands for his friends: he helped to place articles by Beyle in an English review, and among his papers is a list of errands with the eloquent note: "brought from Paris, 20 Octr 1825"

> Ask Southern [Henry Southern, the editor of *The London Magazine*], why he isn't publishing the article on Cuvier's fossils, a really well written piece. And ask him to send me back the article on French

agriculture if he hasn't printed it. Ask him to send me literary reviews
regularly. . . .
   Buy the following things:
   6 flannel waistcoats with sleeves. . . .
   1 doz. cravats
   1 doz. very good razors. . . .
   The rest of *The Edinburgh Review*. . . .

Sutton Sharpe earned the copy of *L'Histoire de la peinture en Italie*
which was given to him by Romain Colomb after Beyle's death. He
himself died in 1843, less than a year after Beyle, at the age of
forty-five.[23]

During his visit to England in the summer of 1826, Beyle accompanied Sharpe on his circuit in the North Country. They visited
Lancaster; on August 9 they found themselves at Manchester, after
which they visited the Lakes. "Fine moonlight with its tender reverie
on the shores of Wendermere. . . ."[24] In his only comment, Beyle
again showed his insensibility to nature and his persistent ignorance
of English. He and Sharpe went on to York, where he admired the
minster, and then—still in August—they went to Birmingham.
Sharpe's uncle, Daniel Rogers (brother of Samuel), was living nearby
at Stourbridge. And near Birmingham, it seems, they admired
Hagley Park.

   The Roman campagna is yellowish, the greenness has completely
   disappeared [Beyle was to write in *Promenades dans Rome*]. . . . One's
   eyes regret the memories of Richmond and Hagley Park. Oh! If the
   English had had a *Palladio*, what would they not have done in the way
   of *towns*, that very rich and aristocratic nation! . . .
   Imagine the Villa Aldobrandini, instead of the square house at
   Hagley [near Birmingham].[25]

On this visit, Beyle met Sarah Austin, who had done much to
introduce German literature into England. His visit had its practical
side: he wanted to ensure further contributions to English
periodicals. These articles—which he continued to write for some
years—offered harsh criticism of France. He probably received his
information from the journalist and government official Jean-Louis
Lingay.[26] His articles were translated by an Irish friend called
Bartholomew Stritch, director of the *Germanic Review* in London.

Stritch was possibly associated with Henry Colburn, the editor and proprietor of journals to which Beyle contributed, and from which he drew about £200 a year. René Dollot maintains, in *Stendhal journaliste*, that for some years two-thirds of his income came to him, more or less regularly, from his English publisher.[27]

In the early autumn of 1826, on his way back to Paris, he passed through Saint-Omer, where he had the final confirmation of his misfortune. Menti had found a new lover: her husband's aide-de-camp, Captain Auguste de Rospiec. This was what Beyle described in his *Souvenirs d'égotisme* as "the terrible misfortune of 15 September 1826."[28] Once again—as he had done when he left Métilde—he thought of ending his crisis by suicide.

On September 18 he reached Paris, and by way of consolation, he took up the draft of *Armance*. By October 10 he had finished it. The next day he reread the impassioned letter in which Menti had expressed her fear of pregnancy, her anxiety, her hatred and her love. "For two years, you avoided a confession, and you dismissed me a week after I had made it to you." He wrote on the letter: "She loved me for two years before 22 May 1824, so from 1822 to the end of 1826, May. Tears and real tenderness, alas! I am writing this on 11 October 1826, after my misfortune." He added: "Quarrels during the first months, later regretted. October 1826."[29]

The author of *De l'Amour* always needed a focus for his emotions, and he did not need, now, to wait for long. Early in 1827 Giulia Rinieri de' Rocchi entered his life. She was twenty-six, and she came from a patrician family in Sienna. Her mother, Anna Martini Rinieri, had followed the general custom by taking a *cavaliere servente;* and when she died in 1824, leaving at least seven children, her *cavaliere,* Daniello Berlinghieri—sometime rector of Siena University—continued to keep a watchful eye on her family. He had shown particular devotion to Giulia, and when, at the end of 1826, he arrived in Paris as the Tuscan minister, he brought her with him. Berlinghieri and Beyle had several friends in common, among them Baron Gérard and the Cuviers, and it was, it was said, at the Cuviers', at the Jardin des Plantes, that Beyle had met Giulia. Now, on January 14, he visited her at the Tuscan legation. He later said that he had begun to love her on February 3.[30]

On February 24 the new edition of *Rome, Naples et Florence* was put on sale. In April or May Beyle signed a contract with Urbain Canel for the publication of *Armance;* on July 17 he sent Canel the introduction, signed "Stendhal," to the anonymous work. *Armance,* in three volumes, was published on August 18. Pierre Jourda claims that, at the dawn of Romanticism, Beyle had created the modern novel.[31]

Twenty-six

To the modern reader, *Armance* seems both refreshing and impossible. It treats the problem of sexual impotence with a delicacy which today appears extraordinary. Indeed, Beyle writes with such restraint that the word "impotence" is not mentioned; and were it not for an explicit letter to Mérimée, many of his readers might not even guess the hero's secret, the "monstrosity" (to use his own word) which wrecks his life and, finally, those of his mother and his wife. Many contemporaries failed to guess the secret of Octave de Malivert. The *Foreign Review and Continental Miscellany* of 1828 ended its review of the novel: "We are sorry, that we cannot gratify [our readers] by telling poor Octave's secret, for we do not know it; and it must therefore remain, with the authorship of Junius, the executioner of Charles I, and the Egyptian hieroglyphs, among the *res incognitae* of the world."[1]

Octave de Malivert, wrote Pierre Brun in 1900, "may be a cousin of René, Werther, Adolphe and Obermann, but he is a cousin of some junior branch. What displeases in him is the physical monster, dragging his abnormal impotence into love. . . . What pleases us, on the contrary, is that he has much of the timid, shy, profoundly tender Stendhal, whom one has not glimpsed often enough."[2] It seems as if

Beyle had wanted to show that the deepest love was the love that was most deeply thwarted. He himself had known that love and pleasure did not always go together. Octave de Malivert knew that he might well make love to casual women, but that if one woman in the world could not arouse his physical passion, it was the woman whom he idolised.

Today, while one admires Beyle's reticence, one also feels impatient. It is not only because the key to the novel has been withheld, but because the suffering of Octave, his mother and Armance all seem perhaps to have been unnecessary. Yet one must not judge *Armance* from the point of view of the twentieth century, for it is so clearly a product of its time. Though Beyle is advanced in his choice of subject, he presents it in a manner which would now be impossible. He also presents the *mal du siècle* which was peculiar to post-Napoleonic society. Octave cannot forget himself, or aspire to glory, in some Bonaparte campaign. He is restricted by his malady, by his social class and by the limited opportunities of the Restoration. He is an aristocrat in a microcosm where social standing and connections seem essential for advancement, where intelligence is dismissed, and merit is less important than assiduous attendance in certain salons, the cultivation of certain *salonnières*. Heart and soul, like intellect, are generally discounted. The only significant factor, beside those of birth and influence, is wealth. *Armance* is the story of an impotent man who finds himself, against all his vows, in love; it is also that of Armance, a girl who is barred from love by this disability, by her own undistinguished birth and her lack of fortune. Beyle describes with cynicism and with clear contempt the petty world in which they move.

Even if one accepts the original premise of the novel, the narrative is a Byronic period piece. The secondary characters have stepped from the boards in some boulevard theatre. It is difficult to accept the duel, the desperate rides on horseback, the depositing of notes in the tubs of orange trees, the forged letter, the fainting fits, the suicide of Octave as his ship comes within sight of Byron's Greece; it is hard to accept the retreat of his mother and widow into a convent.

Yet perhaps one is mistaken to ask for authenticity as one understands it or even to ask for verisimilitude. In this novel, Beyle has endowed his hero with his own timidity, or rather he has made him personify extreme timidity, and he has set him in a situation where decision and audacity mean much. He has made Octave a man of principle in a world where principles are little regarded; he has made him a man of feeling and compassion, intelligence and integrity in a superficial society. He has shown us a man of excruciating sensibility in a pitiless, materialistic world and in an oppressive personal crisis.

Writing to Mérimée, he wondered if *Armance* was too academic. It is indeed an academic exercise, a psychological experiment. One is sometimes impatient with Octave's constant self-analysis, his cerebral approach to life, his tortuous consideration of every problem, sometimes of problems which he has invented. But then Octave is largely Beyle, and Beyle often gained less pleasure and less profit from love itself than he did from anticipation, from calculation, remembrance and regret.

In the summer of 1827 he was not in Paris to observe the reception of *Armance*. On July 20 he had left for Italy. He spent ten days or so at Genoa; then he hastened to Naples and Ischia. There, in solitude, he spent the first "redoubtable anniversary" of his break with Menti. On September 25 he arrived in Rome, where he stayed until October 15. Two days later he reached Florence, where—equipped with an introduction from Mareste—he paid several visits to Lamartine. The author of the *Méditations poétiques* and the *Nouvelles Méditations* was still royalist in sympathy; he was secretary at the French embassy. Beyle did not share his political views or his piety, but he wholeheartedly shared his admiration for Byron.

> At our first meeting [Lamartine was to remember] he said to me:
> "I'm sure that people have told you dreadful things about me; that I was an atheist. . . . I'm not going to try to deceive you. It is true. . . . I have cast the theological baggage—piety, you call it—far behind me. I envy you, for consoling illusions are very sweet truths for those who believe them; but, personally, I don't believe in anything, and I just abandon myself to my taste for literature and the fine arts. . . . Well, there I am!" he said, smiling. . . . "I have come to be nice to you. Let's talk!"
> We talked without mystery and without indignation on either side. I told him [Lamartine continued] that I had been delighted with nearly everything that he had written and that apart from the cynicism which was antipathetic to my nature, and the atheism

which my mind found unacceptable, I had enjoyed all his work. I told him that . . . if he wanted to come at any hour of the evening to end the day with me, we should talk about God, if he liked, or about literature and the arts. He would give me some taste, and I should give him some faith. . . .

And so it happened for two or three months that autumn. I was living in a suburb of the town; every evening, before or after dinner, Beyle would arrive. We threw a handful of sweet-smelling myrtle onto the fire, and we talked with the confidence which solitude and good faith inspire in men. I inspired him with a few doubts about his atheism, and he often enlightened me in my ignorance about music, poetry and the arts.[3]

Beyle left Florence to visit Bologna, Ferrara and Venice. On January 1, 1828, he was unwise enough to arrive in Milan. The political suspicions which he had aroused more than six years earlier had not yet subsided. He was still remembered as the author of *Rome, Naples et Florence,* and he was still suspected as the author of *Histoire de la peinture en Italie.* The police ordered him to leave the Austrian states within twelve hours. Baron de Torresani, director general of police in Milan, reported to Count de Sedlnitzky, prefect of police in Vienna:

> I have also taken the necessary measures to ensure that the frontier remains strictly closed to this dangerous foreigner should he again present himself, and in addition I have warned the directors of the imperial and royal police in Venice and Trieste. . . .
>
> In conclusion, may I humbly add that, during his stay of several years in Milan, Beyle became known as an irreligious, immoral and dangerous enemy of legitimacy, so that it is incomprehensible that my predecessors should have tolerated him for so many years. . . . He is generally considered to be the author of another extremely pernicious work which appeared in Paris in 1817 under the title: *Histoire de la peinture par M.B.A.A.*[4]

The dangerous foreigner spent a fortnight on Lake Maggiore before he took the road home. On January 29 he arrived in Paris.

He found himself in financial straits. Henri Martineau estimates that in 1823 and 1824 he had a total income of 5,000 to 7,000 francs and that in 1825 and 1826 he had 8,000 to 10,000. This was as much as Beyle himself thought necessary for an independent existence. In 1827, however, Colburn's payments became irregular, and in 1828 the half pay, or *demi-solde,* was halved. Beyle was never really poor; but he was accustomed to a comfortable bourgeois standard of living, and according to that standard, he was poor after 1827.[5] On March 23, 1828, he wrote to Sutton Sharpe: "Anything may occur in this world, even an honest publisher. So if chance should ever bring you near this Phoenix, and you could make an arrangement, I should be glad to leave Colburn, who has to be reminded if he is to pay me every three months."[6]

One arrangement had recently been made with *The Athenaeum.* This influential magazine had just been launched by James Silk Buckingham: a journalistic adventurer with independent principles and considerable initiative. On April 4 *The Athenaeum* published "French Society and Literature by a Resident of Paris," the first of a series of foreign correspondences which were to become a distinctive feature of the magazine. The evidence seems to point to Beyle as the writer of these letters. Martineau records that Beyle gave articles to *The Athenaeum* from February 5, 1828, to January 21, 1829.[7]

At this point one may perhaps consider Beyle's contributions to English periodicals. Their most striking and consistent feature is their hostile criticism of French life. In January, 1826, Colburn's *New Monthly Magazine* had published the first of twenty-nine "Sketches of Parisian Society, Politics and Literature." "To be quite honest with you," wrote Beyle, "the King and the royal family have not for three hundred years been so universally scorned as they are to-day; yet no-one wants to run the risk of being guillotined for having tried to get rid of them."[8] It was not only the Bourbons who earned his contempt. In April he explained that "the aristocratic party want us to feel for the French nobility, sold to the ministers, that high degree of respect which people in England naturally feel for men like Lord Holland and Lord Lansdowne. The Jesuits . . . are trying to gain the power and consideration in France which the clergy enjoy in England."[9] The French provincials, continued Beyle, had their heads "stuffed with commerce, and when they had made a fortune, they bought books simply out of vanity."[10] Religious practice had become a form of social life in Paris, and the church of Saint-

Thomas-d'Aquin had become a fashionable meeting place, "and during mass it looks like a crowded salon. . . . Nothing favours the promotion of a young lieutenant more surely than regular attendance at Saint-Thomas-d'Aquin, Saint-Sulpice or any other church which is in vogue."[11] Politically, socially, France remained unstable. "Everything," wrote Beyle, "is uncertain in France to-day. Unlike you in England, we do not have a powerful aristocracy and a clergy worthy of respect, and no-one can say if in 1850 we shall have a republic like America or a monarchy with *lettres de cachet* as in the days of Louis XV."[12] French society had become "very prudish and very dull; it is very dangerous with women to talk more than platitudes, and conversation, once so brilliant, is to-day a *burden* which one would be glad to discard."[13] Nor did elegant social life exist outside Paris. "I suppose that in England the rich enjoy themselves more in the country than they do in town. In France, on the contrary, a château is the most boring thing in the world; in general, people only leave town for reasons of economy."[14]

Beyle's condemnation of modern France was clear in *The New Monthly Magazine* and, again, in *The London Magazine*. In France, he wrote, the great majority of the army were in favour of whoever paid them.[15] Many middle-aged Frenchmen had been reasonable patriots "as long as they saw some hope of establishing a real constitutional government, with two independent Chambers. They have now abandoned their feelings as chimerical, and they are only looking for the chance to sell themselves."[16] Marriage was no more sacred than politics. "The genius of our century is," wrote Beyle, "entirely mercantile, and it makes us consider every marriage as a means of acquiring capital."[17]

If Beyle expressed such views in conversation, it was small wonder that he was mistrusted and disliked in certain salons. French society was still vulnerable after Waterloo; its vanity was more intense than ever. Even artistic questions became questions of national honour —or, to be more precise, of chauvinism. Beyle made no secret of his predilection for Italy; a few years after the appearance of *Racine et Shakespeare,* he also pleaded for the establishment of an English theatre in Paris. "As soon as we find a shrewd businessman, we shall see *Othello, King Lear, Venice preserv'd.* . . . One might perhaps take advantage of the financial straits in which Covent Garden and Drury Lane now find themselves, and secure some good English actors.

Kean enjoys a great reputation in Paris, and his presence would alone ensure the success of the enterprise."[18]

Beyle's remarks on literature are among his more attractive journalistic comments. The future author of *Armance*, he reviews *Olivier* by Latouche—pretending that it is the work of the Duchesse de Duras.[19] The future author of *Le Rouge et le Noir*, he describes the pleasure that he takes in *La Gazette des Tribunaux*, which reports all the *causes célèbres*. "It is," he writes, "highly entertaining, and it gives the most faithful picture of French society."[20] Beyle discusses the passion for Scott; he dismisses "a new novel, called *Cinq-Mars*, . . . by Comte Alfred de Vigny. It is full of affectation."[21] He deplores the official subsidising of the theatres in Paris, and in *The Athenaeum*, turning to the visual arts, he proclaims the "considerable talent" of Delacroix.[22] Such generosity is rare, however; Beyle the cynic more than once condemns "M. Cuvier, the famous naturalist, who has sold himself in turn to all the parties in power."[23] The comment is all the more unpleasant since Beyle himself showed no consistent loyalty in politics and since he often accepted Cuvier's hospitality.

Beyle's contributions to English periodicals were informative, vivacious and often shrewd; they were all too often bitterly aggressive. They offered a *déversoir* to a disappointed man.

As 1828 began, his financial affairs were, as usual, disturbing; his social life remained pleasant enough. He had gone to Florence for a week, he told Sutton Sharpe, but he had stayed there for sixty-eight days. "It was an Englishwoman, a *marquise*, who pleased me most there."[24] The *marquise* was the Countess of Blessington. Now, in June, 1828, she and her husband arrived to spend a few months in Paris. They found a handsome hôtel which had once belonged to Marshal Ney. It stood in the rue Bourbon, and its main windows framed a spectacular view of the Seine and the Tuileries Gardens. The hôtel was duly redecorated; and when the principal drawing room was resplendent with crimson satin curtains, "and sofas, *bergères, fauteuils,* and chairs, richly carved and gilt," Beyle came to pay his respects.[25] In *The Idler in France*, in a passage left undated, Lady Blessington reported: "Mr. H—— B—— dined here yesterday, and he talked over the pleasant days we had passed in Italy. He is an excellent specimen of the young men of the present day. Well-informed, and with a mind highly cultivated, he has travelled much in other countries, without losing any of the good qualities and habits peculiar to his own."[26] Lady Blessington was, it seems, so absorbed by his conversation that she did not see his personal defects. She was certainly generous about the "excellent specimen" of youth. The previous year Henri Monnier, the cartoonist and impersonator, had produced *Les Soirées de Neuilly*, a series of dramatic and historical sketches, "published by M. de Fongeray, with a portrait of the publisher." This lithograph showed an imaginary character, a man of sixty or so, bald and potbellied. Monnier later confessed that it was a sharpened likeness of Henri Beyle.[27]

If Beyle went once to the rue Bourbon, he frequently called at the Jardin des Plantes. Sometimes known as the Jardin du Roi, it had been founded by the physician of Louis XIII, but it owed its beauty and value largely to the labours of Buffon. Its name was not wholly appropriate: a fine botanic garden off the Quai Saint-Bernard, it also contained a large menagerie, a museum of natural history and anatomy, and halls in which public lectures were delivered. During the Restoration the Jardin des Plantes was under the direction of Georges Cuvier. He had largely founded the sciences of comparative anatomy and palaeontology, and the visitor passed through the rooms where he continued his labours. One of the public rooms contained the animal remains of the antediluvian world; among them were the bones "discovered by Cuvier in the plaster-quarries of Montmartre, and of which he had constituted several new genera of extinct quadrupeds."[28] William Hazlitt, that critical observer, considered that the Jardin des Plantes was "delightfully laid out. . . . Every plant of every quarter of the globe is here, growing in the open air; and labelled with its common and its scientific name on it. A prodigious number of animals, wild and tame, are enclosed in separate divisions, feeding on the grass or shrubs, and leading a life of learned leisure."[29]

The tourist admired Cuvier's labours. In the 1820's, Parisian writers and scientists found stimulus in his Saturday evening receptions. Cuvier lived at the Jardin des Plantes. His apartments included a series of rooms in which he kept his library. These led to the drawing room where, after his receptions, a few friends stayed on to supper. They talked of exotic travels, books and pictures; sometimes the conversation continued under an awning in a room which was known as the Tent. It was a lively and elegant world. One summer day Buchon reported to Sutton Sharpe: "Tomorrow Beyle and I and several professors from the Jardin des Plantes are going to meet the giraffe. Mesdemoiselles Cuvier are coming on the steamboat with us. We want to greet the young visitor from abroad, and the Duchesse de Berry, who is excessively bored with the monotonous life at court, has decided to be the first to welcome and compliment the giraffe in Paris."[30]

Beyle had always taken an interest in science; but his intellectual curiosity was counterbalanced by his capricious humour. Even with the Cuviers he could be disconcerting. In 1828, planning an expedition to Saint-Cloud, Sophie Duvaucel explained to Sharpe: "M. Beyle is such a difficult man to *amuse* that I haven't dared to suggest to him that he joined us. But if he were tempted to make the journey with you and to come back and dine at the Jardin des Plantes, we should be really charmed by this heroic resolution."[31]

Twenty-seven

On February 10, 1829, a new figure made her appearance in Beyle's correspondence. "M. Durat is going to do the bust of Madame *Bleue.*"[1] Mme. Bleue, or Mme. Azur, as he sometimes called her, lived in the rue Bleue: hence her pseudonyms. Her real name was Alberthe de Rubempré. She was a courtesan—"an unsublime courtesan à la Du Barry." She was sometime the mistress of the artist Tony Johannot. She was a cousin of Delacroix, and this relationship did not prevent her from being his mistress, too. She was a Romantic, eccentric creature. She was to live on, sadly, for more than forty years. In 1853 Delacroix was to find her "without a fire, in her big alchemist's room, and in one of her curious garbs, which made her look like a sorceress. She has," he wrote, "always had a taste for this magician's apparel, even in the days when her beauty was her true enchantment. I still remember that room hung with black and with funereal symbols, her black velvet robe, and that red cashmere twined round her head. All these kinds of accessories, together with that circle of admirers whom she seemed to keep at a distance did for a moment turn my head. Where is poor Tony [Johannot]? Where is poor Beyle?"[2] Beyle was dead when Delacroix asked the rhetorical question. But Mme. Bleue had not kept him at a distance. On June

21, 1829, she had granted him her favours. Their love affair was violent and brief.

The year 1829 was a golden year for Romanticism. On August 1 Rossini's *Guillaume Tell* had its first performance in Paris. Dumas' *Henri III et sa cour* was staged, and Hugo published *Les Orientales*. During the year, an intrepid foreign visitor descended on Paris to record the cultural scene. Lady Morgan was known as "the Wild Irish Girl," after her famous novel of that name. The daughter of a Dublin actor, she had earned her living as a governess before her writing became remunerative. She owed her social triumph largely to her character. She was tiny and ill-formed; but her eyes flashed fire, and she had "a witty word for everybody." At the age of thirty-five she had married Charles Morgan, an obstetrician. He was knighted on their wedding day, an event which gave her satisfaction. A lively snob, she had scurried across the Channel and produced a book called *France* which went through four editions in a year.

In 1829, after an interval of eleven years, she returned, middle-aged and triumphant, to Paris. She was at once aware of the change in the cultural climate. The contest between Romantic and Classic had almost reached its climax, and Beyle was now famous as one of "the chiefs of the Propaganda, the ardent missionaries who praise Romanticism and preach its mysteries."[3] When the Morgans had left France, in 1818, the word "Romanticism" had—she said—been virtually unknown in Parisian circles. Now, in 1829, "Victor Hugo, De La Martine, Alfred de Vigny, Mérimée, Vitet, Dumas, Beyle, . . . had taken the place of those whom we had left in possession of the public favour."[4]

Lady Morgan did not simply come as a titled tourist. As a celebrated author she moved immediately in literary circles, and she received "a numerous circle of morning visitors." Among them was "the brilliant Beyle, whose travels made me long to know the author, and whose conversation is still more lively and original than his books. . . ."[5] Irish and vivacious herself, she warmed to his vivacity. They discussed Rossini, whom he declared the wittiest man in France, and they discussed the English interpretation of the French language. Beyle maintained—perhaps with a touch of irony—that the English errors were infinitely charming to French readers.

* * *

On September 5 Delaunay published Beyle's *Promenades dans Rome*.
It is a disappointing work. It hardly compares with Gautier's *Voyage en
Italie*. One is constantly aware of the author's lack of visual sense. Nor,
in the *Promenades,* does he use his humour and wit. His two volumes
are a compilation rather than a work of literature. Three-quarters of
this so-called diary, he himself confessed, were judicious extracts from
the best authors.

However, for the student of Beyle, *Promenades dans Rome* has its
interest. "From Paris," he writes, "we went to Basle; we crossed the
most unpleasant country in the world, which noodles call *la belle
France.*" It was not the only time he recorded his lack of admiration for
the French landscape, and repeatedly, he reminds us of his distaste for
his fellow countrymen. No one disliked, more than Henri Beyle, the
superficiality, the hypocrisy and vanity of the French. The Italians,
he maintained, "are not as far as we are from great deeds; they *take
things seriously.* In France, as soon as you have given a witty *explanation*
of a mean action, the action itself is forgotten." And, again, in
Promenades dans Rome, he praised the gravity and the honesty of
Italians: "This *respect for truth,* and the *permanence of desires,* are, we
consider, the two main features which distinguish the Roman from
the Parisian."

Beyle's greatest love in Rome remained the Coliseum. "These
pieces of wall, blackened by time, affect the soul like the music of
Cimarosa." (Here, again, he anticipates the *correspondances* of later
writers.) For Saint Peter's, too, he feels Romantic veneration; he is
tempted to spend the night there, alone. And, speaking of music, he
writes:

> I want to be understood only by those people born for music; I
> should like to be able to write in a sacred tongue.
> The arts are a privilege, and dearly bought! By how many misfor-
> tunes, how many stupidities, how many days of utter melancholy![6]

Promenades dans Rome was, on the whole, judiciously received; it
was accorded seven articles, five of them important, within two
months.[7]

Three days after the book was published, Beyle set out for the south of France and Spain. He travelled by way of Bordeaux and Toulouse, went as far as Barcelona, returned by Montpellier and Grenoble, and arrived in Marseilles. "On the evening sky, in front of the invisible sea, the old fort guarded the entrance to the harbour. . . . All the smells of the Mediterranean mingled with the frowzy smells of the Old Port."[8] It was in Marseilles, where perhaps the smell of tar again recalled an idyll of years ago, where perhaps he thought of Mélanie, where perhaps his senses were heightened, that Beyle had an idea for a novel. During the night of October 25–26 he had "the idea of Julien"—the novel that was to be called *Le Rouge et le Noir.*

He set to work at once. From this moment forward, it has been claimed, his life belongs to the critic rather than the biographer. He tried to understand and to solve in fiction the problems which he had found insoluble in life. Every writer, as Valéry says, makes himself what amends he can for the injustices of destiny. Beylism had not brought its author happiness and success or even the spectacular failure which he would have accepted. Other Beylists, born of his brain, should be more fortunate.[9] Late in November, after a month of intensive work, he took the first draft of his novel back to Paris.

In Paris, on December 2, he saw Alberthe de Rubempré again and realized that Mareste had supplanted him. He was not unduly afflicted. He had chosen to leave Paris for the better part of three months, and he must have known that she would find solace. In any case, he soon discovered consolation. Three years earlier, at the Tuscan legation, he had admired Giulia Rinieri. Now, on January 27, 1830, she made him a declaration of love.

In his *Indiscrétions sur Giulia,* Luigi-Foscolo Benedetto has questioned the spontaneity of her gesture.[10] He suspects that there had been an idyll between Giulia and Peruzzi, the young secretary of legation, who had been living under the same roof since the summer of 1827. Perhaps—as Benedetto says—Giulia was discouraged by Peruzzi or was simply taking her revenge. She wanted to get married, and Beyle seemed a possible husband.

If her declaration of love was calculated, he was not aware of the fact. He was touched, delighted and astonished. For Giulia was eighteen years younger than himself. Her wasp waist and her profusion of ribbons, bows and muslin, her corkscrew curls, her big, dark, melancholy eyes, her pallor—all made her the Romantic heroine. He himself was far from being a Romantic hero. He was four days past his forty-seventh birthday. He was obese, and underneath his wig he was bald. He asked her to decide, at leisure, whether or not she wanted to be his mistress. He needed time, himself, to embellish her in absence, to feel anxiety, to crystallise his passion. But the result was hardly in doubt. On March 22 he became her lover.

His private life was, for the moment, tranquil. His literary life was active. On December 13 the *Revue de Paris* had published his short story "Vanina Vanini," the first of his Italian chronicles. Vanina, a patrician girl, had fallen in love with a carbonaro, Pietro Missirilli. He had set the freedom of Italy above human passion: a gesture which earned the respect of the Cornelian Beyle. One did not always find such nobility in modern literature. On January 10, 1830, writing to Sutton Sharpe, Beyle deplored the triumph of the prolific drama-tist Eugène Scribe. "This Scribe is only interested in money, he has earned 1,500,000 francs in the theatre." And, talking of the theatre, he added: *"Hernani,* a tragedy by M. V. Hugo, . . . is going to cause a battle at the Théâtre-Français on about 6 February."[11]

It was in fact on February 25 that he attended the battle in which the Romantics finally overcame the supporters of Classicism. Hugo's tragedy broke in every way with dramatic conventions; even before it was staged, it had become the symbol of the new literature. But the *bataille d'Hernani* was not merely fought on literary grounds; it was, as the contestants knew, the war between old and young, between past and future, between restriction and absolute freedom. It was a supreme and public occasion for youth to assert itself.

On the first night of *Hernani* the pit and stalls of the Théâtre-Français were therefore filled with supporters of classical drama, and the gallery was thronged with Hugo's garish admirers; among them was Théophile Gautier, refulgent in a pink satin doublet. Etienne Delécluze was among the partisans of tradition, and he took a staid view of the other side: "As for the great majority of the spectators, . . . they could not bear the serene expression of those who did not share their frantic enthusiasm; and if one did not clap one's hands or stamp at every couplet, one was called a stupid fool, and threatened into the bargain."[12] Among the audience was the author of *Racine et Shakespeare.* One suspects, however, that he did not stamp at every couplet. He was far from well (one wonders if his old Milanese ailment had its effect), and on March 1, heavily dosed with opium, he admitted: "I am still very weak. Champagne and *Hernani* have not agreed with me."[13] *Hernani* had not agreed with him. The theories which he had set out in *Racine et Shakespeare* seemed to be, for the moment, at a discount. It was Hugo's name, not Beyle's, which was to rally the innovators. Beyle had urged that tragedies should be written in prose. *Hernani* was, for a time, to rehabilitate verse drama.

Dulled as he was with opium, Beyle continued his reading. One night, unable to sleep, he had taken up Moore's *Memoirs of Lord Byron.* "I knew Lord Byron. How miserable to be handed over after his death to a wretched hypocrite like Moore!"[14] Beyle was eager to find talent, eager to praise. In February, 1830, he announced to Mareste: "I have just discovered a great and true poet. . . . It's M. de Musset, *Contes d'Espagne et d'Italie.* "[15] He was less impressed by the poetry of the young Sainte-Beuve. When he had read *Les Consolations,* he wrote to him with condescension: "I believe, monsieur, that you are intended for the highest literary destiny. However, I still find a little affectation in your verse. . . . I believe that people will speak about you in 1890. But you will do better than *Les Consolations.* "[16] Sainte-Beuve was—so he later maintained—immensely flattered by Beyle's approval. In 1854 he devoted two of his *Causeries du lundi* to Beyle's *Oeuvres complètes* and acclaimed him as one of the first Frenchmen "who had gone abroad, in a literary sense, and made comparisons." He was to acclaim his pioneering work as a critic: "What he did in music for the cause of Mozart, Cimarosa and Rossini, . . . he did in literature against the Augers." With his habitual sureness of touch, Sainte-Beuve defined him: "He was, above all, an exciter of ideas. . . . A Romantic hussar."[17]

Beyle respected Sainte-Beuve. For Hugo, the author of *Hernani,* the accepted leader of the Romantics, he had little sympathy. It was about now—in 1830—that Mérimée brought them together. Sainte-Beuve reported that they were "like two wild cats from two opposite gutters, on the defensive, with bristling fur, only drawing in their claws with infinite precautions."[18] Little love was lost between them. Years afterwards, on a visit to Hugo, Henri Rochefort, the political journalist, attempted to make him read *Le Rouge et le Noir.*

He claimed not to know it [Rochefort recorded], and this astonished me, considering the care he took to keep abreast of modern literature. . . .

"I tried to read it," he told me. "How could you get further than the fourth page? Do you know dialect?"

"Yes," I said, "I know it isn't 'written,' but. . . ."

"Personally," insisted Victor Hugo, "I am not enthralled by errors of French. Every time I try to decipher a phrase in your favourite work, it feels as if someone were tugging out one of my teeth."

And he continued:

"You see, the only works which have a chance of surviving through the ages are the works which are really *written*. . . . M. Stendhal cannot last. He never for a moment suspected what writing meant."[19]

In the first months of 1830, Beyle was nonetheless concerned with his writing. It was probably on January 18 that he took up the manuscript of *Julien,* as he called it, and quickly finished it. On April 8 he signed a contract with Levavasseur for its publication. On May 9 the *Revue de Paris* published his short story, "Le Coffre et le Revenant," and in June it published another, "Le Philtre." "Le Coffre et le Revenant" described the ecstasy of two lovers who met again after an absence which should have been eternal. Beyle sent a copy to the "comtesse nº 2": almost certainly the Comtesse Curial. She acknowledged it by sending him a white rose.[20]

Twenty-eight

On July 28, from his room in Paris, Henri Beyle watched the insurrection that was to be known as Les Trois Glorieuses. The previous year, Charles X had dissolved the Chamber of Deputies for protesting against his reactionary policy. The electorate had shown its discontent by returning a chamber with a much larger opposition party. On July 26, 1830, the king had issued ordinances which again dissolved the chamber, ended representative government by changing the electoral law, and violated the Charter of 1814 by abolishing the freedom of the press. This minor coup d'état provoked immediate resistance among journalists, politicians, and the Parisian populace. Street rioting began next day, July 27, and turned to fighting, which lasted until the twenty-ninth. Charles X abdicated in favour of his grandson the Duc de Bordeaux (later known as the Comte de Chambord), the posthumous son of the Duc de Berry. The Orléanists then contrived the establishment of a constitutional monarchy. On August 7 Louis-Philippe, Duc d'Orléans, was proclaimed King of the French "by the Grace of God and the will of the people."

The *juste milieu* of Louis-Philippe was in time to become obnoxious to the artist in Beyle; as a Romantic, he admired political energy and heroism. However, as a pragmatic realist, he preferred prudence and peace, and only a constitutional monarch could reconcile his aristocratic instincts with his liberalism. He was delighted by the end of the Bourbon Restoration. "Everything that the papers have told you in praise of the people is true [this to Sutton Sharpe]. . . . The king is excellent."[1]

The political change offered him a chance to embark again on an official career. He did not underestimate his worth. On August 3 he asked Guizot to appoint him a prefect. Guizot refused. On August 25 he sent a curiously aggressive note to Comte Molé, Minister of Foreign Affairs.

> M. Beyle is exceedingly grateful that he is still considered good for something, despite his 47 years and his 14 years of service. He must explain that he is completely without means. . . .
>
> M. Beyle would like a place as consul general at Naples, Genoa or Leghorn, if one of the consuls were to leave Italy. If the Consulate is too far above what people seem to want to do for him, he would request the place of first secretary in Naples or in Rome.[2]

His friends were working for him: among them Domenico Fiore, an elderly Italian who was now a French government official. Fiore seems to have had much effect. On September 25, by royal decree, Beyle was granted a consulate. "Dominique is appointed consul at Trieste, in the midst of the barbarians," he announced to Mareste. "The Minister has also, in his kindness, raised the salary to fifteen thousand francs."[3] On September 29 he told Sainte-Beuve: "The first act of my consulate is to invite you to spend six months, or a year, in the consul's house. You will be as free there, monsieur, as you would be at an inn; we should only see one another at table. You could devote yourself to your poetic inspiration."[4] On October 13 he wrote to Comte Molé, announcing his readiness to depart.

Early in November, on the eve of his departure, he told his publisher that he was too preoccupied to correct the proofs of *Le Rouge et le Noir*. He was indeed preoccupied. Now that he had ensured himself a future in Italy, he began to feel that he would miss Parisian society. He had dreamed of consoling himself, among the barbarians, with the conversation of Sainte-Beuve. Now he felt that he would need more permanent and more intimate company. The certainty of his departure gave him sudden courage. The day he left Paris, he wrote to Daniello Berlinghieri, the guardian of Giulia Rinieri, and asked him for her hand.

Monsieur,

It may be great temerity in me, poor and old as I am, to confess that I should consider the happiness of my life assured if I might obtain the hand of your niece. I needed her encouragement. But she told me that your kindness and your affection for her were so great that, even if you did not accept my proposition, you would not deride it too much.

My position is almost my only fortune. I am forty-seven. I am too poor to be concerned with your niece's fortune. If I were rich, I should be no more concerned. I consider it a miracle that I could have been loved at forty-seven.

Your niece would not wish to be separated from you, monsieur, for anything in the world. She would spend six months in Trieste with me and six months with you. I give my word of honour to bring her to Geneva after the first six months and to come and fetch her there six months later. I shall sign the marriage contract without reading it. If mademoiselle has any property, it might be given to the children she might have. In this way, the husband would not be legally concerned. The marriage might take place at Varese, near Lake Maggiore, on 1 May 1831. Monsieur, I have spoken as one gentleman to another. I will part for six months every year from someone who would like to spend her life beside you.

I am with the most profound respect

H. BEYLE[5]

There was no doubt of Beyle's devotion to Giulia, and there was no doubt of the sincerity of his proposal. He was indeed concerned with happiness, not with financial advantage, and to ensure this happiness he offered conditions which, to the average Frenchman, would have seemed extraordinary. One is struck by his real and touching diffidence, by his idealism, by the romanticism of the proposal which he clearly felt was hopeless from the start. He could only trust in Giulia's love for him and in the understanding of her guardian.

Berlinghieri was nearly seventy, and he would have found it hard to be deprived of Giulia's company. No doubt he appreciated the quixotic generosity of the proposal. He must also have questioned the material benefits which such a marriage would bring to his ward. He was accustomed to diplomacy. He sent Beyle a refusal in disguise; he insisted that Giulia must wait before she committed herself to anyone.

On November 6, the day he sent his proposal of marriage, Beyle left for Italy. He was still on his way when, on November 15, the *Bibliographie de la France* announced the publication of *Le Rouge et le Noir*.

Twenty-nine

HENRI BEYLE WAS not a born novelist. He lacked creative power, the ability to devise a situation. He lacked the dynamism and the visual sense of Balzac. He had not trained himself to write novels. He had been forty-three when he embarked on *Armance;* he would clearly not have written it if the Duchesse de Duras had not conceived the story of Olivier, if Latouche had not published a novel on the identical subject. Beyle was not averse to plagiarism in his critical works; he needed to be given a factual basis for his fiction.

In 1829 he had been fascinated by a current murder case. Adrien Lafargue was a young working man at Bagnères-de-Bigorre; he was good-looking, engaging and not uneducated. Betrayed and abandoned by his mistress, he had shot her dead and had then attempted to kill himself. Towards the end of the Restoration, when Dumas *père* was writing *Antony,* the Romantics had some sympathy for a *crime passionnel.* But if Beyle took an interest in Adrien Lafargue and described his case in—of all places—*Promenades dans Rome,* that was because he saw Lafargue as a Frenchman with Italian energy, as an example of French *amour-passion.*

Yet if Beyle gave some of his features to Julien Sorel, he was still aware that his case lacked the necessary significance for a novel; he could see in him only an incomplete sketch of the hero he needed: the young, ambitious, intelligent and inexorable man who would symbolise the antisocial spirit, the spirit of revolt and domination, as well as the ardour and violence of love.

In 1826, in *The New Monthly Magazine,* he had confessed the fascination of *La Gazette des Tribunaux.* Now, in the publication which gave "the most faithful picture of French society,"[1] he found what he needed for his new novel. In the issue of December 28–31, 1827, he found the account of the Berthet affair.

Antoine Berthet had been tried in December, 1827, at the court of appeal in Grenoble—a setting which ensured Beyle's attention. He was twenty-five and (said the *Gazette*) slightly built and dark-eyed. His father was a farrier at Brangues. Since Berthet had shown unusual intelligence, he had been adopted by the local curé and sent to the seminary. Obliged to leave on account of his poor health, he had been recommended to M. Michoud, who had made him tutor to his children. Berthet later admitted that he had been Mme. Michoud's lover. Within a year of his appointment, he had been dismissed and obliged to return to his seminary. He remained there for two years and returned to Brangues in 1825. The Michouds would not employ him again. He seems to have felt persecuted by his former employer; his letters to Mme. Michoud contained violent reproaches and vicious attacks on her husband. Nonetheless, M. Michoud tried to help him, and Berthet became preceptor to the children of a M. Cordon. After a year, M. Cordon dismissed him, apparently on account of some new intrigue. Berthet tried to become a priest, but no seminary would accept him. In his despair he blamed the Michouds. In the church at Brangues, at the moment of communion, he shot Mme. Michoud and then shot himself. He did not kill her, but he was executed.

The parallels between Antoine Berthet and Julien Sorel are remarkable, but if the crime at Brangues remains the main source of the novel, it still only resembles the novel insofar as a skeleton can resemble a living person. As Durand has pointed out, *Le Rouge et le Noir* contains two conflicting sources of inspiration: one is Beyle's concern for *le petit fait vrai,* his interest in *La Gazette des Tribunaux.* The other, charged with all his experience, all his emotion, is the influence we shall find in the *Chroniques italiennes* and, again, in *La Chartreuse de Parme*.[2]

Julien Sorel, a carpenter's son at Verrières, is chosen—as Antoine Berthet had been—as preceptor in a bourgeois family. Despite the actual precedent, it is hard to see how he could be accepted as tutor by the Rênals. He is virtually uneducated; yet he is taken straight from the carpenter's shop (is there, perhaps, some religious undertone?) to assume the educational and moral responsibility for three children. And yet, perhaps, as in the chronicles of the Italian Middle Ages, one has the sense that a destiny is being fulfilled. On many occasions Beyle uses a church or chapel to stress the holiness of love or to dignify prophetic detail. When Julien, on his way to Vergy, enters the church at Verrières, he sits in the Rênals' pew and notices a scrap of newspaper, left there as if it were meant to be read: "Details of the last moments and execution of Louis Jenrel, executed at Besançon. . . ." On the reverse of the paper are the words "The first step." "Who could have put that paper there, thought Julien? Poor wretch, he added, with a sigh, his name ends like mine."[3] It does not merely end like his own: it is an anagram of his name, and as if this blatant omen were not enough, the holy water, spilt on the floor, reflects the crimson curtains in the church like blood.

At Vergy, Julien continues to pursue his destiny. He is the incarnation of the nineteenth-century parvenu. He is the young man who, like Napoleon, rises from humble origins to challenge and to shake the established order. Here is the embodiment of energy (a quality dear to Beyle), the embodiment of ruthless, calculated self-advancement. Julien does not only personify certain qualities and ideals, a persistent theme in the author's mind: he is, very largely, Beyle himself. He has his creator's constant malaise, his sensuality and his utter coldness. He has Beyle's ability to be a hypocrite; he has his snobbery and his hatred of snobbery, his cynicism and his emotional weakness, his arrogance and his physical courage. Above all, like his creator, Julien is cerebral: except at rare moments, in solitude, or under emotional stress, he cannot allow himself to be natural. He analyses his present behaviour and calculates his future. He constantly watches himself as he plays a part. He finds it hard to be spontaneous or emotionally sincere. He cannot command the reader's sympathy.

He is perpetually urged on by his aggressive instinct, by a sense of social injustice, by resentment of inequality; he sees insults where none is intended: in modern parlance, he has a permanent chip on his shoulder. When he was told of his appointment to the Rênal household, his first question had been: *"Avec qui mangerai-je?"* He was already prepared for social discrimination, ready to embark on a class war. Now, when Mme. de Rênal is kind, he resents her kindness as condescension. When he determines to seduce her, he does so to prove himself in his own eyes. When he first takes her hand, he does so according to schedule; when he first makes love to her, he is only afraid of "terrible remorse and eternal ridicule, if he departed from the ideal model which he proposed to follow." When he leaves her, that night, he merely wonders: "Did I fail in anything which I owed to myself? Have I played my part well?"

Mme. de Rênal is the one touching character in the novel. She owes something, perhaps, to Beyle's vision of Métilde: to the ideal which, as he said, predisposed him to goodness and indulgence. She shows how faithfully he could portray the virtues which he himself did not possess: gentleness, unselfishness and innocence. Mme. de Rênal's spontaneity and her goodness of heart are convincing. One has no doubt that her love, at least, is genuine. Yet once again, how Byronic, how contrived the situation becomes! The ladder to the bedroom window, the writing of anonymous letters, the white handkerchief tied to the bar of the window as a sign that her love for Julien was safe: how could Mme. de Rênal have "run up 120 steps" to send her signal, and how could Julien, far away, in hiding, have seen a handkerchief? (But then how, in her anxiety, could she have dropped her steel scissors and broken them?) There remains one's persistent disbelief in M. de Rênal. Two-dimensional though he is, moved only by money or social ambition, it seems impossible that he should not have suspected his wife's liaison. In *Le Rouge et le Noir*, Beyle does not create the first condition demanded of the novel: the willing suspension of disbelief.

Mme. de Rênal suffers from guilt and suspicion as well as love. Julien is obliged to leave Vergy. After a time in a seminary, he is appointed to the household of the Marquis de La Mole, in Paris. Mathilde, the daughter of the house, has the fire and arrogance of Métilde Dembowski—or of one of those sixteenth-century Italian women, fervent and inexorable, whom Beyle admired. She is a sister of Keats' Isabella. (Mathilde, kissing the severed head of Julien, will indeed recall Isabella, kissing the severed head of Lorenzo.) Pierre Brun considers that Mathilde belongs to the melodrama of the boulevard du Crime.[4] There is some truth in this observation, and yet there is also truth in Benedetto's comment that if we need to find a model for Julien and Mathilde de La Mole, we may find it in Beyle and Giulia Rinieri.[5] An important part of the book was written at the finest moment in their liaison. When we recall this, a number of details assume the intensity of lived experience.

Whatever the origins of Mathilde, she is Beyle's most ardent Amazon. But all his heroes are at least touched by moral impotence—and Julien is capable of pleasure but not of passion. We see his latent aggressiveness towards women in all the military terminology with which he invests the pursuit of love. Once again he feels obliged to ensure his self-esteem. Once again the ladder is raised to the bedroom window. But this time he finds his determination, his vanity, his doubts, his regrets, his changing moods are fully matched. Mathilde, like Julien, is moved by pride and energy. In Mathilde he finds an opponent who is worthy of himself.

In this second part of the book, our belief in events is, once again, sorely tried. Mathilde becomes pregnant by Julien; her father has offered him money and secured him a commission in the army. It appears to be only a question of time until he accepts their coming marriage. The carpenter's son has succeeded where the heir to a dukedom has failed. Nothing seems to be wanting for Julien Sorel, now dignified with the title of M. le chevalier Julien Sorel de La Vernaye. It is at this point—or so we are invited to believe—that Julien asks M. de La Mole to write to Mme. de Rênal, and under the influence of her priest, she writes a letter of denunciation. Julien hastens to Verrières, shoots her in church and is promptly arrested. Even now, he might save himself, for she is only slightly injured, and she does not die. Indeed, she and Mathilde both come to visit him in prison and both do their utmost to save him. But Julien is intent on death. In court he asks for death. He is guillotined. Mathilde embarks on an uncertain future, and Mme. de Rênal dies of grief.

In Julien Sorel, Henri Beyle anatomises himself. Père Sorel, the cunning and brutal peasant, is Chérubin Beyle; the violent opening conflict between father and son symbolises Beyle's relationship with *le Bâtard.* Julien's whole career is an attempt to escape his origins, and eventually he escapes by changing his name. Yet even this is not enough: Beyle hints that Julien may be the natural son of some other, superior man. Julien—like his creator—longs to shed the indignity of his birth. He tries to do so in every way. He finds a spiritual father in an old surgeon who had once served under Bonaparte, indeed, one might say in Bonaparte himself. As if this were not enough, he seeks the spiritual paternity of the Abbé Chélan and the Abbé Pirard. Beyle's hostility to his origins is reflected, again, in Valenod, who typifies the detested Grenoblois of his childhood. His minor characters are, again, designed to show his hatred of provincial society: its nouveaux-riches, its petty functionaries. They show his scorn for Restoration politics, the venality of the cleric and the layman (both of them susceptible—or so one surmises—to sexual and financial temptation). The characters in *Le Rouge et le Noir* also show his contempt for Parisian society: its hypocrisy, its fatuity and its false social standards. Here is Beyle's fierce condemnation of his time. In Julien Sorel he sets a Napoleonic figure in the context of the Restoration, an epic figure in a pedestrian society, a Romantic figure in a prosaic world. In doing so he also portrays himself, lonely and out of place, in an unheroic, frustrating age.

The Comtesse Dash recorded that his book was all the rage. "People snatched it from one another, and vied in discussing literature when they weren't discussing politics. . . . That lion of a Stendhal, or Henri Beyle, if you prefer, roused cries of protest from the conventional."[6] Louis Spach went further: he recalled that Beyle's vicious contempt for society and the personal dislike which he inspired were enough to condemn the book. And Spach disagreed with the Comtesse Dash: he maintained that, in aristocratic circles, the verdict was so severe that no woman read the novel, even in secret; no one would have dared to discuss "a picture of manners which was so immoral and in such bad taste."[7] Henri Beyle could not please his contemporaries. Like Julien Sorel, he was too different.

Yet, as Bourget was to write years later: "When this novel does not revolt us, it enchants us. . . . For those who have a mania for this masterpiece, the smallest details are a universe."[8] And Bourget added:

If a character in a novel is to be significant, that is to say, if he is to represent a great number of people like himself, it is essential that an idea necessary to the epoch should have presided at his creation. Now it happens that this feeling of the solitude of the superior man—or the man who believes himself to be so—is perhaps the one that a democracy like our own produces with the greatest facility. . . .

Stendhal said the last word on a whole group of those who, after 1830, were called *les enfants du siècle.* It files past, superbly draped, haloed with poetry, in many of the works of the time: the legion of its melancholy rebels. Victor Hugo's Ruy Blaş belongs to it, like Musset's Rolla, like Dumas' Antony. They suffer from a nostalgia which appears sublime. Stendhal's Julien Şorel suffers from the same nostalgia, but he knows the underlying reason. The cruel, cold passion to succeed wrings his heart, and he knows it. He recognises in himself the implacable ardours of a man declassed and very near to crime. . . . To understand the fires of the Commune, . . . we must reread this book.[9]

Taine read *Le Rouge et le Noir* about eighty times. For him the author was the supreme philosopher of the century. Nietzsche confessed that the discovery of Beyle was among the most fortunate chances in his life. The theory of the superman, the Nietzschean morality, owed much to Beyle. All Beylism was in flower in *Le Rouge et le Noir.*

PART V

The Consul at
Civitavecchia
1831–1842

Thirty

On November 21, 1830, the author of *Le Rouge et le Noir* reached Pavia, on his way to Trieste. At Pavia his political past once again caught up with him. He did not have a visa from the Austrian ambassador in Paris, and the Austrian police seized his passport. The French consul general in Milan was obliged to intervene before he was allowed to continue his journey. He reached Trieste on November 25. On December 4, in Paris, *Le Journal des Débats* announced that the Emperor of Austria had refused to recognise his appointment. The censors and the prefects of police in Milan and Vienna had done their work.

It was some time before the news reached him; in the meanwhile he continued to write reports for Comte Sebastiani, the new Minister of Foreign Affairs. On December 12 he sent Mareste an impression of life in Trieste.

Lodgings cost two thousand two hundred francs, a seven-room apartment on the second floor. Such is my predecessor's apartment, which I do not want to take considering the poverty of the day; everything costs twice as much as it does in my lamented Leghorn....

There is double glazing everywhere here because of the abomina-
ble bora, which puts me in a temper in the evenings. All the streets are
like the *Via larga* in Florence. There are no shutters or blinds.
Everyone has a night-light, so it appears, and they put it between two
panes of glass, so that from ten o'clock at night the town looks as if it
is illuminated. Pavements everywhere, divided from the street by
little pillars. Magnificent sea and hills. . . . I often remember Mme.
Azur's smile.[1]

Consular duties, and attendance at a local salon, did not prevent
him from visiting Venice. He was there from December 17 to 23. On
his return to his consulate he learned that he was *persona non grata.*

He stayed on in Trieste, uncertain of his future. To Virginie
Ancelot he wrote:

Alas! madame, I am dying of boredom and cold. That is the newest
thing I can say today, 1 January 1831. I don't know if I shall stay here.
I read nothing but *La Quotidienne* and *La Gazette.* This diet makes me
thin. . . . Great God! What a dreary century! And how it deserves the
boredom that it feels and exudes. . . . I learned only a week ago of the
appearance of *Le Rouge.* Tell me frankly all the ill you think of this
dull work which does not conform to the academic rules.[2]

He attempted to relieve his boredom and depression by paying a
brief visit to Fiume. On the day he set out, in a copy of *Clarissa
Harlowe,* he noted his first idea for an autobiography:

6 January 1831: departure for Fiume.
I have written the lives of several great men: Mozart, Rossini,
Michelangelo, Leonardo da Vinci. It was the kind of work which
entertained me most. I no longer have the patience to look for
material, assess contradictory accounts, it occurs to me to write a life
every incident of which I know very well. Unfortunately the person is
quite unknown, it is myself.[3]

On January 20 he arrived in Venice, where he remained for a
month. He was still there on February 11, when Louis-Philippe
appointed him consul at Civitavecchia. On March 17 he learned
officially of his new post. It was a marked descent from Trieste.[4] His
salary dropped from 12,000 to 10,000 francs. On March 30 he handed

over the consulate at Trieste to his successor. On April 17, by way of
Florence, he reached Civitavecchia.

Seen from the open sea, Roger Boppe was to write, "under the
Mediterranean light, Civitavecchia offered a coloured picture which
was not without grandeur. Its round pier, its fine crenellated ram-
parts dominating the shore, joined the lazaretto to the arsenal and the
apostolic palace to the buildings of the convict settlement. Beyond,
on the square mass of the fort, stood the octagonal tower which
tradition attributed to Michelangelo."[5] Taine, too, was to admire the
view from the Mediterranean, but his admiration vanished when he
landed. Some thirty years after Beyle's arrival, setting out on the
journey which inspired *Voyage en Italie,* he disembarked at Civitavecchia. He found it

> a dismal town, a mixture of stinking alleyways and administrative
> buildings which reflect the platitude and correctness of their func-
> tion. Some of the alleys are five feet wide. . . . The sun never reaches
> them; the mud is slimy. Sometimes the entrance is an old mediaeval
> building with a porch and some kind of crenellation. One enters the
> passage with hesitation; on both sides one sees black hovels where
> filthy children, wild-haired little girls, slip their stockings on and
> attempt to fasten their rags together. No sponge has ever been over
> the windows, no broom has ever been over the stairways; they are
> impregnated and oozing with human filth; a bitter brackish smell
> assails the nostrils. Several windows seem to be falling in; the broken
> stairways crawl round the leprous walls. In the cross streets, among
> the mud, the cabbage stalks and orange peel, gape the openings of a
> few stalls, below the level of the pavement, and you see shadows
> moving there: a butcher laying out his gory meat and joints of veal
> hung on the wall; a fruiterer who looks like the fiercest of hired
> assassins. . . .
>
> It was here that our poor Stendhal lived for so long.[6]

In April, 1831, not without some apprehension, the Holy See
approved of Beyle's new appointment; his future seemed depres-
singly predictable. He installed himself on the second floor of a
house in the Piazza Camporsino. He was unwell; no doubt his poor
health owed much to depression. "The consul at Civitavecchia has
always been allowed to have a pied-à-terre in Rome," he explained
to Mareste. "[Civitavecchia] is a little bigger than Saint-Cloud and

fever reigns there for two months of the year. It is only fourteen leagues from this fine seaport to Rome."⁷ On July 12 he duly found himself in Rome, where—except for one short break—he remained until the end of July.

Even here he felt frustrated.

> The other day I saw Horace Vernet, director of the Academy of Painting in Rome [Mareste told Sutton Sharpe on August 6]. He told me that the great man was outrageously bored in the Eternal City. He wants to talk freely, as he does in our Paris salons; he discusses, decides and dissertates in his usual fashion. The poor Romans are horribly afraid of compromising themselves with their amiable government; they stop up their ears and run, leaving their interlocutor standing. He doesn't know what will become of him. He needs to have an audience. And so he tells me he's ill, very ill, that he has rheumatism, that he's afraid of the cholera morbus, etc., etc. It simply means: I'm dying of boredom. Not long ago he sent me a fat notebook which contained some pretty comical details about the pimps of the cardinals and the monsignori. If his consular diplomacy is exercised on such subjects, he must clearly have few friends in that country.⁸

Comte Joseph d'Estourmel met the new consul at the French Academy in Rome. He found him outrageous.

> In the evening I went back to the Villa Medici [he recorded in his *Souvenirs*]. The moonlight was enchanting. I was on the balcony, looking at St. Peter's, its dome silhouetted in black against the sky. . . . But the general harmony was somewhat disturbed by a fat man of common appearance, who had a decisive tone—he was full of wit, but the wit was misplaced. He had embarked on a criticism of modern painting, and especially of the institution of the Académie de France. . . . He was holding forth against the school in the school itself, he was talking at Vernet's of suppressing Vernet—who, like Mme. Vernet, showed great dignity in the discussion. Somone told me that this malevolent man was the new consul at Civitavecchia, M. Beyle, better known under the pseudonym of Standall: "The author of *Rouge et Noir*," a woman whispered to me. I confessed to my confusion that I had not read it. "What!" she cried, "you don't know *Le Rouge et le Noir?* But it's as famous as *Plick et Plock* [by Eugène Sue]!" Despite all my pleasure in the music, and in M. de Standall's witty paradoxes, I was obliged to leave early.⁹

Beyle seemed to make a habit of being disagreeable at the Villa Medici, but when Ingres was director, he met his match. Ingres demanded that people should share his artistic tastes, his musical and literary opinions. Legend says that Beyle made the peremptory statement: "There is no melody in Beethoven." Ingres turned on his heel and refused to receive him again.[10]

In August and September, 1831, Beyle visited Siena and Florence. On September 13 he was back at his consulate, where he remained until the end of October. During this time he wrote the short story "San Francesco a Ripa." In November and December he was again in Rome. He and his friend Abraham Constantin, the painter from Geneva, installed themselves in the Palazzo Cavalieri, in the via de Barbieri. On December 28, with the botanist Adrien de Jussieu, Beyle left for Naples. He spent twelve hours, in fascination, studying a crater which, they said, was soon to erupt. It was clearly a tourist attraction, for a ragged young Neapolitan was busy selling wine and baking apples on the edge of the lava. The roving consul also went to a ball at the French embassy; he assessed society women as a connoisseur. He admired the fresco recently discovered at Pompeii. He also recorded happily that, two days earlier, a peasant digging at Misene had found two marble heads. He had recognised one of them as Tiberius. He had acquired it for 4 piastres, and it was thought to be worth at least 100. If, wrote Beyle, he were to die, Fiore must ensure that the bust was sent to Monsieur Dijon. Monsieur Dijon—he could not refrain, even now, from using pseudonyms—was his name for Comte Molé, who had been partly responsible for his appointment. The bust was in fact a bust of an unknown man of the time of Hadrian. It was sent to Molé on Beyle's death.

On January 23 he was back in Rome, where he remained until February 14. Late that month he was once again in Civitavecchia, where he stayed until early in March. On March 8 he found himself in Ancona. French troops under General Amédée-Louis Despans de Cubières had occupied the town, and Beyle was entrusted with new and unexpected functions. On March 15, with some vexation, he addressed himself to the Comte de Sainte-Aulaire, the French ambassador in Rome:

Monsieur le Comte,

For the good of the service I could not refuse to accept, *temporarily*, certain functions which are quite foreign to those of a consul. . . . I must confess that these functions annoy me very much.

As military assistant quartermaster, I am obliged to certify things with my signature which I know nothing about. This morning I signed a mass of papers of this kind.

In the second place, I am paying two thousand men as present and on service; it may be that as a result of some mistakes, of course involuntary, there are only 1,990 men. I know quite well that anything one pays up to the quarterly review is only an instalment, but it will be unpleasant for me, when a military quartermaster arrives, to see everything I have done redone and corrected.

Finally, I am here among the local functionaries, and among soldiers whom I do not have the honour to know; the functions of paymaster and assistant quartermaster give me less official consideration than those of a consul.

For all these reasons, I very much want to return to my post. I would ask Your Excellency to be kind enough to give an account of these new functions to His Excellency the Minister of Foreign Affairs. . . . If Your Excellency is good enough to concern himself about me for a moment, this mission, which is becoming unpleasant, will at least be useful to me.[11]

On March 31 a disgruntled consul was finally able to leave for Civitavecchia. He remained there until the middle of June.

On May 22 he had asked the Minister of Foreign Affairs if he might be granted a month's leave. He had family affairs, he said, to settle in Grenoble. His consular work would not suffer from his absence. He was granted leave, but he did not go to Grenoble. From June 18 to August 7 he was in Rome and Albano. On August 10 he sailed from Civitavecchia for Leghorn. He visited Giulia Rinieri in Siena, and he spent eleven days in Florence. In the first fortnight of September he was once again at his consulate.

He had rarely been there during the year; he had frequently been travelling. Yet he had found time, in June and the first days of July, to write *Souvenirs d'Egotisme*—the autobiography which had crossed his mind. And in Rome, this autumn, he began—and soon abandoned—a novel, *Une position sociale*. It was inspired by the spiritual interest, the *curiosité d'âme*, which he took in the Comtesse de

Sainte-Aulaire. He spent a fortnight travelling in the Abruzzi ("If I were completely free, I should do a hundred leagues a month").[12] On November 6 he found himself again in Siena. He visited Florence and returned to Siena once more. These Sienese visits were spent with Giulia, who had recently returned to her native town. On December 2 he left for Rome. His movements had not passed unobserved. The next day the governor of Siena informed the chief of police in Tuscany:

> According to a report which the police have just handed to me this morning, I learn that the well-known Signor Beyle arrived here from the capital on 27 November last. He spent the night, as usual, at Girolamo Martinucci's house, and next day he went to read the papers in the literary cabinet. He left there in a barouche [*timonella*], accompanied by one of his servants, and went to M. le Commandeur Berlinghieri's villa outside the Pispini gate, where he remained until the first of this month. On the first of this month he returned to Siena. . . . Then he went back again, on foot, to the aforementioned Villa Berlinghieri and had dinner there. . . .[13]

The "well-known Signor Beyle" spent some weeks in Rome. He addressed his official letters, as usual, from Civitavecchia, but it was from Rome, on January 12, that he wrote to Sophie Duvaucel: "I am completely Italian. I don't expect to see Paris until I am destitute. . . . Your Parisian politeness has become a game of chess, which demands continual attention. And the French are not amusing enough."[14] He found no wit in Paris—or, for that matter, in Rome. Writing to Fiore, a few days later, he added: "There's no one to play this battledore and shuttlecock which is known as *being witty.*"[15] He felt himself growing more stupid every day. One consoling thought remained: the thought of Giulia. From January 22 to February 14 he was again with her in Siena.

He was now once more absorbed by his love for her: all the more absorbed as Giulia had other admirers and she confessed that she encouraged them. She was fond of Beyle; despite his plainness, his corpulence, his moods, his lack of purpose and official success, she was still drawn to him. But he was not a possible husband, and she wanted to get married. Beyle understood the situation. He could only accept it; but she was the last woman in his life who was to touch his heart and his senses, and he still liked to keep her in a kind of limbo: unattached and free to be his mistress. On April 9 he received a letter from her which destroyed any hopes for his future. "My dear, don't be angry with me for my sincerity, you have often told me that you liked me to open my heart to you. Well, this heart is now in great peril. . . . Good-bye, my dear. . . . I assure you that I shall always be your affectionate and true friend."[16]

On June 14 she married her cousin, Giulio Martini.[17]

Thirty-one

In the spring, of 1833 the prospect of Giulia's marriage had made Beyle more than ever aware of his loneliness and—for he was just fifty—of advancing age. "Life is getting on," he told Fiore. "Half a century has already passed. Must one let oneself die of boredom? . . . I thirst for a conversation which is something other than a ceremony. . . . I am going to Lutetia to see the streets, the displays in the bookshops and all the theatres."[1]

Late in August he left for Paris, on the month's leave he had long ago been granted. He contrived to stay there until December 4. He went to his old lodgings at 71, rue de Richelieu. He also attempted to revive an old relationship. In November he stayed with Clémentine Curial at her familiar château near Compiègne. The Comtesse Dash was there and left a lively sketch of him in her *Mémoires des autres*. The Comtesse Curial, she added, "had been beautiful; she was then the mother of two sons and of a married daughter. . . . She was still good and amiable."[2] She had now been a widow for four years, but her passion for Beyle was not to be revived. During his leave in Paris, he also saw his friend Mme. Gaulthier. Their meeting was to be more rewarding, for she lent him the manuscript of her novel *Le Lieutenant*.

The "scroll" was no doubt in the chest with all his Parisian purchases when, at last, he left for Italy. The journey was eventful. On December 15, at Lyons, in the steamship going down the Rhône, he encountered George Sand and Alfred de Musset, on their way to Venice. Mme. Sand was to recall the event in *Histoire de ma vie.*

On the steamship which took me from Lyons to Avignon, I met one of the most remarkable writers of the present age: Beyle, whose pseudonym was Stendhal. . . . He was brilliantly witty, and his conversation recalled that of Delatouche, with less delicacy and grace, but with greater depth. At first sight, he was rather the same sort of man as well, fat, with a very fine face under a flaccid mask. . . . I talked with him for some of the day and found him very pleasant. He laughed at my illusions about Italy, assuring me that I should soon have enough of it, and that artists in search of beauty in that country were proper ninnies. I hardly believed him, because I saw that he was tired of his exile and returning to it against his will. . . . His main pose was disdain of vanity; he was always trying to find some pretention to destroy with the running fire of his mockery. But I don't think that he was bad: he took too much trouble to appear so. . . .

We had supper with a certain number of other travellers, in a bad village inn. . . . He was wildly gay there, he grew tolerably drunk, and, dancing around the table with his big fur boots, he became just a little grotesque and far from attractive.

At Avignon, he took us to see the great church. . . . And there, in a corner, an old, painted wooden Christ . . . roused him to the most unbelievable insults. . . . He wanted to punch the effigy with his fists.

Personally, I wasn't sorry to see Beyle take the land road to Genoa. . . . I confess that I had had enough of him. . . . For the rest, he was a distinguished man. . . . He had a genuine and original talent, he wrote badly, but he did so in a way that struck and really interested his readers.[3]

They parted at Marseilles. In 1920, when Beyle's memorial was unveiled in Paris, Paul Bourget observed the irony. It stood near the memorial to the author of *Lélia.* Beyle had disliked Mme. Sand, and she had not liked him.[4]

On December 26 Beyle reached Florence. On January 8 he was again in Rome. He continued to date his official letters from Civitavecchia; but the Marquis de Latour-Maubourg, the new ambassador in Rome, clearly knew where the consul spent his time. On February 22, Beyle had proposed that a young Greek official, Lysimaque Caftangi-Oglou Tavernier, should be chancellor of the consulate; it was a way of making consular duties bearable. On June 7 the ambassador told Beyle: "The confidence which [Lysimaque Tavernier] inspires . . . is the surest guarantee of your continued presence in Rome. If you made the resolution to live at Civitavecchia, don't delude yourself, you couldn't keep it."[5] Beyle had no illusions. "This town [he told Mareste] has 7,500 inhabitants, 7,000 of whom are Neapolitan fishermen, 450 *petits bourgeois,* 6 or 8 bourgeois can give you dinner without trouble. Two are millionaires. You cannot imagine the barbaric state of this place."[6]

And so he spent much of his time in Rome, and here, early in May, he found a task which was congenial. He read the manuscript novel which Julie Gaulthier had lent him.

> I have read *Le Lieutenant,* dear and amiable friend [he reported on May 4]. You must copy it all out again. . . . The language, to me, is horribly noble and emphatic; I have cruelly scribbled over it. . . .
>
>
>
> *Leuwen*
>
> *ou*
>
> *L'Elève chassé de l'Ecole polytechnique*
>
> I should choose this title. . . .[7]

Julie Gaulthier was discouraged, but she was not surprised ("I did tell you that I was a great goose, incapable of laying a good egg"). And since she was not only modest but charming and forgiving, she wrote again, soon afterwards, to tell Beyle that she had been given a copy of his medallion by David d'Angers; it was hanging in her library.[8]

The manuscript of *Le Lieutenant* seems to have vanished; it is an unfortunate loss for the Stendhalien. For Beyle was "absolutely full" of *Le Lieutenant.* He had needed the account of the Berthet case to inspire him with *Le Rouge et le Noir.* He had needed *Le Lieutenant* to inspire him with the novel which he began to write next day: *Lucien Leuwen.*

Early in June came a conflict with Tavernier. It was inevitable that there should be dissension between the absent consul and his *locum tenens,* but the dissension which now arose was serious. On May 19 the new Minister of Foreign Affairs approved of Tavernier's appointment. He also questioned the expenses of the consulate for the first quarter of the year. He asked for a fresh account of receipts and expenses, and he admonished Beyle to avoid further errors. "It is again to you, monsieur, that I owe a reprimand from the minister," Beyle told Tavernier. "I cannot trust you in the least."9 Tavernier retorted that Beyle had approved the accounts himself; he was also dissatisfied with his salary, and he resigned. On June 7, from Rome, Beyle offered the post to his friend Donato Bucci, an antique-dealer in Civitavecchia.

The ambassador understood Beyle's reluctance to live in his consulate. The Minister of Foreign Affairs still considered, with some reason, that he should live there more regularly, and on July 14 he invited him to do so. Whatever the recommendation, Beyle appears to have spent July and August at Albano. His despondency continued.

> I begin to be weary of the job. I envy most profoundly the man who, at fifty, has five thousand francs a year. . . .
>
> So here are two commissions [he told Colomb on September 10]. Try to sell my place to someone else for 4,000 francs a year. Put notices for me in the *Débats* so that I can sell my manuscripts if ever I have the happiness to be able to do so. . . .
>
> Let me tell you that there is not a sad English family, visiting Rome, which does not read the *Promenades;* at the minister-cardinal's, on St. Peter's Day, at the firework display, people talked to me about it without knowing who I was. These fools consider that it lacks gravity. But how happy I should be, on a fourth floor, writing another book like it, if I had my daily bread!10

His only lasting wish, it is said, "except for Saint-Simon and spinach," was to live on a fourth floor in Paris and write. Since he had first left Grenoble, he had never had a home; he had been a stranger in his father's house, and he was always to be a bird of passage.

Late in September, he installed himself in the Palazzo Conti in Rome. On October 23 he was back at his consulate, more dejected than ever. He had amassed 400 books in his library. He lost himself, now, in reading; in his copy of Pascal he noted: "Taken up again at

Civitavecchia in October, 1834, out of respect for the style, in hatred of the affectation of Messrs. de Chateaubriand, Janin and even Courier [Paul-Louis]."[11] He was eager for news of Paris.

> I really must thank you for your good letters [he wrote to Sophie Duvaucel]; I keep them and reread them in the long and solitary evenings. . . . It is a year now since I saw you, since I saw Paris. Must I live and die like this on these solitary shores? I am afraid of it. In that case, I should die completely stupefied by boredom and the non-communication of ideas. I certainly don't pretend that they are good ideas; but, such as they are, if the whole of Civitavecchia clubbed together, they could not understand the simplest of them. Why aren't I a glutton or a huntsman? Why aren't I an antiquarian? But I like the *beautiful,* not the *rare.* . . .[12]

Despite his lack of qualifications, he joined an archaeological survey which planned to excavate some Etruscan tombs at Corneto. But such diversions were transient. On November 1 he lamented to Fiore:

> I am dying of boredom; I cannot make conversation with anyone. I should like a place at 4,000 francs in Paris. . . . What! Grow old at Civitavecchia! Or even in Rome! *I have seen so much of the sun!*
>
> I know that there is something ridiculous in complaining all the time, but can one complain too loudly that one wasn't born with four thousand francs a year? (My father had twelve or fifteen thousand a year, and he went bankrupt in 1818.) What a prospect to live and die here, only able to talk about hunting and money! . . . My soul is a fire that suffers if it is not aflame. I need three or four cubic feet of new ideas a day.

Once he had longed to live in Italy; now he longed for the stimulus of Paris,

> the new ideas that I should find at Mme. de Castellane's, if I went there twenty times in succession. Tuesdays at Mme. Ancelot's, Wednesdays at Gérard's, Saturdays at M. Cuvier's, three suppers a week at the Café Anglais, and I am acquainted with everything that is said in Paris. I also have the *salons* of M. Joseph Bernard, Béranger's friend, those of Mme. Curial, etc.; with that, as M. Hugo would say, I have a *window open* on to life, and all the morning I should work

happily at my octavo volume. . . . M. Guizot should appoint me
professor of the history of the fine arts (painting, sculpture, architecture and music) with five thousand francs. . . . Every year, I should
give sane ideas to two hundred young people, some of whom would
be destined to have *salons* in Paris in about 1850. . . .

Now find me a *friendly* minister.[13]

Beyle's readiness to write commercially seems to have worried
Romain Colomb, who sent him a mild reprimand.

I have no scruples about writing a bad book [came the answer]. . . .
Another reason has prevented me from writing many things for the
past ten years. . . .

Since I have reached the age of reason, or rather, for me, the age of
passion, I have not written what I feel. The shame of seeing an
indiscreet reader read into my soul as he read my papers has
prevented me from doing so. . . .

Experience has taught me that I do not run the danger of being
understood.[14]

Mme. Ancelot underlined his comments. She had found it hard to
discover a copy of *De l'Amour;* when she told him so, "he claimed that
the edition had been put on board a ship to serve as *ballast,* the
publisher being only too happy to rid himself of a work which had
encumbered his shop for five years. . . . He said this gaily, by way of
a joke: 'What would you expect? People are too stupid in France, at
the moment, to understand me.' "[15]

On November 17, 1834, Beyle was back in Rome, where he
remained for a month. He tried to forget his consular task, to lead a
metropolitan life. He continued to dress according to fashion. Indeed,
in 1889, when Henri Cordier was writing *Stendhal et ses amis,* he
learned from a woman who had known Beyle in Rome that "he had
an extremely distinguished manner, that he had small, fine hands
and that he liked to show them, and that he readily looked in mirrors
at his portly figure which did not lack its charms."[16] It was a
charitable picture; against it one might set the picture which Sainte-
Beuve drew of Beyle in his consular years:

His figure was already rotund, like that of Silenus, he had an indefinable *satyresque* air. . . .

He was prematurely stout and thickset, with a short, red neck; his full face was framed with curly brown whiskers and brown hair, and eventually this was artificial. The forehead was fine, the nose *retroussé* and a little Calmuck in shape; the lower lip protruded slightly, with a hint of mockery. The eyes were rather small, but very lively. . . . He became heavy and apoplectic in his final years, but he took great care to hide the signs of his decadence even from his friends.[17]

Berlioz, who saw him in Rome, proved to be no friend of "M. Beile, or Bayle, or Baile, who had written . . . the most irritating nonsense about music." In his *Mémoires* he gave an acid likeness of the author of the *Vie de Rossini:*

"Who is that little man, with a round belly and a malicious smile, who is trying to look important?"

"That is a man of wit who writes about the arts of the imagination. That is the consul at Civitavecchia who believes that *fashion* obliges him to leave his post on the Mediterranean and loll about in a barouche around the sewer of the piazza Navone; at the moment he is meditating a new chapter for his novel, *Le Rouge et le Noir.*"[18]

On December 15, 1834, Beyle was once again at his consulate. It is some measure of his weariness and depression that, the following week, he wrote the first of five testaments on the manuscript of *Lucien Leuwen.* On December 24 he returned, inevitably, to Rome.

He remained there until January 16—although, as usual, he prudently dated his letters from Civitavecchia. He carefully disguised his absences from the ministry. He had worked out the timing of packet boats, but in case of emergency, he had provided Lysimaque Tavernier (now reinstated) with two consular seals. His duties were hardly affected by his absence, for his work was limited. He informed the Minister for Foreign Affairs of the quarantine imposed by the Papal government on vessels coming from the south of France. He asked the French vice-consul in Ancona to report on commerce and navigation; he asked him to forward three copies of a recent speech which contained statistical details. These, he explained, should be sent in a wrapper to economise on postage, an expense which the ministry found considerable. To such minutiae the author of *Le Rouge et le Noir* was obliged to devote his attention.

On January 15, by royal decree, he was accorded the distinction to which he had aspired for some years. He had longed, as he expressed it, to be crucified. Now he was appointed Chevalier de la Légion-d'honneur. It was, apparently, a month before he learned of his decoration. On February 15 he sent his official thanks to François Guizot, who had submitted his name for the cross. It was characteristic of Beyle that his Légion-d'honneur brought him only half satisfaction. He regretted that he had not been decorated as a veteran of the Grande Armée. Yet it was appropriate that he should owe his Légion-d'honneur to the Minister of Public Instruction. He received it, not for his work as a consul—a consul without a vocation—but for his achievement as a man of letters.

Except for three days at Civitavecchia, he remained in Rome throughout January, 1835. On January 30 he returned to his consulate. Desperate for company, he even considered marriage with a young girl in Civitavecchia. Mlle. Vidau was twenty or so; she was plain, uneducated, and (according to Romain Colomb) her mother had been a laundress. Colomb maintained that her pious and well-to-do uncle threatened to disinherit the family if she married a miscreant like Beyle; he was therefore told not to set foot in the Vidaus' house again. Beyle himself gave a different explanation of events. On March 4 he told Sophie Duvaucel, now Mme. Ducrest de Villeneuve: "The marriage is off. The father-in-law wanted to spend his life with me. He finds me agreeable. My character is so ill-made that I broke off at once. Imagine a man of 65 tied to my poor self and believing that he was my father! I shouldn't dine with an old man every day even if he gave me a hundred francs per dinner." [19] Beyle's reluctance to commit himself to a father-in-law was understandable. But now, at fifty-two, he was hardly an attractive proposition. He was a second-class consul, in a second-class consulate, with little chance of promotion; he was poor, he was despondent, and he was unwell. On March 8, from Rome, he wrote to Dr. Prévost in Geneva. He sent him a depressing picture of a now confirmed bachelor.

> Monsieur,
>   I am full of gratitude for the good advice that you gave me in [September] 1833. (I have gout and gravel, I am very fat, excessively

nervous, and I am fifty [*sic*].) You prescribed colchicum wine for me, and avoidance of all acids.

When I came back here, someone suggested a marriage for me; I put off the serious treatment, I contented myself with avoidance of acids. Three times a week, for six months of the year, I take bicarbonate of soda or of potassium. . . . I produce two or three grains (in weight) of gravel every week. . . . I have completely given up coffee for the last eighteen months, the pain in my bowels has almost entirely stopped. . . . When I take coffee again, the pain comes back in the bowels, especially three inches to the left of the navel. I have tea and butter at *déjeuner*. I don't drink much wine; when I drink champagne, I feel much gayer, and I feel less nervous the next day. . . . I am very well, for which I have you to thank. Is there anything to be done? [20]

Beyle's physical condition was, for the moment, better; his depression remained, and it was not relieved by a forbidding letter from the Minister of Foreign Affairs. On February 5 the Comte de Rigny sent him an imperative request to remain at his post.

I have reason to believe, monsieur, that despite the special invitation which my predecessor gave you to conform to article 35 of the decree of 20 August 1833 by an unbroken residence at Civitavecchia, you have continued to absent yourself frequently from that town. I consent to shut my eyes to such a positive and prolonged violation of the decrees only in the hope that it will not occur again. I give you this warning, monsieur, if you have it at heart to keep the post with which his Majesty has entrusted you.[21]

The reprimand was severe, but it did not keep the errant consul in Civitavecchia. He was in Rome from February 9 until March 9 and again from March 12 to 21.

He was not inactive in Rome; he had discovered some manuscript histories which were to become the basis of his *Chroniques italiennes*. Some of the manuscripts, written by contemporaries, were a mere five or six pages long; some of them ran to a hundred pages. He had them copied; each folio volume (and he had twenty) cost him from 90 to 120 francs. He intended to leave them all to M. Molé.

I have discovered many of these things myself, by *physical* work, in archives [he wrote to Romain Colomb and Domenico Fiore]. The volumes left on the tables were covered with dust which had *solidified* with settlement, and was as thick as three ecus. The archivist, to whom I gave presents, ought to have shown me all this, but he usually went away when he had locked me in, and came back at the *Ave Maria.*

My shirt was dark grey every time, and my eyes were nearly always aching. I have discovered some *Confessions* like those of Rousseau, written by a young abbé, the illegitimate son of a great house, at the time of the arrival of Queen Christina of Sweden, in 1655. . . .[22]

In the spring of 1835 Beyle continued to take an interest in archaeology. He was fascinated by the excavation of the tombs of Tarquinia, near Civitavecchia; he went to see some vases at the Princesse de Canino's. The princess, the wife of Napoleon's brother Lucien, was now immersed in beekeeping, and Beyle reported that "the poor princess calculates how much honey and money can be produced by a hundred hives of bees, and her imagination always adds a nought to the result."

Nothing, now, relieved his depression and his apprehension. He wrote, in misery, to Mérimée, saying that "he was hated at the Ministry of Foreign Affairs, and he has a chancellor who denounces him when he absents himself from Civitavecchia. He sees the storm growing over his head," Mérimée recorded, "and he thinks it is impossible to avoid it, or at least he lacks the resignation to avoid it by agreeing to live in the stinking hole into which fate has thrown him. He asks my advice and he wants to change his post. He is thinking of going to Spain or of coming back to Paris to write books." [23]

In April, from Civitavecchia, he wrote again to Fiore:

I am here on the edge of barbarity, I have gout and gravel, I am very fat, excessively nervous, and I am fifty-two! Oh, if I had known, in 1814, that my father was ruined, I should have become an extractor of teeth, an advocate, a judge, etc., etc. I am so stunned by being so bored that I don't want anything, I am dismal; you will appreciate the excess of my decline when I confess that I read the announcements in *La Quotidienne!* I am overwhelmed by being reduced to this way of life! . . .

I'm certainly comfortable, but I am dying of boredom. The animal's real job is to write a novel in an attic, for I prefer the pleasure of writing nonsenses to that of wearing an embroidered coat which costs eight hundred francs. . . .

So see if one couldn't have *two thousand* in Lutèce; a room facing south, on a fifth floor. With an income of five francs and five francs earned with a novel, the little room would be the ultimate happiness. I am made to live with two candles and a desk, and now as I write to you I am happy like that. But I am bored in my swallow's nest!

Good-bye, I should like to hang myself, and leave everything, for a fifth-floor room in the rue Richepanse.

Your bored
BARON DORMANT [24]

He was intolerably bored with Civitavecchia; he was also bored with Rome. He now found its society ponderous; he was weary of the company of scholars, he lamented the lack of music. The visitor who had once been touched by the birdsong in the Coliseum now found that Rome held no romance for him.

During the summer he often escaped the Roman heat by visiting Albano. He continued to write reports on shipping movements and outbreaks of cholera. In September, one suspects, his reports became more legible: he was obliged to wear spectacles. Napoleon's *auditeur,* the impassioned lover of Mélanie and Clémentine, the worshipper of Métilde, was growing old. He was tormented by the thought of ageing and by the fear of forgetting. Jean-Louis Ducis painted his portrait that month; he recorded an ailing man. The sternness of expression is striking, but the eyes suggest that the sitter was presenting a façade.

Thirty-two

"I AM WRITING a novel in two volumes, called *Le Chasseur vert,*" Beyle told the writer and critic Albert Stapfer on September 27. "Have you read *Le Rouge?* Would you be brave enough to tell me *exactly* all the faults you see in it? I shall try to avoid them in *Le Chasseur vert.*" [1]

It was on May 5, 1834, the day after he had read *Le Lieutenant,* that Beyle had begun to write his novel. By March 18, 1835, it already filled four folio volumes. It was, he had recognised, far from orthodox. It was "for freedom of thought, like *Le Rouge;* it doesn't try to shock, but it is severe on the *Rabble.—Le Bois de Prémol,* that is the title." He remained uncertain about the title. At one point he referred to the novel as *Le Chasseur vert;* at another he hesitated between *Lucien Leuwen* and *L'Amarante et le Noir.* But the version which he finally began to dictate on July 28, 1835, was eventually known as *Lucien Leuwen.* [2] *Lucien Leuwen* is the novel of the ageing consul at Civitavecchia. In Lucien he taunts his own youth—a youth impenitent but now condemned for him.

On September 23 he broke off his dictation. Perhaps he was preoccupied by his consular tasks; perhaps for the moment he lacked the energy to continue. *Lucien Leuwen* remains unfinished. There are pages, even chapters, missing from the second part; the third part was never written. Even so, the novel is more satisfying than *Armance* or *Le Rouge et le Noir*. This is largely because Lucien himself remains sympathetic. He is not weak and tortured like Octave de Malivert or calculating and twisted like Julien Sorel. He is high-principled without being inhuman; he is sensitive without being neurotic; he is—at first—innocent without being foolish. He is a rich but engaging young man, and when the novel ends, he has learned wisdom and savoir-faire, he is no longer rich, but he is still an idealist, and he is still engaging.

In the first part of the book, Beyle casts his hero into provincial life, or, rather, he obliges him to leave the privileged life that he leads with his wealthy parents in Paris, and to show his own worth in the army. Lucien is commissioned as a second lieutenant in the lancers, and he joins his regiment at Nancy. He learns to live with, and assess, the philistine, the venal and the common; he discovers the uses and the disadvantages of wealth and the pretentions, ambitions and narrowness of provincial society. He rapidly matures, gains confidence and then, quite suddenly, discovers that he has fallen in love.

Mme. de Chasteller, who bears a strong resemblance to Mme. de Rênal, is one of Beyle's most endearing heroines. She has something of Clémentine Curial about her, and she has much of Métilde. She is twenty-four, but she seems to have a gravity beyond her years; the widow of a general, she has a handsome fortune, and she is the cynosure of local eyes. But her father is unwilling to see her money go beyond his grasp, and he forces a strict life upon her. Inexplicably, she accepts it. Only one admirer is invited to the house: a tedious suitor whom her father knows she would not marry. The advent of Lucien, the young subaltern from Paris, breaks this unpromising and apparently endless round. He marks his arrival in Nancy by being thrown from his horse outside her window; thenceforward he longs to meet her and to redeem himself in her sight. There are one or two encounters where he is silent with self-consciousness, gauche where he hoped to be confident, wretchedly inarticulate (as Beyle himself had been with Métilde); then he comes face to face with Mme. de Chasteller at a ball, and, all at once, he finds himself transformed. His conversation sparkles with intelligence and wit, he feels that she approves, he gains assurance and, suddenly, they talk with utter freedom and find themselves irrevocably in love.

It is the moment which Beyle himself had longed, in vain, to know with Métilde and no one describes more delicately than Beyle the growing, the sudden awareness of passion. He is sensitive to every nuance of emotion, every stage in the progress of feeling. Yet on occasion, his characters behave very strangely. There is, one would think, no impediment to the love of Lucien and Mme. de Chasteller; it is not immoral, it is not even socially unfortunate. It is clearly, from the first, a genuine love, not a transient infatuation. Yet Mme. de Chasteller is horrified that her looks have betrayed her feelings; she is ill with anxiety, she suffers almost from a sense of sin. But their love cannot be denied, and, gently, Beyle intimates their happiness as they stroll through the nearby forest, and—as he had done with Minette, in his Brunswick days—they sit at the café du Chasseur vert, where the Bohemian horns play sweet and simple music as the sun goes down.

To another writer, perhaps, the story would be near its end, but Beyle's hero and heroine continue to run the whole gamut of emotions: apprehension, guilt, felicity, stoic renunciation, jealousy, calculated coldness, devotion. Mme. de Chasteller allows Lucien to visit her; then, alarmed by her forwardness, she actually engages a notorious gossip as her companion, to ensure her own correct behaviour. When Lucien finds her, at last, alone, and kisses her hand, she dismisses him for impropriety. Yet Mme. de Chasteller is no coquette; like Mme. de Rênal, she is strangely innocent, and she is merely afraid of her natural feelings. The complex affair, which could be so simple, is finally broken by Lucien's former friend, Dr. du Poirier. The doctor, anxious to placate the eligible bachelors of Nancy and to remove so serious a rival, convinces Mme. de Chasteller that she is seriously ill. His motive seems as impossible as her behaviour. However, she retires to bed, and while her letters are intercepted (a touch of melodrama), Dr. du Poirier stages a false accouchement in order to destroy Lucien's devotion. Lucien, we are asked to believe, is concealed so that he can hear the doctor's mysterious conversation; he is given a glimpse of a child in swaddling clothes. It does not occur to him that the child is several months old or even that Mme. de Chasteller had not appeared to be pregnant when last he saw her. Victor Brombert sees this false accouchement as a caricature of Beyle's own permanent need to be the dupe of love. Beyle—so he contends—is taking revenge on Lucien for his own want of talent. A note on the manuscript of *Lucien Leuwen* says that Lucien, with Mme. de Chasteller, knows all the calumny which Beyle himself had known when he loved Menti. (And had not Menti been afraid of pregnancy?) Whatever the origins of the situation, however impossible it remains, Lucien is convinced that Mme. de Chasteller has deceived him. He returns at once to Paris, where his influential father arranges matters with the military and civil authorities; he is given a government post.

Here the second part of the novel begins—indeed it is almost a novel in itself. As he had done in *Le Rouge et le Noir,* Beyle shows his hero in Paris and in the provinces. Lucien soon discovers the Parisian forms of hypocrisy, the scheming, the graft and the patent immorality in high places. He agrees to visit a dying man in the hospital, to ensure that he does not talk against the regime; he sees the minister engage in financial speculations; he goes on an electoral mission and witnesses the conflict of ambitions, the violence, venality and intrigue. His father advises him to take a mistress, and Lucien duly pays court to a society hostess; she falls in love with him, but he cannot bring himself to love her. He is wise, now, to the world; but he cannot deny his feelings, and he returns to Nancy in search of Mme. de Chasteller. So we learn from a word or two in the text, for Beyle never wrote the chapter about Lucien's return. The end of this second part of *Lucien Leuwen* has more than one unfinished paragraph; more than one reference is left unexplained. We learn that Lucien's father dies, that Lucien finds himself bankrupt and becomes a diplomat in Madrid. We also know that Beyle intended Lucien to marry Mme. de Chasteller. It would have been an appropriate ending.

As it is, *Lucien Leuwen* is a shapeless, fragmentary book; it reflects Beyle's contempt for most of French society, it is a condemnation of provincial life, of government at work, of the world of politics and finance. Brombert suggests that Beyle was not a genuine cynic, that he was only a hypocrite by vocation. But if Beyle was a democrat by intellectual disposition, he remained an aristocrat by temperament, and if the characters in *Lucien Leuwen* are vivid types rather than individuals, they still remain—like drawings by Daumier—etched on the mind. Yet if the novel is diffuse, if some of the situations are contrived and even absurd, if the multitude of secondary figures are paper-thin, Lucien and Mme. de Chasteller must be indelibly remembered. Lucien is the most endearing idealist among Stendhalian heroes; at times he seems needlessly complex, but

—unlike Julien—we wish him well. Mme. de Chasteller herself is an ideal figure. Like Mme. de Rênal, she is Beyle's dream of the woman who had rejected him.

In *Stendhal et la voie oblique,* Victor Brombert has observed that Beyle's novels are full of traps and hidden springs. Beyle, so accustomed to putting others on the wrong scent, comes to pretend to himself. There are remarkable parallels between his letters to Métilde and *Lucien Leuwen.* When he was writing *Lucien Leuwen,* he was haunted by the memory of his deepest love. And yet it is probable that he himself would have been surprised by the "hallucinating precision" with which certain passages of his novel echo the moral situation and the emotional disorder of 1819.[3]

On September 25, 1835, the author of *Lucien Leuwen* returned from Rome to Civitavecchia. Ten days later, answering a letter from Albert Stapfer, he told him that he had been ill for more than a month.

> I went 27 days without dinner. Then came the great heat. I was overwhelmed by my official writing, I counted on your friendship and waited till I was completely well before I answered you. Today there is a sirocco storm in the air, and I am shaking like an old man. I congratulate you most sincerely on having found a companion in life, one may find moments of impatience in marriage, but never the black and utter boredom of celibacy! [4]

He no longer felt flippant, ironical or antagonistic about marriage. "Think of a husband as a *thing,* and not as a person," he had advised his sister years before. "A dragoon needs a horse if he is to live, and a young girl needs a husband." [5] His attitude to marriage had changed.

Now he often regretted the Sunday visits to Delécluze, in his Paris attic. "How prosaic and stupid my life is, compared to that!" Life, he concluded, was a sad affair, and if one drew the real inferences from things, it became more disagreeable still. Evenings were the most difficult part of provincial life; but in the evening one did not feel inclined to read, and moreover, reading tired one's eyes. And so, he assured another friend, "I spend my evenings looking at the sea and regretting that I have not got a pretty wife." [6]

On October 1 he was back in Rome; on October 7 he set out for Bologna. On October 23 he sent some impressions to Charles-Victor Lobstein, an attaché at the embassy in Rome. "The rain has really settled in today. I took advantage of this fine weather to walk for two miles without an umbrella. First I went under the porticos of Bologna; then along the road of the Madonna de San Luca. . . . The view of the hills near San Luca is admirable. These hills are almost as beautiful as those of Varese, Varese near Milan. Varese is the most beautiful place in the world." [7] Lonely and despondent, he was now recalling the most touching moments of his past. "I think unceasingly of that happy city [Bologna] where you must have been," he had written to Métilde in the summer of 1819. "My spirit wanders through a portico that I have often passed. . . . I see unceasingly those fine hills crowned with palaces which form the view from the garden where you walk. Bologna, where I have received no harsh treatment from you, is sacred to me." [8] Now, sixteen years later, it was still sacred to him. Varese took him back still farther into his past: it took him back twenty-four years to the day, October 23, 1811, when, transported with love for Angela Pietragrua, he had been reunited with her there.

On November 8, 1835, Beyle found himself again in Rome. Soon afterwards there came a more practical reminder of his past. Levavasseur, who had published *Le Rouge et le Noir,* wrote to enquire if he had further literary plans.

> I am really touched, monsieur [answered Beyle], by the kind letter which you have taken the trouble to write to me. . . .
> I have . . . written a novel the style of which, I hope, is less abrupt than that of *Le Rouge,* two large volumes or three small ones. If literature could give me 3,000 francs a year, I should send you *Le Chasseur vert;* because I prefer the pleasure of writing to that of wearing an embroidered coat which costs 800 francs.
> I have bought, at great expense, some old manuscripts in faded ink, which date from the sixteenth and seventeenth centuries. They contain . . . anecdotes of eighty pages each, nearly all of them tragic. I shall call them *Historiettes romaines.* . . . Although love plays a great part in them, in the eyes of an intelligent man these *historiettes* would be a useful complement to the history of Italy in the sixteenth and seventeenth centuries. . . .
> I am now writing a book which may be a great nonsense; it is *Mes*

Confessions, in the same style as Jean-Jacques Rousseau, with more frankness. . . .[9]

In November, two months after he had broken off *Lucien Leuwen,* Beyle had begun to write *Vie de Henry Brulard.*

Early in December he found himself briefly in Civitavecchia. In mid-December he was back in Rome. It was this month that Silvestro Valeri began his portrait of Beyle in the famous embroidered coat. It showed the physical decline that had taken place in the last three months.

In Rome, as the new year began, Beyle continued his *Vie de Henry Brulard.* He was to work at it, erratically, until late in March. As his letters had suggested, as his portraits emphasised, he wanted love, and in his unfortunate way, he continued to seek it. He looked, it seems, not for a wife, but for a goddess who could remain unattainable. He needed an occupation for his emotions and his imagination. His needs had not greatly changed since, thirty years and more ago, he had fallen in love with Victorine Mounier. It was apparently on July 6, 1835, that he had imagined that the Comtesse Sandre took an interest in him. The Comtesse Sandre was his name for Giulia Cini. She was young, gay and frivolous; she was famous for her beauty. She was also the wife of Comte Filippo Cini, who was one of his greatest friends in Rome. This cerebral romance, it is said, inspired him to write *Earline.* It has been suggested that Earline is "a fantastic feminine of the English *Earl*": an appropriate reference to a countess. Beyle's dream of the Comtesse Cini ended in February, 1836, and, with it, his only distraction.[10]

On February 15 he asked the new Minister for Foreign Affairs, the Duc de Broglie, to grant him leave. It was, he said, desirable since he suffered from recurrent bouts of fever; they occurred every year, as soon as the hot weather began. These fevers were always followed by gravel and gout, and he could not take quinine, because it produced internal inflammation. No remedies had done him lasting good, and he wanted to embark on some or other cure "before the final advent of old age." One suspects that the effects of venereal disease remained with him.

He longed for change; on March 14 he told Mme. Jules Gaulthier that he had asked for the consulate at Cartagena. He added: "I should like to see active people. What I should like would be to exchange my place at ten thousand francs for your brother's position at the Cour des Comptes." [11] On April 9 he informed Romain Colomb that he had met a delightful attaché who had spent a fortnight at Gibraltar, "and who swore to me that the said Gibraltar was worth a hundred Civitavecchias. So if one can't have *two thousand* in Lutèce, I'm asking for Gibraltar. . . . But, first and foremost, 2,400 in Lutèce." [12]

On March 28 he learned that his leave was granted. He was so overjoyed, so distracted by the news, that he found himself unable to continue *Vie de Henry Brulard.* It had been a useful bromide in his moments of depression, but his mood had coloured his work. *Vie de Henry Brulard* is the stream of consciousness of a weary man. More than once Beyle repeats himself; sometimes he contradicts himself; often he is unable to disentangle fact from hearsay, a first from a second impression, and he frequently confuses dates. He has no concern for style. He is strangely anxious to fix events and scenes by little sketches; he shows an extraordinary concern for the minutiae of his childhood and his early life. He emphasises the perpetual complexity of his mind, a mind forever turning on itself, a mind tired of the present and permanently bitter about the past.

For *Vie de Henry Brulard* is a cynical account of his early years. His passion for his mother (the word is not too strong) is still outweighed by his hatred for his father. Only one figure is drawn with affection and gratitude: the figure of his grandfather Gagnon; Dr. Gagnon had been the only sympathetic adult in a sombre, loveless world. Beyle's account of his first months in Paris is hardly more charitable than his account of his provincial childhood. *Vie de Henry Brulard* ends with his arrival in Italy in 1800. Here and there, in a phrase, it offers a sudden insight into his character, his books, his dreams, an illumination of the human condition; but, most of all, it suggests a *déversoir.* It suggests a troubled man, wretchedly introspective, rarely satisfied, confessing himself to a psychiatrist. *Vie de Henry Brulard* is a valuable indication of Beyle's literary sources, and it is a sad human document.

Thirty-three

ON MAY 11, 1836, Beyle embarked on the *Pharamond* for Leghorn, Genoa and Marseilles. On May 24 he arrived in Paris, and settled at the hôtel de la Paix, 17, rue du Mont-Blanc. He had come for a matter of months, but he was to stay for three years.

He was conscious of time. On June 8 he made his will, and in it he asked Romain Colomb to buy a fine edition 'of Rousseau as his bequest to Giulia Rinieri-Martini. No doubt he was thinking especially of *La Nouvelle Héloïse* and the Julie of whose loves he had delightedly read as a boy. Now he wanted, above all, to find someone to love. Giulia herself had returned to Paris since her marriage, but she was understandably reticent. On August 24, from Dieppe, Clémentine Curial reminded him that her passion had been dead since 1826, and he must be content to remain a friend.

> I never saw him except in love [so Mérimée was to write], or believing himself to be in love; but he had had two *amours-passions* . . . of which he had never been cured. One had been inspired by Mme. Curial, then in all the brilliance of her beauty. He had many powerful men as rivals, among them a general who was much in favour, Caulaincourt. . . .

In 1836 Beyle told me about this adventure, one evening, under the great trees at Laon. He added that he had just seen Mme. Curial, then forty-seven years old, and that he had found himself as much in love as on the first day. They had both had many passions in the interval. "How can you still love me, at my age?" she said. He had proved it very well, and I never saw him show so much emotion. He had tears in his eyes as he spoke to me.[1]

It seems unlikely that Beyle had, in fact, again proved his love for Menti, and Mérimée maintained that his other great love had been for Angela Pietragrua. He did not even mention Métilde. One should take his comments with caution.

However, in October, once again, Beyle considered marriage. Eulalie-Françoise, the Baronne Lacuée de Saint-Just, was the daughter of the Comte de Réal, who had been *préfet de police* during the Hundred Days. Her husband had been a baron under the Empire, a deputy in the reign of Louis-Philippe, and *auditeur au Conseil d'Etat*. She had now been a widow for two years; she was forty-six. Beyle drafted a proposal of marriage to her.

> For some days I have resisted the urge—rather bold, I agree—to suggest an idea which is perfectly honest in form and in content. So don't be frightened, and don't be afraid of the reputation for singularity which—mistakenly, I think—I enjoy. . . .
>
> It seems to me that both of us have a road to travel. This road leads more or less in the same direction; only you are going farther than I am. Would you accept a travelling companion, a kind of majordomo, entrusted with ordering the relays of horses, and, if necessary, riding them?
>
> . . . This cavalcading groom is a little afraid of you, otherwise he would have asked you in person for association on the journey. . . .
>
> Consider all this in your wisdom, madame, and believe in the interest which, majordomo or not, I shall always take in the journey of an amiable woman endowed with a strong and worthy character. . . .
>
> I am, madame, with true respect, your most humble and most obedient servant,
>
> C. de Seyssel,
> aged 53 years [2]

It is not clear whether this proposal was ever sent to the Baronne

Lacuée de Saint-Just. If it was, she must have dismissed it as a neurotic joke. That year she married Léonor Fresnel, Mérimée's first cousin.[3]

Beyle remained desperate for love. On Christmas Day he made determined advances to the engaging author of *Le Lieutenant*. Mme. Gaulthier was unlikely to be led astray by passion for a friend whom she had known for years. She extricated herself from the situation, but she did so with such tact and kindness that she could not have hurt his feelings. Some have suspected that this sudden "crystallisation" owed as much to Beyle's nostalgia for Paris as it did to genuine love. On September 27, 1837, he was to make the will in which he asked to be buried at the Cimetière d'Andilly or, if that was too expensive, at the Cimetière Montmartre.

Despite his failures in love, he remained, ironically, a counsellor to his friends. Clémentine Curial, anxious to keep a hesitant lover, asked for "learned advice from the author of *De l'Amour.*" "You are necessary to me," she wrote in her old excessive tone, "without you I should rid myself of life, because I rely on you alone to give me a little strength." [4]

The quotation remains, but the letter itself has been destroyed. Menti had written him some 280 letters. He kept them for the rest of his life. After his death, Romain Colomb unforgivably burnt the whole correspondence. One small consolation remains: the Papal police, keeping watch on his mail, had held back a letter which they considered suspect. One single letter from Menti to the consul at Civitavecchia therefore survives in the Vatican archives.[5]

Now, in 1837, overwhelming love was denied him, but he happily resumed his Parisian life. He spent an evening at Baron Gérard's with Balzac, Mérimée, Delacroix and Ballanche. He was invited to dinner by Mme. Victor de Tracy, daughter-in-law of Destutt de Tracy. He joined the Cercle des Arts. He belonged to the little dining club, with a membership of eight, which Mérimée mentioned in his correspondence with the Comtesse de Montijo. The other members were Sutton Sharpe, Delacroix, Mareste, Viel-Castel, Koreff and possibly Victor Jacquemont. They usually met at the Café Anglais and enjoyed entertainments which Mérimée took care not to specify to his correspondent. On March 29 Beyle wrote gaily to Comte Cini, in Rome:

We have had infamous weather from 2 September until today. Apart from that, Paris is a celestial place. Nothing can equal the ball at the Tuileries in magnificence. The suite of illuminated rooms is six times as long as the façade of the palazzo Chigi on the square.

As for the cost of living:

A superb room with two small rooms in the fashionable districts

	−65 fr.
Cost of blacking, boots, etc.	−12 fr.
Dinner	− 5 fr.
Déjeuner at 2 fr.	− 2 fr.

My passions are very like Mme. Martini, who was in Rome two years ago, and they cost me 120 francs a month. It is true that I don't claim miraculous fidelity.

The Salon is dull.[6]

Since he had arrived in Paris, Beyle had resumed his writing. In November, 1836, he had begun his *Mémoires sur Napoléon* (he abandoned them in April, 1837). Now that middle age was upon him, he looked back with increasing favour on the great adventure of his youth. One summer day, at Civitavecchia, he had reread the *Mémorial de Sainte-Hélène* by Las Cases, and he had scribbled on the cover a note which would have satisfied Julien Sorel: "Real *boock* to read on the eve of one's execution. Reread, moved, with the sharpest emotion." [7] He had added the comment that Napoleon's mistake at Saint Helena had been not to have an English officer in attendance. Napoleon—said Beyle—would have charmed him and gained a chance of escape. Now, in the late 1830's, Beyle regretted that the emperor had not attempted a second Hundred Days.

He was not only writing on Napoleon. On March 1, 1837, he published "Vittoria Accoramboni" in the *Revue des Deux Mondes*. This violent and meaningless chronicle was taken (he maintained) from a manuscript written in Padua in 1585. Vittoria Accoramboni came from a noble family in Urbino. Her parents chose Felix Peretti, the nephew of Cardinal Montalto, as her husband. The cardinal bestowed great favours on her family. Felix was then murdered—on the orders, it appears, of the cardinal or of Prince Orsini. Vittoria married Prince Paolo Orsini; but soon afterwards he died, and she herself was brutally murdered. Beyle was fascinated by crude violence—or what he thought heroic energy. On July 1 the *Revue des Deux Mondes* was to

publish "Les Cenci." Beatrix Cenci's father had repeatedly attempted to have intercourse with her; she had hired assassins to knock a nail
into one of his eyes and another into his throat, and she herself was
duly executed.

The author of *Promenades dans Rome* had also decided to describe a
journey in France. He needed to document himself, and he dutifully
toured the provinces. From April 17 to 22 he visited Le Havre. On
May 25 he set out for western France; he went to La Charité-sur-
Loire, Bourges, Tours, Nantes, Le Havre—again—and Rouen. On
July 5 he was back in Paris, where he settled at 8, rue Caumartin. In
August and September he was probably travelling in Brittany and
the Dauphiné. On September 28 he was back in Paris.

On March 8, 1838, he embarked on a second grand tour. On March
11 he reached Bordeaux. He felt no haste to leave it for, as he told
Fiore, he had found "a gay friend, who makes me dine with the pretty
women of the neighbourhood. I didn't know what Bordeaux wine
was like before this journey. . . . I am amusing myself by doing, or
rather writing, my travels in the south." [8] He continued his journey to
Agen, Toulouse, Bordeaux again and Bayonne and crossed the
Spanish frontier to Irún. The Spanish, like the Italians, had a splendid spontaneity; they, too, satisfied his aesthetic demands. From Irún
he returned to France, travelled on to Fontarabie, Hendaye, Pau,
Carcassonne, Montpellier and the familiar Marseilles. Then he spent
three days at Cannes, among the orange trees, and June found him in
Valence, Grenoble, Chambéry and Geneva. In Geneva he called on
Dr. Prévost, who advised the occasional use of leeches and the cure at
Vichy. From Geneva he went to Berne, where he was stricken with
gout. By July 2 he was in Strasbourg, where he unburdened himself to
Fiore:

> The sight of me walking in the street with the help of a stick, and
> swearing when I stub my left foot on a sharp paving stone, must
> certainly amuse the Strasbourgeois. . . . I should go back to Paris with
> the greatest pleasure; but I am so near the triumphant church at
> Cologne! . . .
> Tomorrow, 3 July, at Baden; on 5 July I return to Kehl, to take the
> steamship; on the 6th, I sleep at Mayence, on land; on the 7th, at
> Cologne; on the 9th I shall be in Brussels, doing twenty-seven leagues

by railway from Liège to the said Brussels. One day for the Rubens
pictures, and on the 11th or 12th I leave for Paris.[9]

He returned to Paris on July 22 and settled, once again, at 8, rue
Caumartin. On August 3, his ill health was forgotten: he resumed
his love affair with Giulia.

André Billy maintains that Beyle's fourth visit to London can
probably be dated August, 1838.[10] There may be evidence for this in
a note which Joseph Primoli discovered in Beyle's *Histoire de Napoléon.*
After some comments on English politics, Beyle adds: "Said by S the
15 août evening 1838 fine sight of this friend." [11] It is tempting to
identify the friend as Sutton Sharpe and the occasion as an evening in
London. However, Doris Gunnell, in *Stendhal et l'Angleterre,* suggests
that all the evidence points to the end of the year. Colomb says that
Beyle also went to Scotland and Ireland, but if so, it is strange that he
made no allusion to the fact. However, Colomb remains the only
source of information about this final visit to London. It was a short
visit, during which Sutton Sharpe took Beyle to the Athenaeum, and
Beyle struck up an acquaintance with Theodore Hook, the wit and
man of letters.[12]

On June 30 the *Bibliographie de la France* had announced the two
volumes of *Mémoires d'un touriste.* "Nothing is more exhausting," Pierre
Brun confessed, "than these two thick volumes, a kind of compact
encyclopaedia." [13] It is hard to write a travel book without vitality,
without an eager visual sense, without affection for the country in
question. Yet this, in fact, is what Beyle has done. *Mémoires d'un touriste*
reflect the more disagreeable side of his nature: his cynicism, bitterness and contempt. They are Baedeker memoirs, enlivened with
occasional anecdotes and with autobiographical details which may
be of a certain interest. They add nothing to Henri Beyle's literary
reputation.

When he had written his travel book, he thought of making
another novel out of the youth of Alexander Farnese. Almost at once
it occurred to him to turn it into a modern chronicle. On September 1
he wrote the description of the Battle of Waterloo, which was to be the
first episode of *La Chartreuse de Parme.*

On August 15 "La Duchesse de Palliano" had appeared in the
Revue des Deux Mondes. It was another story of gratuitous violence. A
servant was stabbed to death by the Duc de Palliano for confessing

that he had slept with the duchess; the duchess protested her innocence, but nonetheless she was strangled. On September 12–13 Beyle wrote the first part of "L'Abbesse de Castro." The story, again, is set in the sixteenth century. Hélène de Campiréali, the daughter of a patrician in Albano, is loved by Jules Branciforte, a plebeian soldier of fortune, and she duly falls in love with him. Jules kills her brother, Fabio, in a skirmish between the partisans of the Colonnas and the Orsinis. Hélène is taken to the convent of the Visitation at Castro. Jules tries in vain to storm the convent and to rescue her. She is told that he has died, and "out of boredom, or, if you prefer, libertinage," she has a love affair with a bishop. In time she gives birth to a son. She learns that Jules is, after all, alive. She has loved only him. She makes her confession to him, and kills herself.

"L'Abbesse de Castro" suggests a boulevard melodrama—and in fact, the theatre was to exploit it. On April 4 "L'Abbaye de Castro" earned a success on the boards. Nonetheless, the story is the most accomplished of Beyle's short stories; its characters and action have the vigour and spontaneity which he admired in the Italians. The *Chroniques italiennes,* though hardly more than a skillful adaptation of melodramatic chronicles, carry some of Beyle's most insistent poetic themes: the rebellion of the outlaw, the double point of view on morality, the ambiguous clash of private virtues with public vices, the themes of tragic happiness, of love as a *coup de foudre* and, as an impossibility, of the immurement of the beloved. Translated into terms of sixteenth-century Scotland, this might have been a world for Sir Walter Scott.

On November 4 Beyle began in earnest to write *La Chartreuse de Parme.* He finished it on December 26. On January 24, 1839, he signed a contract for it with the publisher Dupont. He was hardly idle while he waited for the novel to come out. On February 1 the first part of "L'Abbesse de Castro" appeared in the *Revue des Deux Mondes.* From February 19 to 21 he wrote the second part; this appeared on March 1. On March 8 he attended a reading of Balzac's play *L'Ecole des ménages* at the Marquis de Custine's. Another theatrical event had recently roused Beyle—indeed, all Paris—to enthusiasm. In January, in a letter to Comte Cini, he had described the advent of Rachel. "Mlle. Rachel is a poor little beggar girl of eighteen, very thin, who

acts tragedy as if she were inventing what she said; she has caused a
revolution at the Théâtre-Français. . . . She has a genius which con-
founds me with amazement every time I see her perform; for two
hundred years there has not been such a miracle in France." [14]

It was in March that Beyle moved to 30, rue Godot-de-Mauroy. He
had no doubt been led to this address partly because it was almost
opposite the house where his cousin Romain Colomb was living. He
had a happy relationship with Romain and his wife; Félicien Colomb
became his *adorable cousine*. And expressing his concern about
Romain's health, Beyle added: "Anyway, console yourself: if you lose
him, I will marry you." [15]

It was from the rue Godot-de-Mauroy that, on March 29, he wrote
to Balzac:

> I wanted to send *La Chartreuse* to you, as the king of novelists of the
> present century. My porter will not go to 1, rue Cassini; he pretends
> that he doesn't understand my directions. . . .
> Sometimes, Monsieur, you venture into Christian territory, give
> me a straightforward address. . . .
> Or else send for the said novel.[16]

> Monsieur [replied Balzac],
> I have already read in *Le Constitutionnel* an article taken from *La
> Chartreuse* which led me to commit the sin of envy. Yes, I was seized by
> an attack of jealousy at that true, superb description of a battle which I
> was dreaming of for the *Scènes de la vie militaire*, the most difficult part of
> my work, and this passage charmed me and vexed me and enchanted
> me, and it made me despair. I say so candidly. It is done like Borgog-
> none and Vouvermans, Salvator Rosa and Walter Scott. So don't be
> surprised if I leap at your offer, and send for the book.[17]

On April 5 he wrote again:

> Monsieur,
> One must never delay giving pleasure to those who have given us
> pleasure. *La Chartreuse* is a great and noble work.[18]

The next day the novel was announced by the *Bibliographie de la*

France. On April 13 Emile Forgues, writing in *Le Commerce,* declared it "a work of the first importance, a real *camera oscura* which reproduces life with incomparable fidelity." [19] On April 14 Balzac assured Mme. Hanska: "Beyle has just published what I think is the finest book to have appeared in the last fifty years. It is called *La Chartreuse de Parme....* If Machiavelli wrote a novel, it would be this." [20]

Thirty-four

In 1821, FROM La Poretta, Beyle had written to Sir Walter Scott, expressing his admiration for *The Abbot*. "What a pity," he added, "that the author did not have to paint the Middle Ages in this admirable Italy!" [1] It is doubtful whether this letter was ever sent to Scott, but Scott was not averse to the idea which it contained. In May, 1832, Sir William Gell, the topographer, recounted the novelist's visit to Rome:

> We all dined at the Palace of the Duchess Torlonia. . . .
> It was at this entertainment that Sir Walter met with the Duke and Duchess of Corchino. . . . The Duke told him he was possessed of a vast collection of papers, giving true accounts of all the murders, poisonings, intrigues, and curious adventures of all the great Roman families during many centuries, all of which were at his service to copy and publish in his way as historical romances. . . . Whoever has read any of these memoirs of Italian families, of which many are published and very many exist in manuscript, will acknowledge how they abound in strange events and romantic stories, and may form some idea of the delight with which Sir Walter imagined himself on the point of pouncing upon a treasure after his own heart. [2]

Scott was to die at Abbotsford on September 21, but Beyle, it appears, delighted in the treasure. Maurice Barrès suggests that these manuscripts were among those which he was to copy the following year.[3] Whether or not this is true, it was certainly an account of the origins of the Farnese family, sovereigns of Parma in the sixteenth century, which contained the basic plot of *La Chartreuse de Parme*. Beyle translated the action into terms of the nineteenth century. *La Chartreuse de Parme* is a picture of life and intrigues at a small Italian court between 1815 and 1830.

Julien Sorel, in the first part of *Le Rouge et le Noir*, had represented Beyle as he was; Fabrice del Dongo represents, fairly exactly, what Beyle would have liked to be. Partly French by birth (it is tacitly implied that his father was a young French officer), Fabrice is fired by his admiration for Napoleon. When he learns that the emperor has escaped from Elba, he determines to join him. Unbeknown to the Marquis del Dongo, and aided by his mother, the marquise, and her sister-in-law, Gina Pietranera, he escapes from Grianta, on Lake Como, travels north to Paris and finds himself, an eager innocent, dressed in the uniform of a dead hussar, equipped with a stolen cartridge box and musket, on the periphery of Waterloo.

Beyle's description of Waterloo owes something to his experience at Bautzen; he had heard rather than seen, guessed rather than known, that a battle was in progress. No doubt much of the detail which Fabrice observed had been observed by Beyle in Italy, in Prussia and Russia, as he followed the emperor's campaigns. Whatever the origin of these pages, they are the most remarkable in any of his novels or short stories. Wide-eyed, quixotic, bold and timid, frightened but determined, too young to wield a sabre or to see a corpse without anguish, Fabrice wanders, like a lost child, in and out of the battle. Fabrice is the Beyle of seventeen who had ridden into Italy in the wake of the Napoleonic armies—or, rather, he is Beyle *en beau*, generous, warm, spontaneous and unbitter. He is at the mercy of the quick-witted and unscrupulous, he is disillusioned by the roughness and cunning of the soldiery, he is a boyish idealist who hates to be disappointed; he is also driven by exaltation, by a sense that he is present at the making of history. At the turn of the century Augustin Filon, once tutor to the prince imperial, observed: "There is something epic in the air, epic by suggestion, and we divine that, behind those clouds of dust and smoke, great things are happening, prodigious destinies are being fulfilled. I prefer Stendhal's Waterloo in *La Chartreuse de Parme* to Victor Hugo's in *Les Misérables*, and . . . I prefer it to Zola's Sedan in *La Débâcle.*" [4] Max Nordau observed that Beyle was the first novelist who had spoken of war as a cool but disgusted spectator. Tolstoy's *War and Peace* had, he said, been modelled on *La Chartreuse de Parme*.[5]

Maurice Barrès wrote of *La Chartreuse:* "There is colour and atmosphere. But the book is overweighted with complex intrigues. The only excellent thing in it is the account of the Battle of Waterloo." [6] There was a certain truth in the comment. The description of Waterloo was written with verve, perception, brilliance, even humour, but it remained an extravagance: it could be removed from the book without damage, and the rest of the novel was indeed extraordinarily complex. After Waterloo (of which he saw little), Fabrice returned to Italy, somewhat suspect because of his French escapade. His "aunt," Gina Pietranera, now the Duchesse de Sanseverina, was the mistress of Count Mosca, chief minister at the court of Parma. Beautiful, resourceful, dominant, she was much enamoured of Fabrice. There seemed little future for an ardent youth, now that Waterloo was fought and lost, but through her influence, he now found himself on the threshold of a career in the church. Count Mosca's enemies, aware that La Sanseverina loved Fabrice, plotted to remove him from the capital, for it was clear that she would follow him and that Mosca would go with her. The plot succeeded, thanks to his imprudent love affair with a young actress. He was imprisoned but escaped with the aid of La Sanseverina, Count Mosca and Clélia Conti, the daughter of the prison governor. If La Sanseverina belongs to the family of Mathilde de La Mole, of the heroines of the *Chroniques italiennes,* Clélia is the sister of Mme. de Chasteller, Mme. de Rênal and Armance. She is the gentle, selfless figure, innocent and utterly devoted, whom, in his tranquil and more reasonable moments, Beyle admired. Clélia does not command the same sympathy or affection as Mme. de Rênal or Mme. de Chasteller, but she is cast in the same mould.

La Sanseverina contrives to have the reigning Prince of Parma poisoned; through her influence, again, the new prince pardons Fabrice, who becomes an eminent cleric and renews his love affair with Clélia Conti, now the Marchesa Crescenzi. Their son, Sandrino, is born, and two years later, he is kidnapped by Fabrice, who wants to have his child to himself. The boy dies. Clélia believes that his death is punishment for her sins (one recalls the anguish of Mme. de Rênal at her son's sickbed). Pierre Martino has emphasised that Alexander Farnese and Cleria, his mistress, had had a child; Beyle has remained faithful to detail. No doubt he had also remembered Menti's fear of pregnancy and the illness and death of Bathilde. In *La Chartreuse de Parme*, the death of Sandrino is soon followed by the death of his mother. Fabrice retires to the Carthusian monastery of Parma and dies a year later. La Sanseverina (now married to Mosca) does not long survive him.

The book, as Maurice Barrès said, is overweighted with intrigues, but it is full of colour. In the antiquated court, which seems a perpetual parody of Versailles, Ranuce-Ernest IV, Prince of Parma, apes the majesty of Louis XIV and allows the liberal Beyle to express his detestation of absolute monarchy, his antipathy to the Bourbons and the Hapsburgs. The Marquis del Dongo, nominal father of Fabrice, and his elder son, the Marchesino Ascanio, represent the pro-Austrian Italians whom Beyle abhorred. The Marquise Raversi, flamboyant virago and intriguer, owes something, one suspects, to Mme. Traversi, the opulent and scheming cousin of Métilde. Beyle is no kinder to the middle class than he is to the nobility: he shows his contempt for the magistrates, especially for Rassi, the cynical, dishonest grand judge of the state of Parma. Cool and appraising, he observes the aspirations and vanities, the emptiness and pretentions of courtiers and bourgeois as they further their careers. Sometimes the colour is heightened, but the portraits have the authenticity of lived experience. *La Chartreuse de Parme* is pullulating, too, with plebeian characters: jailers, gendarmes, customs officials, actors, tavernkeepers and beggars. We see them in the mass, but we remember them as sharply defined individuals.

Fabrice del Dongo is, in many ways, Beyle himself. His birth reflects the dilemma of Beyle, the would-be Milanese; Fabrice, the illegitimate son, asserts Beyle's lifelong wish to dissociate himself from his own father. Fabrice, like Beyle's other heroes, inherits the mythology of the veteran soldier: if he is not the incarnation of Renaissance Italy, he is the spiritual son of Napoleon. *La Chartreuse de Parme* deliberately opens, *allegro con brio*, with the entry of the French troops into Milan in 1796. Beyle creates his favourite son Fabrice from the memory of the huge and unparalleled happiness of his own seventeenth year. As Gilbert Durand rightly observes, in *Le Décor mythique de la Chartreuse de Parme,* Fabrice is the child of Beyle's dream: the son of the young cavalry subaltern, Henri Beyle, and of Angela Pietragrua.[7]

In *La Chartreuse de Parme,* Beyle has presented not only his youth, but his maturity. The name of Count Mosca, director general of police and friend of Rossini, had long ago appeared in *Rome, Naples et Florence* and in the *Journal.* Balzac claimed to recognise Beyle's Mosca as a likeness of Metternich; Beyle denied that he had had Metternich in mind. Possibly some of Mosca's features were taken from Comte Saurau, sometime governor of Lombardy, whom he had often seen in Milan; possibly Mosca owed something to Guillaume-Louis Dutillot, Prime Minister of Parma in the eighteenth century and lover of Anna Malaspina della Bastia, lady-in-waiting to the Duchess of Parma. But if certain details were taken from history, the character was that of Beyle himself, or, rather, the mature Beyle as he would have liked to be. Mosca had the dreams of the ageing consul at Civitavecchia. He was the mentor of Fabrice; he was well informed and wise, expert at intrigue, a consummate man of the world. In the romanticised memoirs which form a large part of *La Chartreuse de Parme,* Mosca is the man who is not a dupe or a fool but wants, to the end, to pursue felicity, to follow *la chasse au bonheur.* Mosca is Henri Beyle himself, wanting to see himself in his young heroes, mastering his disenchantment by art, by irony, by self-analysis, exorcising his lost illusions. Fabrice and Mosca are developments of their creator, much more than likenesses; they owe their vitality to the fact that they synthesise so much of his life, they are a bittersweet compensation for so many of his reverses. They attain sharp relief; they are endowed with a remarkable presence, because they sum up, between them, the realities and dreams, the hopes and disappointments, of a lifetime. Fabrice and Mosca are not only their creator in youth and in maturity; they represent the Italian soul. Mosca is the Italian who has passed the age of enthusiasm; he is the conservative attached to his privileges. Fabrice has the spontaneity, the tenderness and generous warmth, the honesty, panache and chivalry which are lacking in Beyle's French heroes. He symbolises his creator's nostalgia for Italy.

So does La Sanseverina. For Angela Pietragrua is here the source for a Beyle who is writing not only a chronicle, but his romanticised memoirs. La Sanseverina has Angela's powers of seduction, her considered coquetry; she has the same refinements of cruelty. Yet she has candour, too, and nobility; she has romantic sensibility, a capacity for exaltation. Like Fabrice, she belongs to an elite which is marked by *virtù*, by energy of spirit. Her prototype may be Vandozza Farnese, she may reflect La Pietragrua, but she symbolises Italian passion. So does Clélia Conti, who owes something to Métilde Dembowski: her patriotism, her illuminating spiritual beauty. Clélia has, too, the fervent and innocent piety of the Italian and an Italian sense of filial duty. She is, perhaps, the ideal compensation which Beyle allows himself for his rejection by Métilde.

Beyle had always wanted to escape from his own time and place. "It seems to me," he had written, "that one must get out of one's century and make oneself a citizen of that which has been most favourable to the work of genius. . . . One must become contemporary with Corneille." [8] And again: "I must get completely out of my century, and imagine myself in the sight of Louis XIV. Always work for the twentieth century." [9] So he had written as a youth. In 1838, a disillusioned middle-aged man, he had dreamed about Napoleon's campaigns and reflected sadly: "I have fallen into an age of transition, that is to say, an age of mediocrity, and it will hardly be half gone before time, which goes so slowly for a nation and so fast for a human being, will make a sign to me that I must go. I was much wilder, but much happier when . . . I was always dreaming of the passions which I felt about to feel and perhaps to inspire." [10] In *La Chartreuse de Parme,* as Fabrice del Dongo, he recalled the ardour and the sensibility of youth; as Mosca he continued his pursuit of happiness. All novelists, it is said, make themselves amends for the injustices of fate. *La Chartreuse de Parme* is Beyle's declaration of love for Italy. It is also his escape from nineteenth-century France, his fulfilment of his own persistent dreams.

The characters in Beyle's novels sometimes give the sense of being duplicates or recurring types. This is perhaps because he approached his fiction in a scientific manner, performed psychological experiments. He had trained himself to write plays by means of dissection and reconstruction; in a sense, he wrote his novels in a laboratory. The characters which he created, partly from documents and partly from experience, came to be symbols rather than human beings. They lived through situations which were symbolic, too. Fabrice learns of Napoleon's landing in the Golfe Juan; almost immediately he sees an imperial eagle, flying at a great height towards Switzerland and France. "And I, too, I said to myself at once, will cross Switzerland with the speed of an eagle. I shall go and offer that great man something very small, but in fact all that I possess—the power of my frail arm." The moment recalls a moment in *Le Rouge et le Noir* when Julien, on a mountaintop, had watched a sparrow-hawk in flight. More than once Beyle sets his heroes at a symbolic height: Julien astride the beams in the carpenter's shop, Fabrice in the bell tower, overlooking Grianta. Fabrice is imprisoned, as Julien had been, and Fabrice is imprisoned at the top of a tower, as if to emphasise his superiority and his isolation. Yet prison, in the novels of Beyle, is not oppressive. As Gilbert Durand has emphasised, the theme of prison occupies the same ambivalent place in his works as the gardens of Armide in the works of Tasso.[11] There are the terrors of the labyrinth and the delights of claustrophilia. Julien Sorel had found his ideal life in prison, away from the vexations of the world. It was there, awaiting death, in the presence of Mme. de Rênal, that he had known the meaning of love. In *La Chartreuse de Parme* the Farnese Tower is the symbol of secret happiness, of perfect intimacy. It is in the solitude of this "enchanted world" where Clélia lives that Fabrice understands love for the first time. The tower, austere though it is, becomes the symbol of time rediscovered. The world of prison is a world in which night is day; like the churches and convents, the caves and grottoes, the mountains and enclosed gardens which so often figure in Beyle's fiction, it emphasises the isolation and, in a sense, the sacredness of love. In the decor of Waterloo, Fabrice had shown heroic exaltation; in the decor of the Farnese Tower, he had come to experience love. The Charterhouse of Parma is, for him, the ultimate and inevitable retreat.

Beyle's heroes are not sentimental figureheads like Werther and René; they belong to a later generation. They owe something, perhaps, to Dumas' Antony and much to Byron's Childe Harold and to Byron himself: idealistic, ardent and occasionally cynical. They sometimes strike an attitude from the Ambigu-Comique. They also reflect the philosophy and the lived experience of their creator. *La Chartreuse de Parme* was written by Beyle three and a half years before his death; it is both a testament and the final spiritual maturing of his life.

Thirty-five

BEYLE HAD RARELY been so creative as he was in the early months of 1839. On March 16 he had begun "Suora Scolastica." On April 8 he had drafted the short story "Trop de faveur tue." On April 22 he sketched out another short story, "Le Chevalier de Saint-Isnier." On April 13, more significantly, he had had the first idea for *Lamiel.*

Lamiel—which he was not to finish—was a kind of counterpart to *Le Rouge et le Noir.* Lamiel, a foundling, is adopted by a bourgeois couple at Carville, in Normandy. Brought up in innocence and piety, she becomes reader to the Duchesse de Miossens, who lives in a closed world in the local château. The young girl earns the devotion of the lonely, middle-aged widow, and she discovers the pettiness and the endless boredom of social life; she attracts the attention of Dr. Sansfin: a sinister hunchback who is seeking power to console himself for his deformity. She becomes slightly enamoured of a poor young abbé (the only sympathetic character in the novel), and she pays a local youth fifteen francs to initiate her into love. Disillusioned by the experience and contemptuous of society, she captivates the young Duc de Miossens and then abandons him in Rouen. Taking half his available money, she sets off for Paris, to assert her powers of attraction. The innocent foundling has become a female Julien Sorel, determined to make herself amends for her early years. Lamiel has the energy which Beyle admired in men and women: the inflexible independence, the uncompromising will to succeed. In *Lamiel,* as in *Le Rouge,* he wanted to show how an independent spirit reacted to the vulgarity of a stupid world. Lamiel discards morality even more completely than Julien had done, and even more than Julien, she learns the need to be a hypocrite. In *Lamiel,* Beyle had set himself a more difficult task than he had done in *Le Rouge.* He had chosen a girl to embody a masculine ruthlessness and sense of purpose. He also hoped to present French society in the early years of Louis-Philippe, and he did not seem to see that lives of great adventure were now impossible for women. He worked, sporadically, at *Lamiel;* he was working at it only a few days before his death. It remained an unfinished draft, and it was published only in 1889. It remains of interest to the student of his methods, and Lamiel herself clearly belongs to the family of his creations. Like her creator, she is still unsatisfied, even in pleasure, and Beyle intended her to abandon a comfortable life and—still in search of love—to end her unhappy existence in the company of bandits.

On June 24, 1839, Beyle himself left Paris to return to his distant consulate. He was energetic, happy, and recognised by his peers as one of the most remarkable writers of the day. To one of these admirers he had sent a farewell note: "Fabrice has called several times. He is desolate to leave Paris without seeing Monsieur de Balzac. That amiable man is begged to remember that he has an admirer—one might dare to add a friend—at Civitavecchia." [1]

Beyle had asked for six weeks' leave; he had been away for more than three years. Even now, he lingered on his journey back to Italy. On June 27 the chancellor of the consulate at Leghorn wrote to a colleague at Genoa: "M. Beyle is in Florence. I expect him to arrive here at any moment, that is, if he remembers that he has a post to occupy. A man of genius finds it hard to accept consular monotony in such a beastly hole as Civitavecchia." [2] From Leghorn, Beyle went on to Siena, where he again saw Giulia. On August 10 he resumed control of his consulate and blandly explained to the Minister of Foreign Affairs: "I was delayed at Genoa, and then at Leghorn, by attacks of gout." [3]

The following month he moved to Rome, where he lived with his old friend Abraham Constantin at 48, via Condotti. His boredom had already begun to return. "I hardly believe in *energy*, in Rome or anywhere else," he reported on September 26. "Boredom is giving me nervous excitement and I cannot write." [4] A few days later he took M. de Gasparin, a former Minister of the Interior, on a conducted tour of Civitavecchai, and de Gasparin agreed "that one must have killed both father and mother to live in such a hole. The cafés," Beyle observed, "do half their business in the morning by the light of execrable lamps, and everyone goes to bed at eight o'clock. All this would be nothing if I had colleagues, but I am the only animal of my species." [5]

On October 10 his exile was lightened by the arrival of Mérimée. In Civitavecchia, Rome and Naples they spent the next month together. On November 10 he found himself alone, once more, in Civitavecchia. He had moved now to a third-floor apartment at 7, piazza di Porta Romana, where he was to stay until 1841. The monotony of life was a little relieved by the presence of the Duc de Bordeaux in Rome. The Pope had chosen not to receive the legitimist claimant to the French throne. For the officials of Louis-Philippe—still afraid of a Bourbon coup d'état—the position was delicate, and Beyle felt obliged to ask the ambassador how he should behave if the duc should embark at Civitavecchia. "If," came the answer, "you have reason to suspect a clandestine embarkation, . . . then I request you to do all in your power to enlighten the Papal authorities." [6]

The Duc de Bordeaux was not tempted to embark from Civitavecchia. As the new year opened, he was enjoying the eulogies of Roman society. On January 4, from Rome, Beyle assured Fiore: "The young man in whose honour so many lies are told is a copy of the Duc d'Angoulême, he is always slouching from foot to foot. . . . He is continually choked with flattery." [7] Beyle had not lost his lifelong aversion to the Bourbons.

On January 20 he was back at his consulate, and there, it seems, he learned that a distant cousin had recently disembarked at Civitavecchia, on his way to Rome. Ernest Hébert, born in Grenoble in 1817, had won the *grand prix* for painting, and he was about to begin his four years' residence at the Villa Medici. The French Academy in Rome was now directed by Ingres, and among the prizewinners were Lefuel, one day to be an architect of the Tuileries, and Gounod, the future composer of *Faust*. In his eagerness to get to Rome, Hébert had not called on the ageing consul at Civitavecchia. His social lapse brought a swift rebuke. Nonetheless, Beyle urged Constantin to take an interest in his young cousin, "who might perhaps have a soul." [8]

Beyle appears to have shown more generosity than Hébert. In 1885, Maurice Barrès recorded Hébert's comments on his relative.

> "You like Stendhal? He was a very witty old man, but he was crotchety. I knew him well. Yes, Monsieur Barrès, he was my cousin, and when I was sent to the villa [Medici], at your age, my parents told me to go and pay my respects at Civitavecchia. He was bored to death there; he spent the evenings with the one and only local publisher. I really believe that the Pope had forbidden him to enter Rome. Why? No doubt his *Promenades* had caused displeasure. Monsieur Barrès, I don't know if you would have found my cousin as entertaining as his books!"
>
> And M. Hébert recalled that Stendhal did not accept that he was growing old, and he showed himself very touchy with young people. He had a mania for disconcerting loving couples. . . .[9]

The reminiscences, set down nearly half a century later, are not entirely accurate, and they bear the stamp of malice. And yet, from time to time, they sound authentic.

As the new year, 1840, opened in Civitavecchia, Beyle attempted to keep up his spirits. "Out of a hundred foreigners who pass through here, . . . fifty want to see the famous brigand Gasparone, and four or five M. de Stendhal. This consulate was nothing before 1831; now it is one of the busiest, it's a post office. This morning I was woken at five o'clock by a courier coming from Rome, and it was so warm that I received him in my nightshirt." And writing to Fiore, he added: "If you approve of the letter, put it in the post or deliver it at the ministry." [10] The letter in question was addressed to the Minister of Foreign Affairs, and it asked if he would raise the consulate to first-class status or increase the consul's salary. Since Beyle was now busy with excavations in the Roman campagna and since he had never been an orthodox consul, he also sent the Minister a report on the statues recently discovered at Cerveteri. No doubt he hoped that the French government would try to acquire them.

He tried to find literary distraction. *Lamiel* did not emerge from limbo, but he was shaping Constantin's notes on Italian pictures and corresponding with Vieusseux, in Florence, about the printing of the work *Idées italiennes sur quelques tableaux célèbres*. He spent most of April in Rome and all of May in Civitavecchia. He was in Rome from June 3 to 21. He returned briefly to Civitavecchia before he left for Florence on June 30. He was doubtless concerned with the proofs of *Idées italiennes*. He was certainly concerned with Giulia. She had now moved to Florence, and on this visit, from July 1 to 18, and on his later visit, from August 19 to September 15, they resumed their consoling and remarkably persistent love affair.

A minor source of pleasure and consolation was Beyle's continuing friendship with the Montijos. On his last visit to Paris, Mérimée had introduced him to the Comtesse de Montijo, the wife of a Spanish grandee. Beyle could be delightful to children, and he had earned the devotion of her two young daughters, Paca and Eugénie, by telling them the story of Napoleon: "that wonderful story which he had lived." Many years afterwards, Joseph Primoli asked Eugénie if she remembered Beyle.

> Remember M. Beyle [she cried]! He was the first man who made my heart beat—and beat violently! . . . He came to my mother's every Thursday; that evening, in honour of our great friend, we went to bed at 9 instead of 8, we didn't have dinner, we were so impatient to hear him! Whenever the bell rang we rushed to the door. . . . At last we brought him back, in triumph, into the salon, each of us holding one of his hands, and we settled him in his armchair by the fire. . . . He used to take one of us on each knee; we didn't give him time to breathe before we reminded him of the victory where he had left our emperor, the emperor we had thought about all the week. . . . He had inspired us with his fanaticism for the only man whom he admired. . . . We wept and laughed and shuddered, we went mad. . . . He showed us the emperor radiant in the sun of Austerlitz, pale in the snows of Russia, dying at Saint Helena. . . .
>
> My mother used to intervene and admonish us: "Leave him in peace!" . . . "It doesn't matter," he used to say, as he embraced us. "Only little girls understand great things; their approval consoles me for the criticisms of fools and bourgeois."

When he returned to his post and we made our way back to Spain, a regular correspondence kept us in touch.[11]

Now, on August 10, 1840, from his consulate, Beyle addressed himself to Eugénie, for whom he felt avuncular affection. His affection was clearly returned, for she had already ventured, more than once, to write to him.

Your letters are too short and they aren't dated [so he informed her]; mine have the opposite fault. Because of you I can't think of anything except the events in Barcelona. I observed a long time ago that every state that changes its government gives itself troubles for forty years. You will not enjoy peace in Spain until all the positions are occupied by men who are fifteen years old today, four years older than you. Aren't you eleven or twelve? Perhaps thirteen?

All your life, you will see a small accident, like the one in Barcelona, happen every four years. Would you rather have been born in about 1750, in the ridiculous reign of. . . . (This king is so obscure that I don't know his name.) As for me, I give thanks to God that I entered Berlin, with my pistols carefully loaded and primed, on October [27], 1806. Napoleon put on the full-dress uniform of a general of division to make his entry. That is perhaps the only time I saw him wear it. He went in twenty yards ahead of the troops; the *silent* crowd were only two feet from his horse; they could have shot at him from every window. . . .

The revolution which followed the death of Ferdinand VII reduced your fortune to half. . . . It is not in your power to regain those million reals; it's better not to think about it. You will have an effort of this kind to make when you are forty-five. . . . So contrive an occupation for your old age. Think of all these things ten years before they happen.[12]

It was strangely sombre advice to give to a child, but perhaps, in 1870, at the age of forty-four, Eugénie remembered it. She was then the wife of Napoleon III, and the Second Empire had fallen.

I have had a careful watch kept on M. Beyle, consul at Civitavecchia, who has now been staying in Rome for a week [reported Captain Nardoni, of the Papal police, on October 10]. It seems that he often goes to the Académie de France and more often to his minister. . . .

The liberals in Rome, those of the middle class, do not know him. Some who belong to the aristocracy consider him to be a *freemason* because of *the publication of the antireligious work which he published before 1831,* but nobody thinks (at least in Rome) that he is busy conspiring.

He is returning to Civitavecchia early next week.[13]

He was, it seems, still in Rome when, on October 15, he received a copy of *La Revue parisienne,* which contained Balzac's article on *La Chartreuse de Parme.*

> I had [wrote Balzac] met M. Beyle twice in society, in twelve years, until the moment when I met him in the boulevard des Italiens, and took the liberty of congratulating him on *La Chartreuse de Parme.* On no occasion did his conversation belie the impression which I had formed of him from his works. . . . At first his physique—he is very stout—conflicts with the delicacy and the elegance of his manners, but he triumphs over that at once. . . . He has a fine forehead, bright and piercing eyes, a sardonic mouth; in fact, he has exactly the physiognomy of his talent. . . .
>
> M. Beyle is one of the superior men of our time. It is difficult to explain how this observer of the first order, this profound diplomat who . . . has so often proved the loftiness of his ideas and the breadth of his practical knowledge, should find himself merely consul at Civitavecchia. No one would be better equipped to serve France in Rome.

Balzac acclaimed Beyle as a novelist, but he also reproached him for writing badly. "The weak side of this work is the style. . . . Sometimes the tenses of verbs don't agree, sometimes there is no verb; sometimes there are *c'est*'s and *ce que*'s and *que*'s which tire the reader and make the mind feel as if it is travelling in a badly slung carriage." [14]

Beyle was delighted by the praise, but he could not accept the rebuke: he considered that he had a style of his own. He found it difficult to reply. He made three drafts of his answer, the last of them on October 28 and 29.

> I don't think [he wrote] that anyone was ever treated like that in a review, and by the best judge of the matter. . . . I have responded to

this kindness in a fitting manner. I read the review yesterday evening
[*sic*], and this morning I reduced to 4 or 5 pages the first 54 pages of
the work which you are launching into the world. . . .

I abhor a convoluted style and I must confess that many pages of
La Chartreuse were printed according to the original dictation. . . .

When I wrote *La Chartreuse,* I read 2 or 3 pages of the *Code civil*
every morning to get the tone. . . .[15]

The fair copy of Beyle's letter has not survived, and we do not even
know when the recipient read it. However, Beyle spent the rest of the
year following Balzac's advice and correcting his work.

On October 23 he was once again in Civitavecchia, where the
inhabitants "were only interested in earning money, and in selling
articles at two or three times their worth to the travellers brought in
by the steamships." A lithograph of Napoleon on the wall of his
apartment reminded him, bitterly, of his past. Donato Bucci later
recalled how Beyle had criticised the government of Louis-Philippe.
"It is a very bad government, it has no solidity, it may be overthrown
any day. If we live another few years, I think that we should see one
of the Bonaparte family in power. Whatever they say, the Empire
has left a profound impression in France." [16] Beyle was more
prophetic than he knew.

He spent the first months of 1841 between Rome and Civitavecchia. His health became more disturbing every day. On March
15 he had an attack of apoplexy.

I too have fought with nothingness [he told Fiore on April 5]. It's
the transition which is unpleasant, and the horror of it comes from all
the nonsense that they put into our heads when we were three.

Don't say anything to Colomb, I didn't intend to write anything;
but I believe in the interest you show me. Well, then, [I had] horrible
migraines for six months; then, four attacks as follows:

Suddenly I forget every word of French. I can no longer say: *Give me
a glass of water.* I observe myself with curiosity; except for the use of
words, I enjoy all the natural properties of *the animal.* This state lasts
from eight to ten minutes; then, little by little, the memory of words
comes back, and I remain tired.

I have little trust in medicine, and especially in doctors, so I only
consulted one after six months of terrible migraines.—M. Séverin is a
homeopath from Berlin, and he has performed some fine cures in

Rome; he recited a phrase or two, after which I guessed that it was a question of *nervous,* not sanguine, apoplexy.

I am going to write to the excellent M. Prévost, of Geneva, but I don't believe in anything, except in the profound attention which M. Prévost pays to illness.

M. Séverin . . . made me take aconite to liven the circulation, and, in the spring, he wants to make me take sulphide. . . .

I have had four losses of memory of French in the last year. . . . The ideas come all right, but without the words. Ten days ago, dining at the tavern with Constantin, I made incredible efforts to find the word 'glass.' I still have a faint headache, which comes from the stomach, and I am tired because I have tried to write these three pages less badly.[17]

On April 10 he wrote again:

I came to Rome on the first of this month, to profit from the enlightenment of the brusque Dr. Dematteis. He shows me marked kindness; he treated me for gravel in 1833.

The doctor didn't want to bleed me a third time; he dismissed my swollen tongue, though yesterday this disagreeable phenomenon recurred. . . .

M. Dematteis is hard-headed; he has no time for homeopathy; he maintains that my complaint is gout. As it doesn't go to the feet, it resorts to the head. Four or five times a day, I am on the point of suffocation; but dinner half cures me and I sleep well. I have made the sacrifice of life a hundred times, as I went to bed, firmly believing I shouldn't wake again. . . .

I have hidden my ailment quite well; I think there is nothing ridiculous in dying in the street, when you don't do it on purpose. . . .[18]

Rome [Monday], 19 April 1841.

Yesterday they put an exutory on my left arm; this morning, they bled me. The most unpleasant symptom is the difficulty with the tongue, which makes me stammer.

The excellent Constantin comes to see me twice a day; M. Alertz, of Aix-la-Chapelle, the Pope's doctor, comes to see me. Constantin gilds the pill very well for me, and it isn't too bitter. I certainly hope to recover. But anyway, I want to say my farewells to you, in case this letter should be the last. I really love you, and I don't love all that many.

Good-bye, take things gaily.[19]

He recovered slowly and continued his consular activities, but on June 15, sending his commercial report to the Minister of Foreign Affairs, he emphasised that "the sending of this document has been delayed by an attack of gout; this has been counteracted by eight bloodlettings, and it has almost deprived me of the faculty of thinking." [20] The constant thought remained with him: the need to give affection. On June 19 he told Colomb: "I have two dogs which I love tenderly. One is black, an English spaniel, beautiful, but sad and melancholy; the other, *Lupetto,* café-au-lait, gay and lively, in fact the young Bourguignon; I was sad to have nothing to love." [21]

He was still capable of human love. On July 21 Cecchina Lablache, Mme. François Bouchot, arrived at the consulate. She was the daughter of the celebrated singer, and the wife of a young French artist, and she was later to marry the pianist Sigismund Thalberg. She had come to Civitavecchia for sea bathing. Hébert had introduced her to Beyle. She was tall and slim, Italian-looking. It was a happy diversion. On August 2 the author of *De l'Amour* proved his prowess for the last time.[22] But little strength remained to him, now, to spend on his affairs of the heart. A few days later, Mme. Bouchot's lover, the German painter Henri Lehmann, arrived at Civitavecchia. On August 8 he made a pencil drawing of the consul. This, the last known likeness of him, shows the process of degeneration. He is fighting, still, with nothingness.

Lysimaque Tavernier was now on leave in Constantinople. He was due to return to the consulate early in September. On August 9 Beyle wrote to the Minister of Foreign Affairs: "I am in the first days of a painful convalescence, after an illness of four months. Gout threatened a congestion of the brain. I had to have nine bloodlettings; I am convalescing in the unhealthy climate of Civitavecchia. . . . I should like a change of air, and I should like to go to Geneva, to consult M. Prévost." [23]

On September 15 Guizot granted him permission to leave his consulate as soon as Tavernier had returned. On October 21, when he had resigned the administration to Tavernier, Beyle wrote his last official letter, a letter of thanks. Then he embarked on the steamship *Leopoldo II,* bound for Marseilles.

Thirty-six

On October 31 he was in Geneva. On November 8 he was back in Paris, and, with his friend Vincenzo Salvagnoli, an advocate from Florence, he settled at the hôtel de l'Empire, 49, rue Neuve-Saint-Augustin. "I may stay on a little," he told Bucci on December 8. "My health has been better since 20 November. . . . I was delighted with the first performance of *La Chaîne.*" [1] Scribe's latest comedy had been launched on November 29. Beyle had been known to fulminate against the commercialism of Scribe. Illness and time had made him more tolerant. On this last visit to Paris, his friends found him physically very changed and intellectually dull. Emile Forgues, the critic, used to see him in the evening at the Cercle des Arts. "Beyle seemed tired and ill, he could not finish his dinner, he already had warnings of apoplexy. The end was approaching." Romain Colomb observed that his speech was slow and difficult; he was less aggressive, more thoughtful and affectionate. "Perhaps the premonition of his approaching death had some secret influence upon him." [2]

In mid-December he and Salvagnoli moved to 78, rue des Petits-Champs, near the rue de la Paix. In January he travelled to Le Havre and went on a shooting expedition. He returned to Paris early in February, and almost at once, he set out for Compiègne, where he expected to stay for a fortnight.

I often thought of you [he assured Comte Cini], when I was shooting in the fine forests round Compiègne. A friend of mine had a very old husband who was also a great shot; he died, and the formalities obliged her to go and live in her château. She invited her friends to come and keep her company in this sad situation. In my capacity as a shot, I inherited a magnificent shoot; for five days a week, at least, I did 5 or 6 leagues with the local shots, who very soon became my friends. Would you believe it? I often regretted the solitudes of Civitavecchia; politeness obliged me to make good conversation almost continually, . . . and I couldn't abandon myself to the thoughts which I should have delighted in finding in these magnificent forests.[3]

The châtelaine near Compiègne has not been identified. André Billy suggests, not very plausibly, that Beyle invented the episode to excuse his delay in answering a letter from Comte Cini.[4] There is certainly an inconsistency in the letter: Beyle maintains that he went shooting "for five days a week, at least"; he also says that his visit to the château had lasted only four or five days. Unforeseen circumstances had, he said, brought him back to Paris rather earlier than he had expected. Whatever the length of his stay, however, he came back feeling well, he thought of visiting London in mid-March, and he now planned to return to his post. "Look after the apartment and the gun," he instructed Bucci on February 25. "I enjoy good health. Send me details about Civitavecchia. . . . I shall see you again in May."[5] One wonders if his health was now as good as he claimed. On March 25 Charles Defly, then in charge of the consulate at Malta, wrote to Lysimaque Tavernier: "Is it true that M. Beyle had a fit of apoplexy which left him completely paralysed, and that there is a question of replacing him?" If Defly could write this from Malta on March 25, the news could hardly have left Paris after March 5. This premature news is somewhat disturbing, and it makes one wonder if Beyle did have an attack late in February or early the following month.[6]

In March, however, he was working at *Lamiel* and at "Suora Scolastica." In mid-March, considering a new edition of *De l'Amour*, he drafted a third preface for it and recalled how he had been led to write it. On March 21 he signed a contract with the *Revue des Deux Mondes*. He agreed that, within the next year, he would hand in the manuscript of two volumes of novels and short stories. Every month he would deliver a short story, signed *Stendhal*, which might appear in the paper. The collected works would finally be published in two volumes. He was to be paid, in all, 5,000 francs; he received 1,500 francs as an immediate advance.

Next day, March 22, he spent the morning working at "Suora Scolastica." At seven o'clock that evening, leaving a dinner given by Guizot, he had another attack of apoplexy. It struck him down on the pavement of the rue Neuve-des-Capucines, near the entrance of the Ministry of Foreign Affairs: once the hôtel where Bonaparte had lived. It was a few yards from the attic in the rue de Chabanais where Beyle had attended the Sundays of Etienne Delécluze.

He was taken back to his lodgings. He died at two o'clock next morning, March 23, without regaining consciousness. "He always told me that he wanted to die without knowing," wrote Félix Faure. "It was as he had wished." [7] The next day there was a funeral service at the Eglise de l'Assomption. Three friends—one of them Mérimée—followed his coffin, and there was no oration by the grave. He had wanted to be buried beside Shelley, at the foot of the Pyramid of Caius Cestius, in Rome. Destiny decreed that *Arrigo Beyle, Milanese* should lie in the Cimetière Montmartre, and later, as a final insult, in the shadow of the railway viaduct. It was only on March 23, 1962, the hundred and twentieth anniversary of his death, that his tomb was moved to another site in the cemetery—out of the shadow of the Pont Caulaincourt.

PART VI

Stendhal and Posterity

Thirty-seven

FOR SOME YEARS after Stendhal's death, his reputation remained a subject of contention. In 1843 Liszt observed to Mme. d'Agoult that some books could only be appreciated among friends. "Very few copies of Stendhal's *Vie de Rossini* were sold, and the subject and the book were quite interesting." [1] In 1845, in a critical essay on Stendhal in *Le Commerce,* Arthur de Gobineau concluded: "The qualities of his style, like those of his mind, go more directly to the intelligence than to the heart. That, after all, may be the main reason for the little popularity which his name has so far acquired." [2] The same year, Elizabeth Barrett urged Miss Mitford "to order and read 'Le rouge et le noir' by a M. de Stendhal. . . . It has ridden me like an incubus for several days." [3]

In 1848, when Francisque Sarcey, the future dramatic critic, entered the Ecole normale, he and his fellow students had not heard of Stendhal. It was one of his professors, M. Jacquinet, who mentioned *La Chartreuse de Parme.* In 1849, in a box of 20-sou books, Sarcey found the novel and innocently bought it. "Even today, after so many years," he wrote in 1883, "I cannot recall without a kind of retrospective pleasure the wild enthusiasm that took possession of me and my friends, when we read that book. We were seized by a passion which is inconceivable to me today, for Stendhal's heroes, and Stendhal himself. . . . I went round everywhere, like St. Paul, spreading the good news that a genius had been refound." [4]

No one worked more effectively than Sarcey and his fellow Normalien Hippolyte Taine for the glory of Stendhal. Mérimée was also determined to make amends for the neglect which had been shown by Stendhal's contemporaries. "It isn't a plot of ground he asks for," he explained, "it is a memory." In 1850 he published his essay *H.B.* His recollections—which seem reserved today—were greeted with cries of outraged modesty. But henceforward the name of Beyle, or Stendhal, had passed beyond the circle of his friends. Reparation had begun.

Romain Colomb, Beyle's cousin and executor, was diligently working on his papers; like all creators of myths, he was determined not to spoil an image, and he sometimes abused his discretionary powers. He destroyed the great mass of Clémentine Curial's letters to Beyle, to the lasting regret of posterity. However, he also published an edition of Beyle's works, and on January 21, 1854, *Armance* was put on sale with a biographical notice by Colomb. "My ambition," he wrote, "will only be to have been an honest chronicler for him." [5] His notice, more complete than Mérimée's, was not uncritical.

In 1874 Andrew Paton produced his *Henri Beyle,* the first full-length biography of Stendhal to appear in any language. "He is, to a certain extent, *caviare to the general,*" Paton confessed in his preface, "and [he] is more enjoyed by those who have a certain social and intellectual culture than by the great outer public." Paton, one of the inner circle, one of the happy few, paid tribute to Beyle's part in Romanticism. "He was, perhaps, more than any other man, the writer who brought home Shakespeare to the public that had hitherto adored Racine." [6] Paton had access to the Beyle family correspondence, but he did not know of the *Journal, Vie de Henry Brulard, Souvenirs d'Egotisme* or the other Stendhalian manuscripts which began to appear in print after 1888, thanks to the labours of Chuquet, Stryienski, Paupe and Cordier. "I shall be understood in about 1880," Beyle had said. The statement had seemed outrageous. Now it appeared like a prophecy.

In 1881, in *Les Romanciers naturalistes,* Zola observed that Stendhal still remained "rather in the state of a legend. . . . But Stendhal's rôle in our modern literature is," he wrote, "so considerable that I must commit myself, although I may not shed as much light as I should wish on the complex works which, with those of Balzac, have deter-

mined the present naturalistic evolution." [7] Zola's essay on Stendhal
was one of the most perceptive and generous appraisals ever made of
him, and he drew his own unarguable conclusions.

> Stendhal is first and foremost a psychologist. M. Taine has defined
> his domain very well, by saying that he was interested only in the life
> of the soul. For Stendhal, man was composed of the soul alone. . . .
> There, in brief, is his whole formula: the study of the mechanism of
> the soul. . . .
> One always feels him there, coldly attentive to the working of his
> machine. Each of the characters he creates is a psychologist's
> experiment which he ventures to try on man. . . . Stendhal does not
> write a novel to analyse a corner of reality, people and things; he
> writes a novel to apply his theories of love, to apply Condillac's
> system on the formation of ideas. That is the great difference between
> Stendhal and Balzac. . . .
> In short, Stendhal is the real link that joins the modern novel to the
> novel of the eighteenth century. . . . Thanks to him we can leap across
> Romanticism and join the old French genius. . . .
> Stendhal is the transition, in the novel, between the metaphysical
> conception of the eighteenth century and the scientific conception of
> our own.[8]

Four years later, Maurice Barrès, novelist, essayist and politician,
talked to Ernest Hébert about Stendhal. Barrès admired the
Romanesque in Stendhal. He respected him for portraying the
outsiders, the *déracinés:* the men who did not live in their natural time
and place. For Barrès, Stendhal seemed to be a necessary completion
of himself: "Baudelaire, Stendhal, Balzac are glorious in my eyes
because my spirit needs them, is completed by them." [9]

Beyle, the sceptic, had found his believers, and one of the most
fervent was the novelist and critic Paul Bourget. In 1889 Bourget
reviewed a new edition of *Le Rouge et le Noir.*

> The enigmatic writer who signed so many pages of such rare
> originality with the pseudonym Stendhal is one of those who inspire
> devotion or aversion. . . . Those who love him love his very faults;
> those who are repelled detest his very virtues. Sainte-Beuve refused
> him any talent as a storyteller. M. Taine repeatedly proclaims *La
> Chartreuse de Parme* to be among the greatest novels of this century.
> Poor Léon Chapron, whose last work was to write this preface, ad-

mitted only *Le Rouge et le Noir*. But his enthusiasm for the book reached devotion. He knew every phrase of it by heart. If he met you in the street, or in an interval on a first night, he began to talk about Julien Sorel and Mme. de Rênal, . . . just as Balzac used to talk about Eugénie Grandet or Baron Hulot. . . .

And so [continued Bourget] Beyle's literary ambitions have been more than fulfilled; and yet it is another strange fact about his strange renown that *La Chartreuse de Parme*, *Le Rouge et le Noir* and *Les Chroniques italiennes* should be works which are at once very famous and very isolated, I was about to say very ineffectual. . . . [Stendhal] is claimed as an ancestor by the modern tellers of tales, for the same reason as Balzac; but we seek in vain for a trace of his influence in the work of his contemporaries. . . . In his curious work on the writers of the Naturalist novels, M. Emile Zola wrote: "Stendhal is the father of us all. . . ." But that is an official and as it were an honorary paternity. Neither in the novels of Flaubert, nor in those of the Goncourt brothers, nor in the studies of M. Zola himself or of M. Daudet, nor in those of M. de Maupassant and M. Huysmans, can one discover a feature which suggests, even faintly, the very special and very recognisable "hand" of the author of *Le Rouge et le Noir*. . . .

And yet it seems that only in our day have people professed the theory of observation for the sake of observation, and without any concern for beauty or morality. To study the human soul . . . just for the pleasure of stating and describing a reality, like a naturalist who considers the habits of an animal species or the development of a flower—that is a new point of view, and one which seems more suited to our age of analysis without metaphysics. M. Taine gave the clearest formula of this conception when he defined literature as "a living psychology". . . . Stendhal was among the first to perceive this possible marriage between the imagination and the psychological search, and he was among the first to apply himself, to use one of his expressions, "to looking clearly at the facts." In his eyes, this was the ultimate aim of the art of writing.

What is remarkable in Stendhal . . . is that he takes account of all the psychological truths acquired in his time, and also of those which he has divined. In this he is like the great English novelist, George Eliot. Both have perceived the action of the great known laws upon the mind. This action is the very stuff of the novel of characters, and none of those who attempt it will be able to ignore *Le Rouge et le Noir* and *La Chartreuse de Parme,* any more than *Silas Marner* and *The Mill on the Floss.* Is that not enough for the glory of Beyle? [10]

In 1890 Henri Cordier opened *Stendhal et ses amis* with a confident affirmation.

> Stendhal is in fashion.
>
> Luxury editions, critical studies, the publication of unpublished documents, nothing is wanting for his glory. People talk about him, perhaps, more than they read his work. It is good style to be a *rougiste* or a *chartreux* and not to talk of love without discussing *crystallisation*. . . .
>
> To talk of Stendhal, one needs to have a little of the scepticism which was characteristic of his mind. Those who want to make a great man of him do not understand him: Beyle would have been desolate to be a great man, unless the state of a great man had procured him a fine uniform and a handsome fortune. . . .
>
> Beyle seems to me to have had only one great passion and only one great weakness: the excessive love of women, and the immoderate desire for gold braid.[11]

In 1900 Stendhal was assessed by Emile Faguet. "Displaced people," wrote that shrewd and formidable critic, "are as curious to study as those people who are declassed. Stendhal was a bit of both. . . . The need to contradict, vanity, epicureanism, those are the fundamental traits, the deep and intimate forces of Stendhal's nature. He cultivated them carefully." There was also, considered Faguet, a certain vulgarity about him. In Stendhal there was always an exhibitionist, a commercial traveller. He had a bad style that he never lost. Stendhal was, above all, said Faguet, "an explorer of the middle and lower classes, rather than an observer of the human heart. . . . He was a Saint-Simon of the table d'hôte. . . . Apart from these qualities as an observer, Stendhal's intellect is very insignificant. He was very little of a philosopher, almost incapable of general ideas." What he called energy was simply violence. He had the conception "of a subscriber to a reading room, or a regular visitor to the Ambigu." From the height of his academic rostrum, Faguet observed and coolly analysed Stendhal's weaknesses, but he also recognised his strength. "He is original, . . . he is loyal, sincere, conscientious in his task of observation. He had the taste for the accurate detail, *le petit fait vrai*, seen close to and faithfully reported, and he gave us back this taste which, astonishingly, we had lost." [12]

In 1900, in *Henry Beyle-Stendhal,* a Grenoblois, Pierre Brun, made his

assessment. He wrote wisely: "Emile Zola has made Stendhal one of
the fathers of the Naturalist School. . . . Stendhal is not the father of
anything; he is an observer, a man of the world, listening, if need be,
at the doors of drawing rooms and coming back to tell the literati in
the anteroom the secrets he has been told or discovered." Brun
continued:

> Henri Beyle, I repeat, is in no way the leader of a school. He is
> isolated by his habits of mind and his introspection; his fixed aim is
> never to speak like an author. He is the lost child of criticism: writing,
> as he says, what *he* thinks and not what *people* think. . . . He is an
> amateur of art rather than an artist. He is impressionistic rather than
> dogmatic; he is an ideologist and inquisitive on his own account
> rather than an initiator. He is cosmopolitan rather than French. He is
> in some ways behind his century, rather than a precursor of the
> century to come. Stendhal, this "displaced man," as Emile Faguet
> calls him, could not penetrate the multitude and make disciples. . . .
> He has profoundly studied himself; and having spent a long time
> contemplating his navel, he has nothing of the pastor of flocks about
> him.
>   And so he remains a curious but attractive figure. . . . And he has
> had all the glory to which he was entitled. . . . And, in the Elysian
> fields, . . . this neurotic should feel as happy as he felt at the fireworks
> at Frascati.[13]

Some still considered that Stendhal deserved more honour. In
1905 a committee was formed to erect a memorial to him.[14] In 1909,
in *La Vie amoureuse de Stendhal,* Jean Mélia declared him to be one of
the most popular and glorious writers in France.[15] In 1913, when
Henri Cordier was asked for an essay on Stendhal, he could already
ask: "What can be said that one doesn't already know? People have
talked about Stendhal the diplomat, Stendhal the mathematician,
Stendhal the socialist, Stendhal the soldier, Stendhal the economist,
Stendhal the Academician—he only had the 41st Chair in the
Académie-Française—Stendhal here and Stendhal there. How many
Stendhals! My God! How difficult it is for me!" [16]

In 1914 Léon Blum, the critic and Socialist politician, published
Stendhal et le beylisme, an affectionate and penetrating study of the man
"for whom friendship was posthumous, like glory." Stendhal, he
wrote, "is perhaps the only writer who, misjudged or misunderstood

during his lifetime, has found himself in intimate understanding, in close relationship, with the feeling and thought of another age. For thirty years, a whole series of young people and of adult men have recognised him not only as a nearer predecessor or a dearer ancestor, but as a friend and something like a brother." Yet even now, Blum recognised that Beylism might be dangerous. "A self-sufficient imagination, a distaste for everything which one considers beneath oneself, a lazy reverie, out of humour with real life. . . . The drug was heady, to say the least, and the future will judge, according to the results, if one must consider it as tonic or toxic." He himself was in no doubt. Beylism, he wrote, "or, as M. Bourget has called it, analytical romanticism, has incurable effects when it is administered to the requisite subject, in favourable conditions." [17]

On May 20, 1914, the plinth of Stendhal's monument was inaugurated in the Jardin du Luxembourg. Six years and a Great War later, on June 28, 1920, the monument was finally unveiled. Its plinth was now adorned with a profile of Stendhal, sculpted by Auguste Rodin after the medallion by David d'Angers. In this medallion, two worlds of admirers met. Eighty years after Stendhal's death, with affectionate perception, Paul Bourget traced his significance for posterity:

> Because he had the courage of his complications and the talent to define them, the passionate ideologist of Civitavecchia appears to us as one of the ancestors who most resembles us. He recognised this duality in himself, and delighted in it. On one hand was the abuse of the analytical spirit; on the other was the appetite for strong emotion. One one hand was the taste for feeling, on the other was the need to watch himself feeling. Is this not among the most touching features of modern youth? . . . Is it surprising if the victims of this conflict have recognised Stendhal as a precursor? And what a precursor, how brilliant, how generous, how virile and courageous! For this master of almost morbid introspection and sentimental refinement remains, despite it all, a professor of energy.[18]

By 1924 Emile Henriot could observe that "the little chapel of the *happy few* for whom alone he was tempted to write has become an enormous church, where the faithful jostle one another, often with less piety than is seemly." And Henriot felt obliged to add: "Being a *Stendhalien* is not a profession." [19] Stendhal's books had earned him only 5,700 francs in twenty-two years, but when, that year, a memorial plaque was unveiled in Civitavecchia, even Clovis Bucci, the grandson of the friend of the sometime consul, was awarded the Légion-d'honneur.[20]

In 1930 Paul Valéry assessed the author of *Le Rouge et le Noir:*

> There is much of the actor in this author [Valéry decided]. His work is full of words aimed at the gallery. . . . On his private stage, he gives the unceasing performance of Himself. . . .
>
> Beyle played, in himself, a dozen characters. . . . Just as a touring actor carries his wigs and beards and belongings, Beyle carried in his bag his *Bombet,* his *Brulard* and his *Dominique.* . . . This temperament which engendered a perpetual scenario made him, in return, consider all human things from their theatrical aspect. . . .
>
> Stendhal's own sincerity . . . was mixed with an act of sincerity which he was performing to himself.[21]

In 1931, in *Stendhal. Sa vie, son oeuvre,* Maurice David explained:

> I have sought *my* Stendhal, or rather . . . the Stendhal of my generation. . . .
>
> If today Stendhal counts so many passionate partisans, it may not be because we are superior to the readers of 1830. . . . But history has shown us the downfall of so many regimes and governments, of so many Schools and Chapels, that our critical sense has become refined, our taste has broadened, and, as a result, we are more capable of appreciating at his true worth a writer who is "truly free." [22]

One wonders if he was in fact truly free. His moments of abandon had been rare. Perhaps his modernity consisted partly in the fact that he displayed his complex maladjustment more freely than most authors before his time. Stendhal's maladjustment was itself a subject for study. In 1938, in *Le Cas Stendhal,* Rémi Bosselaers made it clear that he himself was no passionate partisan.

> Beyle-Stendhal [he concluded] is a man with every contrast. These contrasts may largely be reduced to the alternation of his syntone, hypomaniac and depressive states, crossed by schizoid elements. . . .
>
> It is very wrong to see him as a professor of energy. Humanity has no use for this morbid violence; on the contrary, it must be saved from it. . . . We do not learn morality from psychopaths. . . .

The man deserves our pity, as much as—and more than—our blame. But it was important not to hide the psychological defects of a writer who, thanks to a great and well-earned literary vogue, exercises a fatal moral influence.[23]

Stendhal will be reassessed by every generation, and since there are many Stendhals in Stendhal, each generation may find him curiously modern, unexpectedly significant. For us, in the second half of the twentieth century, he is not distinguished as a critic. Poetry was a closed book for him. He was no true critic of art (he took a superficial, literary view), yet he had learned from the Abbé Dubos the idea of relative art which Taine was to develop with effect. Destutt de Tracy had written: "I turn the ideas of colour and sound into the more general idea of feeling...." [24] Beyle had remembered the words, and tentatively suggested the theory of *correspondances* which later writers were to explore. As for his criticism of music, Berlioz destroyed any pretention that it was enlightened. His writing on Rossini brought a smile to the face of Anatole France. And, as Jytte Ditlivsen writes, Stendhal appears unable to distinguish between *musichetta* and great music.[25]

Stendhal could never speak or write the English language correctly, but his appreciation of English literature was considerable: more extensive, no doubt, than that of most of his contemporaries. He spoke Italian rather badly, and wrote it even worse, but he read it fluently. He has, however, been called the greatest French Italian since Napoleon. Italy was, after ideology, the ferment which acted most on the development of his taste and his ideas. Loving Italy as he did, he gave French writers a new source of inspiration. Yet having said this, we must repeat that Stendhal was more than *Arrigo Beyle, Milanese:* he was one of the first of the Europeans. "I do not say," he once wrote, "that our sculptors should copy Canova, one must not copy anybody; but one should certainly try to please all Europe, like that celebrated Italian." [26]

Today he seems, perhaps, less remarkable as a novelist than he is as a student of psychology. We may have reservations about his powers of invention, his ability to create a character or a situation, or to write French prose with elegance. His delicate sensibility was incompatible with his critical intellectualism. He was a Romantic at heart, a

Classic in the rigour of his mind. Yet he did not, like Flaubert, write with the distinctive merits of both schools. "Although he liked writing," Collignon observed in 1868, "Stendhal was never what one calls *a man of letters*. He was always more a man of the world and a dilettante than a literary man, more an amateur than a professional author." [27] He showed an indifference to his work which, to Flaubert, would have been sacrilegious. "Form," insisted Gustave Lanson, "does not exist, in Stendhal, as an art form. It is only the noting of ideas." [28] The observation is fair. And so, perhaps, is Paul Hazard's comment: "What he cannot do, he writes." [29] Almost alone among the great French writers, Stendhal does not earn the title of *maître*.

"In Stendhal's lifetime," wrote Léon Blum in 1914, "nearly everyone wore rouge, and that is why his style appeared colourless and dull. . . . But, thanks to this bareness, Stendhal's style has not aged at all, and, over the years, he has been able to regain his real public. . . . His style is timeless, so to speak, and it has nothing to fear from fashion or from time." [30]

His style might remain beyond fashion; his beliefs might perhaps come to seem unsatisfying. Sarcey wondered if perhaps Stendhal had belonged to a certain age. When he came to reread *De l'Amour,* he found that he had lost the emotional key. All his generation had known these oscillations of taste.[31] Stendhal might voice the creed of the angry young man, the rebel and the outsider, but he might not speak for conventional men, successful men in their maturity. As Fineshriber observed in 1932:

> Many of the most ardent Stendhalians have forsaken the idol of their youth, once they have found their place in society. . . . The Léon Blum of today, journalist, orator, and political leader, writes in the preface to his 1930 edition of *Stendhal et le beylisme* that he hardly recognizes the passionate admiration for Stendhal which he had expressed in his articles of 1914.
>
> It is impossible to find one's place in society and at the same time remain a Julien Sorel. These original Stendhalians did what Beyle was never able to do. They matured fully.[32]

We turn to Stendhal for certain studies of character which, by chance, we find in his novels. We turn to him for certain *aperçus*, certain insights into human nature, certain moments of emotion which he records with a delicacy which anticipates Verlaine. The poet, he wrote, needed a treasure hoard of emotions. Throughout his adult life, Stendhal deliberately set out to amass this treasure: to experience every situation, every nuance of emotion, to make himself perpetually responsive. He needed not only to feel, but to know, to analyse himself, to plan and follow his emotional progress. As Jean Mélia writes: "He deliberately makes himself the slave of passion, . . . and he is therefore less of a slave than he might let us suppose." [33]

His novels, like his letters and his journals, are largely records of psychological experiments. Julien was his clear, cold mind, incisive and dangerous. Fabrice was the heart of Stendhal, fundamentally good. "Unfortunate Fabrice," wrote Pierre Brun, "turned into a vast field for Beylist experiments!" [34] Stendhal pursued these experiments all his adult life, with the precision of a scientist. "Passions are not identical in direction," he noted in his journal in 1805, "and only higher or lower like a thermometer. . . . To appreciate the passion of a man, one must know the value in his eyes of everything that he sacrifices to this passion." [35] He himself sacrificed conventional happiness in the search for ideal happiness, *la chasse au bonheur*.

In a copy of Saint-Simon, he wrote: "M. de Saint-Simon has only depth enough to turn a nice phrase in the way of Tacitus. . . . His depth does not touch the bottom of things." [36] He himself touched the rocks on the sea bed. His self-analysis was ruthless, but in compensation, how intense the pleasures he enjoyed! The moment at Frascati when the fireworks had been lit, and Adèle had leant against him, was intense enough to stay with him for life; an engraving of Milan could move him unbearably more than thirty years after he had first been there.

He was not merely a profound psychologist; he was above all a complex, disagreeable and engaging man. The vicissitudes of his emotions, his intellectual progress and his career are more fascinating than any fiction he wrote. He reflected the politics and the social changes of his era. He had the restlessness, the cosmopolitan tastes, the melancholy and the fervour of the Romantics; he had all the ambition which the cometary rise of Napoleon inspired. The nineteenth century was an age for the parvenu, for brilliant and original careers. Stendhal enjoyed remarkable success; he might have achieved some eminence had he shown more consistency of purpose.

He was largely formed by the Bonaparte epic; he was also that

Napoleonic but strangely modern figure, an outsider. He was a provincial born outside the Establishment, enjoying none of the privileges of birth, wealth or education. His sense of inequality and grievance led him, bitterly, to make himself amends. He despised authority, he professed to scorn nobility, and yet—like Julien Sorel—he wanted to conquer them. He ridiculed the dignitaries in the Tuileries, and yet, with monotonous persistence, he tried to ensure himself a barony. He professed to despise ambition, but all his life he was conscious of status. He was bourgeois and self-made, but he longed to be an aristocrat, with inherited wealth and position. He was a man supremely of his time, and yet he gives us an anticipation of contemporary sensibility. In his political changes, in his lack of religion, his shifting purpose, his intense and unremitting introspection, he is modern man. Stendhal, wrote Léon Blum in 1914, "is the man of moments of confusion, of social mixing, of periods of disorder. . . . With the return of the Stendhalian elements; personal anxiety, conflicting influences, alternatives of duty and pleasure, we shall see the Stendhalian faith revive." [37]

His spirit was so free [wrote Pierre Martino in 1950], so careless of contemporary fashions, that every generation readily finds in him the reflection of its own preoccupations. After 1830 people loved him because he had "invented Romanticism"; in about 1860, it was because he had fought against it. Then he became the father of Naturalism and, almost at once, the godfather of the psychologists. Later he became a preacher of the energy of the individual. . . . It seems that today he is often preferred because of a taste which had certainly been noticed, but perhaps insufficiently recognised. . . : an intellectual cosmopolitanism.[38]

It is above all his art which corresponds to modern temperament and to modern taste [so Victor Brombert wrote in 1954]. Mistrust in the face of emotion, a sense of embarrassment towards the world of dreams, the ambiguous and unstable attitude of the artist before his work, the need to break the romantic impulse, the fear of the cliché and of sentimentalism: there are some characteristic symptoms of our age. Every day, we disavow our romantic heritage. But this disavowal is itself a sign that this heritage is with us, that we rebel perfidiously against ourselves.

It is in this sense that, as Maurras said, Stendhal is the most living and the most active of our masters. There is no need at all for an intermediary between him and ourselves.[39]

There seemed no need. In 1955 a Japanese admirer visited the house at Furonières which had once belonged to Chérubin Beyle. He asked to see the tree under which Henri Beyle used to sit and read. He sat beneath it, motionless, for four hours.[40]

We cannot learn from Stendhal unless we learn from his mistakes and learn, above all, to look out as well as in. He constantly defeated his ends by excessive introspection. "Dominique's character," he noted in about 1840. ". . . He is constantly dreaming. His greatest difficulty is to detach himself from this reverie." [41] He lived too much in his own mind and not enough in the lives of other men. He was intensely self-absorbed. He thought too little of what he could give.

Reading his journals and his letters, one is also constantly aggravated by the way in which he complicates his life, puts obstacles in his own path. Leaning over his shoulder, one repeatedly feels the urge to encourage, warn and condemn. He is frequently unpleasant; he is sometimes needlessly crude. But he is never for a moment dull, and though at first we may not be in sympathy with him, we gradually become involved in his life. We know him far better than his contemporaries knew him, and "the reality which emerges from the pages of *Brulard* is more continuously fascinating than any fantasies he was able to create, the man more intriguing than any of the roles he allowed himself in imagination to play. He had never quite succeeded in transforming the personal into the universal. . . . But *Henry Brulard* takes its place with the great confessions." [42] Gide declared that he would sacrifice everything else for *Henry Brulard*.[43] "Henri Beyle is, in my eyes, a type of mind much more than a man of letters," wrote Paul Valéry. And he added: "There is no end to Stendhal. I see no greater praise." [44]

Stendhal's main interest, without doubt, lies in his study of the human heart—in what he used to call his profession. And by studying his own, he deepens our general insight. "As we watch the intellectual and sentimental movement working in this man of glass, . . . it is really ourselves whom we learn to know." So said André François-Poncet.[45] As we follow Stendhal, observing, analysing and deducing, we refine and sharpen our awareness and feel ourselves at last his friends and his accomplices. We are among the *heureux peu nombreux,* among the happy few.

Notes

ABBREVIATIONS

Works by Stendhal

CA = *Courrier anglais*
Corr. = *Correspondance*
De l'A = *De l'Amour*
P d R = *Promenades dans Rome*
RNF = *Rome, Naples et Florence en 1817*
R & S = *Racine et Shakespeare*
SE = *Souvenirs d'Egotisme*
V d R = *Vie de Rossini*
VHB = *Vie de Henry Brulard*

LM = *The London Magazine*
NMM = *The New Monthly Magazine*

Notes

1

1. Bourget, *Stendhal: Discours...*, p. 19.
2. Barrès, *Mes Cahiers*, Vol. III, p. 19.
3. Stendhal, *VHB*, pp. 26–27.
4. *Ibid.*, p. 31.
5. *Ibid.*, p. 32.
6. *Ibid.*, p. 32.
7. *Ibid.*, pp. 38, 40.
8. *Ibid.*, p. 58.
9. *Ibid.*, pp. 60–62.
10. *Ibid.*, p. 63.
11. *Ibid.*, p. 80.
12. Dugas, *Les Grands Timides*, pp. 124, 114.
13. *VHB*, pp. 93–94.
14. *Ibid.*, p. 104.
15. *Ibid.*, p. 113.
16. *Ibid.*, p. 195.
17. For Virginie Kubly, see Martineau, *Petit Dictionnaire stendhalien*, pp. 277–80.
18. Blum, *Stendhal et le Beylisme*, pp. 25, 27.
19. *VHB*, p. 209.
20. *Ibid.*

21. *Ibid.*, p. 212.
22. *Ibid.*, pp. 217–18.
23. For Beyle's aversion for Grenoble, see also *VHB*, pp. 81, 86, 282, 301.
24. Brun, *Henry Beyle-Stendhal*, p. 120.
25. Blum, *op. cit.*, p. 13.
26. *VHB*, p. 311.

2

1. *VHB*, p. 314.
2. *Ibid.*, pp. 314–15.
3. *Ibid.*, p. 317.
4. *Ibid.*, p. 339.
5. *Ibid.*, p. 348.
6. [April 10, 1810]: *Corr.*, Vol. I, pp. 3, 4.
7. [April or May, 1800]: *Corr.*, Vol. I, p. 5. In his *Bibliographie stendhalienne, 1956,* Del Litto records (p. 8) that in 1953 six letters from Beyle to Pauline were sold in Paris for 280,000 francs.
8. *VHB*, pp. 387, 388.
9. *Ibid.*, p. 389.
10. *Ibid.*, p. 393.
11. June 29, 1800; *Corr.*, Vol. I, p. 7.

12. Quoted by Billy, *Ce cher Stendhal*, pp. 38–39. In *Stendhal; ou la double vie de Henri Beyle*, p. 41, Boncompain and Vermale note Beyle's comment on his two years in Italy "without women." This, as they observe, was written thirty years later, when his memories were magnified by regret.

13. *VHB*, p. 393.

14. December 7, 1800; *Corr.*, Vol. I, p. 13.

15. *Journal*, pp. 414–15.

16. November 18, 1801; *Corr.*, Vol. I, p. 28.

17. *Journal*, p. 427.

3

1. *Journal*, p. 429.

2. Arbelet, *Trois solitaires*, p. 130.

3. *Journal*, pp. 429–30.

4. June 6, 1801; *Corr.*, Vol. I, p. 31.

5. *Journal*, p. 430.

6. *Ibid.*, pp. 430–31.

7. *Ibid.*, p. 431.

8. *Ibid.*, p. 434.

9. January 1, 1803; *Corr.*, Vol. I, pp. 40–41.

10. *Ibid.*

11. February 7, 1806; *Corr.*, Vol. I, p. 283.

12. February 8, 1803; *Corr.*, Vol. I, p. 53.

13. March 3, 1803; *Corr.*, Vol. I, pp. 58–59.

14. March 18, 1803; *Corr.*, Vol. I, p. 60.

15. May 1, 1803; *Corr.*, Vol. I, p. 70.

16. June 28, 1803; *Corr.*, Vol. I, p. 77.

17. July 31, 1803; *Corr.*, Vol. I, p. 79.

4

1. February, 1804; *Corr.*, Vol. I, p. 86.

2. *Ibid.*, p. 88.

3. April 12, 1804; *Corr.*, Vol. I, pp. 91–92.

4. *Journal*, p. 452.

5. *Ibid.*, p. 466.

6. June 7, 1804; *Corr.*, Vol. I, p. 98.

7. June 26, 1804; *Corr.*, Vol. I, p. 113.

8. *Journal*, p. 482.

9. Lemaître, *Les Contemporains*, pp. 14–15.

10. *Journal*, p. 523.

11. August 21, 1804; *Corr.*, Vol. I, p. 146.

12. *Ibid.; Corr.*, Vol. I, pp. 146–47.

13. August 29, 1804; *Corr.*, Vol. I, p. 149.

14. *Journal*, p. 541.

15. *Ibid.*, p. 576. For Mélanie Guilbert (and Joseph Hilarion Blanc de Volx), see Arbelet, *Louason, ou les perplexités amoureuses de Stendhal*.

16. *Journal*, p. 578.

17. *Corr.*, Vol. I, pp. ix–x.

18. May 11, 1804; *Corr.*, Vol. I, p. 93.

19. [July] 1804; *Corr.*, Vol. I, p. 129.

20. February 14, 1805; *Corr.*, Vol. I, pp. 176–77.

21. February 26, 1805; *Corr.*, Vol. I, pp. 181–82.

22. April 11, 1805; *Corr.*, Vol. I, p. 1098.

23. April 15, 1805; *Corr.*, Vol. I, p. 189.

24. April 29, 1805; *Corr.*, Vol. I, pp. 197–98.

25. Arbelet, *Stendhal épicier*, pp. 14–15.

26. April 30, 1805; *Corr.*, Vol. I, p. 200.

27. May 4, 1805; *Corr.*, Vol. I, pp. 1100–1.

28. May 23, 1805; *Corr.*, Vol. I, pp. 1102–3.

29. [June 18–20, 1805]; *Corr.*, Vol. I, p. 201.

30. *Ibid.*, p. 205.

31. [June, 1805]: *Corr.*, Vol. I, p. 1105.

32. June 22, 1805; *Corr.*, Vol. I, p. 1106.

33. June 27, 1805; *Corr.*, Vol. I, pp. 1106–8.

34. July 26, 1805; *Corr.*, Vol. I, p. 208.

5

1. August 8, 1805; *Corr.*, Vol. I, pp. 210–12.

2. [Early August, 1805]; *Corr.*, Vol. I, p. 112.

3. August 20, 1805; *Corr.*, Vol. I, pp. 213–14.

4. *Ibid.; Corr.*, Vol. I, pp. 214–15.

5. For further details about Mélanie, see Arbelet, *Louason, ou les perplexités amoureuses de Stendhal.*

6. August 22, 1805; *Corr.*, Vol. I, pp. 215, 219–20.

7. August 27, 1805; *Corr.*, Vol. I, p. 222.

8. September 4, 1805; *Corr.*, Vol. I, p. 1114.

9. September 9–13, 1805; *Corr.*, Vol. I, pp. 225–26.

10. September 17, 1805; *Corr.*, Vol. I, p. 227.

11. *Ibid.*

12. *Ibid.*, p. 228.

13. September 21, 24, 1805; *Corr.*, Vol. I, pp. 1118, 1119.

14. October 1, 1805; *Corr.*, Vol. I, p. 233.

15. October 7, 1805; *Corr.*, Vol. I, p. 1121.

16. [About October 10, 1805]; *Corr.*, Vol. I, p. 1123.

17. November 15–17, 1805; *Corr.*, Vol. I, p. 247.

18. Destutt de Tracy, *Projet d'éléments d'idéologie*, Vol. I, pp. 2–3, 49, 74.

19. December 5, 1805; *Corr.*, Vol. I, p. 1151.

20. December 17, 1805; *Corr.*, Vol. I, pp. 259–60.

21. December 28, 1805; *Corr.*, Vol. I, pp. 1163–64.

22. January 4, 1806; *Corr.*, Vol. I, p. 265.

23. January 8, 1806; *Corr.*, Vol. I, pp. 266–67.

24. January 14–15, 1806; *Corr.*, Vol. I, pp. 266–67.

25. January 16, 1806; *Corr.*, Vol. I, pp. 1117–18.

26. January 26, 1806; *Corr.*, Vol. I, pp. 1183–84.

27. January 27, 1806; *Corr.*, Vol. I, p. 1185.

28. February 6, 1806; *Corr.*, Vol. I, p. 281.

29. February 25, 1806; *Corr.*, Vol. I, pp. 1203, 1204.

30. *Ibid.*, p. 1205.

6

1. March 4, 1806; *Corr.*, Vol. I, p. 291.

2. March 5, 1806; *Corr.*, Vol. I, pp. 294–95.

3. [March 6, 1806]; *Corr.*, Vol. I, p. 1206.

4. *Journal*, p. 759.

5. *Ibid.*, p. 767.

6. *Ibid.*, pp. 773, 776, 777, 781.

7. *Ibid.*, pp. 792, 794.

8. 21 [May, 1806]; *Corr.*, Vol. I, p. 1211.

9. [June 1, 1806]; *Corr.*, Vol. I, p. 325.

10. June 2, 1806; *Corr.*, Vol. I, p. 1222.

11. Brun, *op. cit.*, p. 21. June 10 [1806]; *Corr.*, Vol. I, pp. 1226–28.

12. *Journal*, p. 809.

13. *Ibid.*, p. 812.

14. *Ibid.*, p. 825.

7

1. [October 18, 1806]; *Corr.*, Vol. I, p. 328.

2. November 8 [1806]; *Corr.*, Vol. I, p. 331.

3. [1807]; *Corr.*, Vol. I, p. 337.

4. François-Poncet, *Stendhal à Brunswick*, p. 99.

5. March 16, 1807; *Corr.*, Vol. I, pp. 338–39.

6. *Ibid.*, p. 338.

7. March 24, 1807; *Corr.*, Vol. I, p. 342.

8. *Ibid.*, p. 343.

9. April 30, 1807; *Corr.*, Vol. I, p. 346.

10. June 9, 1807; *Corr.*, Vol. I, pp. 353–54.

11. *Journal*, pp. 829–30.

12. *Ibid.*, p. 833.

13. *Ibid.*, p. 834.

14. July 10, 1807; *Corr.*, Vol. I, p. 357.

15. September 2, 1807; *Corr.*, Vol. I, pp. 360–61.

16. October 3, 1807; *Corr.,* Vol. I, pp. 364, 365.

17. *Journal,* p. 841.

18. January 24, 1808; *Corr.,* Vol. I, p. 379.

19. *Journal,* p. 850.

20. For Beyle in Brunswick, see François-Poncet, *op. cit.*

21. March 26, 1808; *Corr.,* Vol. I, pp. 441-43.

22. [End of May] 1808; *Corr.,* Vol. I, p. 484.

23. Billy, *op. cit.,* p. 74.

24. September 19, 1808; *Corr.,* Vol. I, pp. 512-13.

25. October 29, 1808; *Corr.,* Vol. I, pp. 514-15.

8

1. *Journal,* pp. 867, 868.

2. April 19, 1809; *Corr.,* Vol. I, p. 520.

3. April 21, 1809; *Corr.,* Vol. I, p. 521.

4. May 18, 1809; *Corr.,* Vol. I, pp. 531, 532.

5. June 15, 1809; *Corr.,* Vol. I, p. 532.

6. July 14, 1809; *Corr.,* Vol. I, p. 534.

7. October 14 [1809]; *Corr.,* Vol. I, p. 541.

8. *Journal,* p. 892.

9. *Ibid.,* p. 898.

10. *Ibid.,* p. 901.

11. May 13, 1810; *Corr.,* Vol. I, p. 569.

12. Victorine Mounier (1783-1822) eventually married M. Achard; see Martineau, *Petit Dictionnaire stendhalien,* p. 355.

13. May 24, 1810; *Corr.,* Vol. I, pp. 572-74.

14. June 4, 1810; *Corr.,* Vol. I, p. 574.

15. *Journal,* p. 942.

16. *Ibid.,* pp. 944-46.

17. *Ibid.,* p. 955.

18. *Ibid.,* p. 957.

19. *Ibid.,* pp. 958-59.

20. [August 5, 1810]; *Corr.,* Vol. I, p. 583.

21. August 7, 1810; *Corr.,* Vol. I, p. 584.

22. August 11 [1810]; *Corr.,* Vol. I, pp. 585-86.

23. *Journal,* p. 965.

9

1. *Journal,* p. 977.

2. October 9, 1810; *Corr.,* Vol. I, p. 592.

3. December 10, 1810; *Corr.,* Vol. I, pp. 597-98.

4. *Journal,* p. 986.

5. *Ibid.,* p. 996.

6. Angelina-Marie Béreyter, said to be of Jewish origin, was born in Lyons on May 10, 1786. In his *Petit Dictionnaire stendhalien,* pp. 52-54, Martineau records that she was the daughter of Louis-Jean Béreyter, a printer. She appeared in the opera buffa lists until 1818. In 1820 Beyle asked Mareste to embrace her for him. A death certificate, reconstituted after the fires of the Commune, records that "Marie-Angélique Béreyter, musicienne," aged fifty-five, a spinster, died in the rue du Chantre, Paris, on March 23, 1841.

7. *Journal,* pp. 999, 1003-4.

8. *Ibid.,* pp. 999-1000.

9. *Ibid.,* p. 1018. The Charavay catalogue for November, 1959, includes an unpublished fragment of the *Journal;* its date is given as March, 1811, and also as March, 1813.

10. *Journal,* p. 1019.

11. May 15 [1811]; *Corr.,* Vol. I, p. 610.

12. *Journal,* p. 1023.

13. *Ibid.,* p. 1586 *note.*

14. *Ibid.,* p. 1024.

15. *Ibid.*

16. *Ibid.,* p. 1032.

17. *Ibid.,* p. 1042.

18. June 26, 1811; *Corr.,* Vol. I, pp. 611-12.

19. *Journal,* p. 1051.

20. August 17, 1811; *Corr.,* Vol. I, p. 611.

21. *Journal,* p. 1060.

22. *Ibid.,* p. 1079.

10

1. *Ibid.,* pp. 1079–80.
2. *Ibid.,* p. 1080.
3. *Ibid.,* pp. 1084–85.
4. Morgan, *Italy,* Vol. I, pp. 95, 97.
5. *Journal,* p. 1090.
6. *Ibid.,* p. 1093.
7. *Ibid.,* pp. 1094–95.
8. *Ibid.,* p. 1098.
9. *Ibid.,* p. 1102.
10. *Ibid.,* p. 1118.
11. *Ibid.*˙
12. *Ibid.,* p. 1140.
13. *Ibid.,* p. 1146.
14. *Ibid.,* p. 1147.
15. *Ibid.,* p. 1148.
16. *Ibid.,* pp. 1160–61.
17. *Ibid.,* p. 1166.
18. *Ibid.,* p. 1178.

11

1. *Journal,* p. 1184.
2. February 27, 1812; *Corr.,* Vol. I, pp. 632–33.
3. July 14, 1812; *Corr.,* Vol. I, p. 649.
4. July 23, 1812; *Corr.,* Vol. I, p. 650.
5. July 23, 1812; *Corr.,* Vol. I, pp. 652–53.
6. August 24, 1812; *Corr.,* Vol. I, pp. 656–57.
7. *Ibid.,* p. 657.
8. October 4, 1812; *Corr.,* Vol. I, p. 664.
9. October 15, 1812; *Corr.,* Vol. I, p. 674.
10. October 16, 1812; *Corr.,* Vol. I, p. 675.
11. November 7, 1812; *Corr.,* Vol. I, p. 681.
12. November 7, 1812; *Corr.,* Vol. I, p. 678.
13. November 7, 1812; *Corr.,* Vol. I, p. 679.
14. November 10, 1812; *Corr.,* Vol. I, p. 686.
15. December 7, 1812; *Corr.,* Vol. I, p. 688.

12

1. February 4, 1813; *Corr.,* Vol. I, p. 692.
2. *Journal,* p. 1197.
3. *Ibid.*
4. *Ibid.*
5. *Ibid.,* p. 1198.
6. *Ibid.,* p. 1205.
7. *Ibid.,* p. 1207.
8. *Ibid.,* pp. 1209–10.
9. April 13, 1813; *Corr.,* Vol. I, pp. 693–94.
10. April 26, 1813; *Corr.,* Vol. I, p. 696.
11. April 29, 1813; *Corr.,* Vol. I, p. 696.
12. *Journal,* p. 1227.
13. July 26, 1812; *Corr.,* Vol. I, p. 704.
14. September 1, 1813; *Corr.,* Vol. I, p. 705.

13

1. *Journal,* pp. 1240–41.
2. Galt, *Life of Lord Byron,* pp. 347 sqq.; 356.
3. *Journal,* p. 1241.
4. *Ibid.,* pp. 1243, 1244.
5. *Ibid.,* p. 1248.
6. October 8, 1813; *Corr.,* Vol. I, p. 708.
7. *Ibid.,* pp. 707–8.
8. October 15, 1813; *Corr.,* Vol. I, pp. 708–9.

14

1. December 27, 1813; *Corr.,* Vol. I, p. 717.
2. Quoted by Jourda, *Stendhal raconté par ceux qui l'ont vu,* p. 18.
3. March 12, 1814; *Corr.,* Vol. I, p. 760.
4. April 15, 1814; *Corr.,* Vol. I, p. 767.
5. May 23, 1814; *Corr.,* Vol. I, p. 772.
6. *Journal,* p. 1256.
7. Boncompain et Vermale, *op. cit.,* p. 211.
8. Jourda, *op. cit.,* pp. 19–20.
9. *Journal,* p. 1259.
10. For Angelina Béreyter, see Ar-

belet, *Stendhal et le Petit Ange,* and Martineau, *Le Coeur de Stendhal,* Vol. I, pp. 251 sqq.

11. *Journal,* p. 1259.

15

1. August 22, 1814; *Corr.,* Vol. I, pp. 780–81.
2. *Journal,* p. 1263.
3. *Ibid.,* pp. 1263–64.
4. October 6, 1814; *Corr.,* Vol. I, pp. 788–89.
5. *Journal,* pp. 1265–66.
6. October 17, 1814; *Corr.,* Vol. I, p. 790.
7. October 28, 1814; *Corr.,* Vol. I, p. 791.
8. December 3, 1814; *Corr.,* Vol. I, p. 796.
9. September 30, 1816; *Corr.,* Vol. I, p. 824.
10. January 14, 1815; *Corr.,* Vol. I, pp. 799–800.
11. *Ibid.,* pp. 800–1.
12. April 1, 1815; *Corr.,* Vol. I, p. 804.
13. April 4, 1815; *Corr.,* Vol. I, p. 805.
14. May 6, 1815; *Corr.,* Vol. I, pp. 805–6.
15. *Ibid.,* p. 80t.
16. *Journal,* p. 126y.
17. *Ibid.,* pp. 1274, 1275, 1277.
18. Quoted by Gunnell, *Stendhal et l'Angleterre,* pp. 172–73.
19. *Journal,* p. 1277.
20. *Ibid.,* p. 1278.
21. Boncompain et Vermale, *op. cit.,* pp. 161–62.
22. Bellanger, *Notes stendhaliennes. Suivies du H.B.* de Mérimée, p. 165.
23. December 1, 1815; *Corr.,* Vol. I, p. 1241.
24. *Ibid., note.*

16

1. *Journal,* p. 1279.
2. September 28, 1816; *Corr.,* Vol. I, p. 819.
3. Strauss, *La Fortune de Stendhal en Angleterre,* p. 44 and *passim.*

4. September 30, 1816; *Corr.,* Vol. I, p. 825.
5. October 1, 1816; *Corr.,* Vol. I, pp. 827–28.
6. Broughton, *Recollections of a Long Life,* Vol. II, pp. 46–47.
7. October 20, 1816; *Corr.,* Vol. I, p. 832.
8. Broughton, *op. cit.,* pp. 52–56.
9. *Ibid.,* pp. 56–57.
10. December 26, 1816; *Corr.,* Vol. I, p. 843.
11. January 6, 1817; *Corr.,* Vol. I, p. 850.
12. January 13, 1817; *Corr.,* Vol. I, p. 852.
13. March 5, 1817; *Corr.,* Vol. I, pp. 857–61.
14. *Journal,* p. 1286.
15. Gunnell, *Stendhal et l'Angleterre,* p. 73.
16. *Ibid.,* p. 97.
17. *Ibid.,* p. 30. In a note on this page, Doris Gunnell queries the meeting with Lewis, but in 1817 Lewis was staying with his sister, the wife of Sir Henry Lushington, at Naples. He gave a ball at which Beyle was said to be one of the guests.
18. Jourda, *Stendhal, l'homme et l'oeuvre,* p. 111, note, says that Beyle paid a second visit to England in 1819. This is not mentioned by Martineau, in *L'Itinéraire de Stendhal.*
19. August 27, 1817; *Corr.,* Vol. I, p. 1249.

17

1. For details of Beyle's plagiarisms, see Arbelet's preface to his edition of this work, pp. I, xxxv sqq.
2. Mérimée, *Portraits historiques et littéraires,* pp. 185–86.
3. Arbelet, *loc. cit.,* Vol. I, pp. i–ii, iv.
4. *Ibid.,* p. lxxxiv.
5. *Histoire de la peinture en Italie,* ed. Arbelet, Vol. I, p. 13.
6. *Ibid.,* p. 44.
7. *Ibid.,* p. 54.
8. *Ibid.,* pp. 41–42.

9. *Ibid.*, p. 106.

10. Jacoubet, *Les Romans de Stendhal,* pp. 13–14; François-Poncet, *op. cit.,* pp. 73–74.

11. RNF, Vol. II, p. 286.

12. *Ibid.*, Vol. I, p. 161.

13. *Ibid.*, Vol. I, p. 157.

14. *Ibid.*, pp. 155–56.

15. *Ibid.*, p. 15.

16. *Ibid.*, p. 54.

17. *Ibid.*, pp. 70–71, 183.

18. Quoted by Maurras in his preface to *RNF*, Vol. I, pp. xvii–xviii.

19. Lumbroso, *Vingt jugements inédits sur Henri Beyle (Stendhal)*, pp. 35–36.

18

1. Martineau, *Le Coeur de Stendhal,* Vol. I, p. 385.

2. *Ibid.*, note.

3. *Armance,* précédé d'une notice biographique par R. Colomb, p. lxviii.

4. December 1, 1817; *Corr.,* Vol. I, pp. 878–80.

5. Martineau maintains *(L'Oeuvre de Stendhal*, p. 198) that "Stendhal really invented an historical method, which Taine was later to use much to his advantage. This experimental method consists of drawing general rules from small significant details, carefully chosen and minutely noted." Albert Claveau of *Le Figaro* wrote in 1898: "When it is a question of great men, the microscope, trained on a dressing gown and slippers, becomes the most deceptive of instruments. What is certain is that Sainte-Beuve, that king of analysts, often expressed in my presence, with great force, his lack of confidence in Stendhal's very personal optics." (Lumbroso, *op. cit.,* pp. 57–58.) However, Claveau added that Stendhal's character inspired him, instinctively, with aversion. "Perhaps where I find only egoism, vanity, and a systematic mind, I should see particular sagacity and penetration." *(Ibid.,* p. 57.)

6. January 25, 1818; *Corr.,* Vol. I, p. 890.

19

1. Arbelet, *Trois solitaires,* pp. 162–64; Billy, *op. cit.,* p. 135. See also Arbelet in *Le Figaro,* March 4, 1933. Martineau, in *Petit Dictionnaire stendhalien,* p. 175, records Carlo Dembowski's dates as 1808–63 and Ercole Dembowski's as 1812–81. On January 22, 1839, George Sand wrote to Charlotte Marliani that she had had a visitor from Paris who was known to Chopin: "M. Dembowski, Italiano-Polonais." This was Métilde's elder son, then an engineer, who had had to leave Milan after killing Comte Grisoni in a duel at Lodi. (Sand, *Corr.,* Vol. IV, p. 559.)

2. Arbelet, *Le Figaro, loc. cit.* Martineau, *Petit Dictionnaire stendhalien,* p. 178, notes that Métilde was put under house arrest in December, 1822, and questioned on her relations with the carbonari.

3. Morgan, *Italy,* Vol. I, pp. 71, 95, 159.

4. Quoted by Martineau, in his introduction to *De l'Amour,* p. xiii.

5. *SE,* p. 1395.

6. *Ibid.*, pp. 1403, 1409, 1489.

7. August 8, 1804; *Corr.,* Vol. I, p. 139.

8. Henriot, *Stendhaliana,* p. 23.

9. Martino, *Stendhal: Del Romanticismo nelle arti,* pp. 4–6.

10. *Ibid.*, p. 22.

11. April 14, 1818; *Corr.,* Vol. I, p. 909.

12. May 4, 1818; *Corr.,* Vol. I, pp. 921–22.

13. *Journal,* p. 1291.

14. August 26, 1818; *Corr.,* Vol. I, p. 931.

15. September 3, 1818; *Corr.,* Vol. I, p. 933.

16. Edgeworth, *Letters from England, 1813–1844,* p. 101.

17. Letter from Mareste, September 26, 1818; *Corr.,* Vol. I, p. 1263.

18. [October 4, 1818]; *Corr.,* Vol. I, p. 940.

19. November 16, 1818; *Corr.,* Vol. I, pp. 947–48.

20. [May 12, 1819]; *Corr.*, Vol. I, pp. 964–65.

21. June 11, 1819; *Corr.*, Vol. I, p. 970.

22. *Ibid.*, pp. 970–71.

23. June 7, 1819; *Corr.*, Vol. I, pp. 965–66, 968.

24. June 11, 1819; *Corr.*, Vol. I, p. 972.

25. *Ibid.*, p. 969.

26. July 20, 1819; *Corr.*, Vol. I, p. 981.

27. August 15, 1819; *Corr.*, Vol. I, pp. 985–86.

28. *Ibid.*, pp. 987–88.

29. Billy, *op. cit.*, p. 139.

30. See also Beyle's letter of June 30, 1819: "I do not hope, madame; but the corner of the earth where I am least unhappy is beside you." *Corr.*, Vol. I, p. 976.

31. Del Litto, *Première journée du Stendhal-Club*, p. 61.

32. Martineau published the existing fragment of the *Roman de Métilde* in his edition of Beyle's works, in the first volume of *Mélanges de littérature*.

33. Martineau emphasised that love gave Beyle a pleasure like that of music. (*De l'Amour.* Avertissement, p. xiv.)

20

1. March 21, 1820; *Corr.*, Vol. I, p. 1009.

2. Martino, *Stendhal: Del Romanticismo nelle arti*, p. 12.

3. March 21, 1820; *Corr.*, Vol. I, pp. 1009, 1010.

4. March 25, 1820; *Corr.*, Vol. I, p. 1012.

5. March 25, 1820; *Corr.*, Vol. I, pp. 1012–13.

6. March 26 [1820]; *Corr.*, Vol. I, p. 1017.

7. February 8 [1820]; *Corr.*, Vol. I, p. 1000.

8. June 12, 1820; *Corr.*, Vol. I, pp. 1024–26.

9. July 12, 1820; *Corr.*, Vol. I, pp. 1029–30.

10. July 23, 1820; *Corr.*, Vol. I, pp. 1030–31.

11. Boncompain et Vermale, *op. cit.*, p. 185.

12. Billy, *op. cit.*, pp. 141–42.

13. October 20, 1820; *Corr.*, Vol. I, pp. 1040–41.

14. November 4, 1820; *Corr.*, Vol. I, p. 1042.

15. November 13, 1820; *Corr.*, Vol. I, pp. 1043, 1044.

16. February 23, 1821; *Corr.*, Vol. I, p. 1057.

17. *"To send the* 3 janvier 1821"; *Corr.*, Vol. I, p. 1055.

18. April 1, 1821; *Corr.*, Vol. I, p. 1059.

19. April 2, 1821; *Corr.*, Vol. I, pp. 1060–61.

20. April 14, 1821; *Corr.*, Vol. I, p. 1061.

21. June 6, 1821; *Corr.*, Vol. I, p. 1065.

21

1. *SE*, pp. 1395–96.

2. *Ibid.*, p. 1398.

3. *Ibid.*, p. 1403.

4. *Ibid.*, pp. 1404, 1407.

5. *Ibid.*, p. 1409.

6. *Ibid.*, p. 1431.

7. *Ibid.*, p. 1436.

8. *Ibid.*, p. 1438.

9. *Ibid.*, pp. 1438–39, 1440; *Mélanges de littérature*, Vol. II: "Sur l'Angleterre." In *L'Itinéraire de Stendhal*, p. 72, Martineau dates this visit from September to December, 1821.

10. Smiles, *Memoir and Correspondence of the late John Murray*, Vol. I, pp. 264–65. In *La Fortune de Stendhal en Angleterre*, p. 143, Strauss notes that the English translation of the life of Haydn was published in 1817. Seven hundred and three copies were printed in June, 1817, and 1,263 copies in October, 1818, and the last copies were sold in 1823.

11. [May, 1810]; *Corr.*, Vol. I, p. 578.

12. [November 18, 1821]; *Corr.*, Vol. II, p. 1.

13. *SE*, pp. 1444–47.

14. Redding, *Fifty Years' Recollections*, Vol. II, p. 321.

15. Martineau, *L'Oeuvre de Stendhal*, p. 252.

16. *SE*, p. 1454.

17. Galpin, *Fauriel in Italy*, pp. 32–33.

18. Delécluze, *Souvenirs de soixante années*, pp. 156–58.

19. Baschet, *E.-J. Delécluze*, pp. 103, 126; Delécluze, *op. cit.*, pp. 242–45.

20. In his commonplace book (Sharpe Papers, p. 86), kept in the Library of University College, London, Sutton Sharpe noted:

> Une des plus belles prérogatives de l'esprit, c'est qu'il donne de la considération à la vieillesse.
>
> Beyle - de l'Amour Vol. 2 p. 146.
>
> Instance the present Lady Holland &c.

One wonders if Sutton Sharpe—the nephew of a habitué, Samuel Rogers—presented Beyle at Holland House. In *Armance* (pp. 104–5), Octave de Malivert asked: "How could one go to England and not have oneself presented to the Marquess of Lansdowne, Mr. Brougham and Lord Holland?" However, in his notes to *Armance* (p. 1447), Martineau says that Beyle had failed to be presented to them, though he had his works sent to them.

22

1. Quoted by Martineau in his introduction to *De l'Amour*, p. xiv.

2. Brombert, (ed.), *Stendhal. A Collection of Critical Essays*, pp. 12–13.

3. In his *Stendhal*, p. 62, Clewes observes that the chapter "Des Fiasco" was omitted from an English transiation published as late as 1915.

4. Sainte-Beuve, *Causeries du lundi*, Vol. IX, p. 269.

5. The explanatory anecdote, "Le Rameau de Salzbourg," was not written until 1825, and it first appeared in the edition published after Beyle's death, by Colomb. But it does not matter when—or whether—Beyle went to Salzburg. Even before the episode of "Le Rameau de Salzbourg," his theory of crystallisation was already present in *De l'Amour*.

6. *De l'A*, p. 11.

7. *Ibid.*, p. 25.

8. *Ibid.*, pp. 36, 37.

9. *Ibid.*, p. 39.

10. *Ibid.*, pp. 58–59.

11. *Ibid.*, p. 101.

12. *Ibid.*, pp. 215, 216.

13. Billy, *op. cit.*, p. 168.

14. Galpin, *op. cit.*, pp. 53–54.

15. Hazlitt, *Notes of a Journey through France and Italy*, p. 314 sqq.

16. Quoted by Martineau, *L'oEuvre de Stendhal*, pp. 200–1.

17. Gourmont, *Promenades philosophiques*, 3e serie, p. 192.

18. Coffe, *Chronique stendhalienne*, pp. 5–6; Del Litto, *Bibliographie stendhalienne, 1953–1956*, p. 9.

23

1. Martineau, *L'OEuvre de Stendhal*, p. 254.

2. Gunnell, *Stendhal et l'Angleterre*, pp. 71–72.

3. *R & S*, p. 62.

4. *Ibid.*, p. 69.

5. Lemaître, *op. cit.*, pp. 14–15.

6. May 3 [1823]; *Corr.*, Vol. II, p. 14.

7. Jourda, *Vieusseux et ses correspondants français, passim*.

8. May 29, 1823; *Corr.*, Vol. II, pp. 779–80.

9. June 23, 1823; *Corr.*, Vol. II, pp. 16–18.

10. Prothero, *The Works of Lord Byron*, Vol. VI, p. 284.

24

1. For Clémentine Curial, see Mar-

tineau, *Dictionnaire,* pp. 149–55. Born on May 5, 1788, she died on June 14, 1840. Philibert Curial, born on August 21, 1774, was created comte by the emperor, March 22, 1814, and peer of France the following June by Louis XVIII. He died on May 30, 1829, "as the result, it is said, of a carriage accident which occurred at the coronation of Charles X." André Billy *(Ce cher Stendhal,* pp. 184–85), says that Philibert Curial was the model for Octave de Malivert in *Armance.* Possibly he provided some of the hero's features; but since the theme of the novel was the impotence of the hero, it is hard to identify De Malivert with a notorious philanderer who was also the father of several children. Martineau *(op. cit.,* p. 154) mentions the Curials' *three* children: Napoléon-Joseph (1809–61); Marie-Clémentine (1812–89); Adolphe-Philibert (1813–73). She had also lost another daughter, Bathilde. Martineau fails to mention Claire-Charlotte.

2. *Journal,* p. 1306.

3. *V d R,* Vol. I, p. 24.

4. *Ibid.,* Vol. II, pp. 265–66.

5. Mérimée, *op. cit.,* p. 182.

6. December 5, 1823; *Corr.,* Vol. II, pp. 22–23.

7. January 13, 1824; *Corr.,* Vol. II, pp. 24–25.

8. Against this comment one might set the comment of Liszt, quoted in Chapter 37, that Stendhal's *Vie de Rossini* was "quite interesting."

9. April 3, 1824; *Corr.,* Vol. II, p. 782.

10. December 5, 1823; *Corr.,* Vol. II, pp. 22–23.

11. May 18, 1824; *Corr.,* Vol. II, pp. 30–31.

12. May 20, 1824; *Corr.,* Vol. II, p. 783.

13. *SE,* p. 1404.

14. 1824; *Corr.,* Vol. II, pp. 32–33.

15. 1824; *Corr.,* Vol. II, p. 33.

16. Boncompain et Vermale, *op. cit.,* pp. 209–10.

17. *Ibid.,* p. 210.

18. June 24, 1824; *Corr.,* Vol. II, p. 35.

19. Mélia, *La Vie amoureuse de Stendhal,* p. 17.

20. [July 4, 1824]; *Corr.,* Vol. II, pp. 790–92.

21. July, 1824; *Corr.,* Vol. II, p. 796.

22. July, 1824; *Corr.,* Vol. II, p. 792.

23. August 10, 1824; *Corr.,* Vol. II, p. 792.

24. Billy, *op. cit.,* p. 182.

25. Mélia, *op. cit.,* p. 27.

26. *Ibid.,* p. 361.

27. Billy, *op. cit.,* p. 184.

28. For a detailed account of the liaison, see Martineau, *Le Coeur de Stendhal,* Vol. II, p. 69 sqq.

25

1. [April 26, 1824]; *Corr.,* Vol. II, pp. 27–28.

2. April 30, 1824; *Corr.,* Vol. II, p. 942 note.

3. Morley, *Henry Crabb Robinson on Books and Their Authors,* Vol. I, p. 343.

4. [March, 1825]; *Corr.,* Vol. II, p. 800.

5. March 25, 1825; *Corr.,* Vol. II, p. 801.

6. [March 31, 1825]; *Corr.,* Vol. II, p. 59.

7. Simon, *Les Souvenirs du Baron de Strombeck et de Louis Spach sur Stendhal,* pp. 10–11.

8. Delécluze, *op. cit.,* p. 129.

9. Baschet, *op. cit.,* pp. 231–33.

10. Delécluze, *op. cit.,* pp. 140–41.

11. Ancelot, *Les Salons de Paris,* p. 47 sqq.

12. *Ibid.*

13. *Ibid.,* pp. 68–69.

14. [August, 1824]; *Corr.,* Vol. II, p. 40.

15. October 11, 1825; *Corr.,* Vol. II, p. 813.

16. November 13, 1825; *Corr.,* Vol. II, p. 814.

17. Gunnell, *Stendhal et l'Angleterre,* p. 16; Chuquet, *Stendhal-Beyle,* pp. 179–80.

18. François Michel: "Bathilde

Curial. Une Enfant à travers l'oeuvre de Stendhal," in Martineau et Michel, *Nouvelles soirées du Stendhal-Club*, p. 14 sqq.

19. *Ibid.*

20. Gunnell, *Stendhal et l'Angleterre*, p. 22.

21. *P d R*, Vol. I,

22. *Ibid.*, Vol. I, p. 209.

23. Sharpe Papers folio 83 (pp. 20–21); 86.

24. Gunnell, *Stendhal et l'Angleterre*, p. 21.

25. *P d R*, Vol. I, p. 51.

26. Lingay (1791–1851) had entered journalism in 1815, and in 1820 he became secretary to the president of the Conseil des ministres; after a period out of office, he was reinstated after 1830. He played an important part behind the scenes in the July Monarchy.

27. Dollot, *Stendhal journaliste*, p. 74.

28. *SE*, p. 1399.

29. [July 4, 1824]; *Corr.*, Vol. II, pp. 790, 792 notes.

30. For Giulia Rinieri, see Martineau, *Le Coeur de Stendhal*, Vol. II, p. 172 sqq.

31. Jourda, *Stendhal: l'homme et l'oeuvre*, p. 7; in August, 1828, Auguste Boulant announced a second edition of *Armance*. It was, in fact, the remaining sheets of the first edition, with new title page and new binding.

26

1. Quoted by Strauss, *op. cit.*, p. 204.

2. Brun, *op. cit.*, p. 57.

3. Lamartine, *Cours familier de littérature*, pp. 420–24.

4. Simon, *Stendhal et la police autrichienne*, pp. 3, 14–15.

5. Giraud, *The Unheroic Hero*, pp. 88–89.

6. March 23 [1828]; *Corr.*, Vol. II, p. 140.

7. Martineau: *L'Oeuvre de Standhal*, p. 266.

8. *NMM*, January, 1826; *CA*, Vol. II, p. 394.

9. *NMM*, April, 1826; *ibid.*, Vol. III, p. 8.

10. *Ibid.*, pp. 23–24.

11. *Ibid.*, p. 28.

12. *NMM*, May, 1826; *ibid.*, p. 39.

13. *CA*, Vol. III, p. 146.

14. *Ibid.*, pp. 145–46.

15. *LM*, February 1, 1825; *CA*, Vol. IV, p. 51.

16. *Ibid.*, p. 106.

17. *LM*, October, 1826; *CA*, Vol. IV, p. 292.

18. *NMM*, July, 1826; *CA*, Vol. III, pp. 136–38.

19. *NMM*, February, 1826; *CA*, Vol. II, p. 426.

20. *NMM*, May, 1826; *CA*, Vol. III, p. 43.

21. *NMM*, July, 1826; *CA*, Vol. III, pp. 128–29.

22. *The Athenaeum*, May 28, 1828; *CA*, Vol. V, p. 307.

23. *NMM*, October, 1826; CA, Vol. III, p. 170, see also Vol. III, p. 125.

24. March 23 [1828]; *Corr.*, Vol. II, p. 140.

25. Blessington, *The Idler in France*, Vol. I, p. 115.

26. *Ibid.*, pp. 219–20.

27. Asselineau, *Bibliographie romantique*, pp. 257, 307.

28. Planta, *A New Picture of Paris*, p. 348.

29. Hazlitt, *op. cit.*, pp. 139–40.

30. Gunnell, *Sutton Sharpe et ses amis français*, p. 151.

31. *Ibid.*, p. 228.

27

1. February 10 [1829]; *Corr.*, Vol. II, p. 161.

2. Joubin, *Journal d'Eugène Delacroix*, Vol. II, pp. 116–17.

3. Morgan, *France in 1829–30*, Vol. I, p. 206.

4. *Ibid.*, pp. 258–61.

5. *Ibid.*, pp. 320–21.

6. *P d R*, Vol. I, p. 5 and *passim*.

7. *Ibid.*, p. cxi sqq.

8. Arbelet, *Stendhal épicier*, pp. 64–65.

9. Valéry, *Variété,* Vol. II, p. 84. Krutch, *Five Masters,* pp. 227–28. The Berthet affair, on which *Le Rouge et le Noir* was partly based, had been recorded in the *Gazette des Tribunaux,* December 28–31, 1827. For the origin of the novel, see also Claude Liprandi, *Au Coeur du Rouge.*

10. Benedetto, *Indiscrétions sur Giulia,* pp. 39–43.

11. January 10 [1830]; *Corr.,* Vol. II, p. 172.

12. Delécluze: *op. cit.,* pp. 431–32.

13. March 1, 1830; *Corr.,* Vol. II, p. 176.

14. [February 19, 1830]; *Corr.,* Vol. II, p. 175.

15. [February, 1830]; *Corr.,* Vol. II, p. 175.

16. March 26, 1830; *Corr.,* Vol. II, p. 180.

17. Lamartine, *op. cit.,* pp. 417, 404; Sainte-Beuve, *Causeries du lundi,* Vol. IX, p. 241 sqq.

18. Quoted by Henriot, *op. cit.,* p. 12.

19. Rochefort, *Les Aventures de ma vie,* Vol. II, p. 54 sqq. Maurice Barrès observed: "If Hugo said that, he was a fool."

20. Benedetto, *Indiscrétions sur Guilia,* p. 108.

28

1. August 15, 1830; *Corr.,* Vol. II, p. 187.

2. August 25, 1830; *Corr.,* Vol. II, p. 188.

3. [September 26, 1830]; *Corr.,* Vol. II, p. 190.

4. September 29, 1830; *Corr.,* Vol. II, p. 190.

5. November 6, 1830; *Corr.,* Vol. II, pp. 193–94.

29

1. *NMM,* May, 1826; *CA,* Vol. III, p. 43.

2. Durand, *Le Décor Mythique de la Chartreuse de Parme,* p. 38 and *passim.*

3. *Le Rouge et le Noir,* p. 240.

4. Brun, *op. cit.,* p. 61.

5. Benedetto, *op. cit.,* p. 119 and *passim.*

6. Quoted by Jourda, *Stendhal raconté par ceux qui l'ont vu,* p. 112.

7. Simon, *Les Souvenirs du Baron de Strombeck et de Louis Spach sur Stendhal,* p. 10.

8. Bourget, *Essais,* pp. 309–10.

9. *Ibid.,* pp. 313–14, 319–20.

30

1. December 12, 1830; *Corr.,* Vol. II, pp. 198–99.

2. January 1, 1831; *Corr.,* Vol. II, p. 205.

3. Boyer, *Les Lectures de Stendhal,* pp. 21–22.

4. March 31, 1831; *Corr.,* Vol. II, p. 266.

5. Boppe, *Stendhal à Rome,* pp. 1–2.

6. Taine, *Voyage en Italie,* Vol. I, p. 11 sqq.

7. For Beyle in Rome, see Boppe, *passim.*

8. Gunnell, *Sutton Sharpe et ses amis français,* p. 213.

9. Estourmel, *Souvenirs...,* pp. 295–96.

10. Beyle, however, recognised Ingres' distinction and thought he might be spoken of in 1935 *(VHB,* p. 8).

11. March 15, 1832; *Corr.,* Vol. II, pp. 407–8.

12. However, writing to Fiore on September 14, 1831, he observed: "I go to Rome when I want. Yet really one must keep at one's post." *(Corr.,* Vol. II, p. 345.)

13. Benedetto, *op. cit.,* p. 140.

14. January 12, 1833; *Corr.,* Vol. II, p. 494.

15. January 20, 1833; *Corr.,* Vol. II, p. 497.

16. April 1, 1833; *Corr.,* Vol. II, pp. 1126–27.

17. In his *Indiscrétions sur Giulia,* pp. 60 sqq. and 151, Benedetto records that there were two children of the marriage, Anna and Daniele. Berlinghieri helped

to foster Martini's career. In time he became the minister resident accredited to the King of Sardinia; in 1859 he was Minister of Public Instruction. He retired the following year. Giulia survived him, and she was still alive in 1876. She was one of the three women to whom Beyle bequeathed a copy of his works.

31

1. April 30, 1833; *Corr.*, Vol. II, pp. 514, 515.
2. Martineau quotes this in his *Dictionnaire*, p. 154.
3. Sand, *Histoire de ma vie*, Vol. IV, pp. 184–86.
4. Bourget, *Stendhal: Discours*, p. 10.
5. [June 7, 1834]; *Corr.*, Vol. II, p. 918. Chuquet *(op. cit.,* p. 532) says that Tavernier had a Greek father and a French mother.
6. July 13 [1834]; *Corr.*, Vol. II, pp. 665–66.
7. May 4, 1834; *Corr.*, Voi. II, p. 643.
8. Doyon et Du Parc, *Amitiés parisiennes de Stendhal,* pp. 42, 43.
9. 3 [June 1834]; *Corr.*, Vol. II, p. 647.
10. September 10, 1834; *Corr.*, Vol. II, pp. 692, 693.
11. Boyer, *Bibliothèques stendhaliennes à Civitavecchia et à Rome,* p. 11.
12. October 28, 1834; *Corr.*, Vol. II, pp. 711–12.
13. November 1, 1834; *Corr.*, Vol. II, pp. 718, 719, 720.
14. November 4, 1834; *Corr.*, Vol. II, pp. 721, 722.
15. Ancelot, *op. cit.,* pp. 68–69.
16. Cordier, *Stendhal et ses amis,* p. 130.
17. Sainte-Beuve, *Causeries du lundi,* Vol. IX, pp. 259, 272–73.
18. Berlioz, *Mémoires,* p. 139 and note.
19. March 4 [1835]; *Corr.*, Vol. III, p. 13.
20. March 8, 1835; *Corr.*, Vol. III, pp. 14–15.
21. February 5, 1835; *Corr.*, Vol. III, p. 524.
22. March 18, 1835; *Corr.*, Vol. III, p. 19.
23. [April, 1835]; *Corr.*, Vol. III, p. 31.
24. [April] 1835; *Corr.*, Vol. III, pp. 57–58.

32

1. September 27, 1835; *Corr.*, Vol. III, p. 129.
2. For the various titles of *Lucien Leuwen*, see Martineau's introduction to the novel, pp. 750–51.
3. Brombert, *Stendhal et la voie oblique,* pp. 2, 5, 116–17.
4. September 27, 1835; *Corr.*, Vol. III, p. 129.
5. April 30, 1807; *Corr.*, Vol. I, p. 348.
6. September 27, 1835; *Corr.*, Vol. III, pp. 129, 130. September 27, 1835; *Corr.*, Vol. III, p. 133.
7. October 23, 1835; *Corr.*, Vol. III, p. 135.
8. August 15, 1819; *Corr.*, Vol. I, p. 986.
9. November 21, 1835; *Corr.*, Vol. III, pp. 139–40.
10. February 15, 1836; *Corr.*, Vol. III, p. 170.
11. March 14, 1836; *Corr.*, Vol. III, p. 195.
12. April 9 [1836]; *Corr.*, Vol. III, p. 203.

33

1. Bellanger, *op. cit.,* pp. 163, 164.
2. [October, 1836]; *Corr.*, Vol. III, p. 221.
3. *Corr.*, Vol. III, p. 750 *note.*
4. [1837?]; *Corr.*, Vol. III, p. 537.
5. For the history of this letter, see: Durry, *Une Passion de Stendhal: Clémentine.*
6. March 29 [1837?]; *Corr.*, Vol. III, p. 230.
7. Boyer, *Stendhal et les historiens de Napoléon,* pp. 4, 6.
8. March 24, 1838; *Corr.*, Vol. III, p. 259.
9. July 2, 1838; *Corr.*, Vol. III, p. 261.

10. Billy, *op. cit.*, p. 253.

11. Primoli, *Une Promenade dans Rome sur les traces de Stendhal*, pp. 62–63.

12. Gunnell, *Stendhal et l'Angleterre*, pp. 23, 24–25; Beyle was not a member of the Athenaeum, and the club has no knowledge of him (letter from the secretary to the present author, January 16, 1973).

13. Brun, *op. cit.*, p. 114.

14. January 3, 1839; *Corr.*, Vol. III, pp. 271, 272.

15. June 9, 1839; *Corr.*, Vol. III, p. 279.

16. [March 29, 1839]; *Corr.*, Vol. III, p. 277.

17. [End of March, 1839]; *Corr.*, Vol. III, p. 555.

18. [April 5, 1839]; *Corr.*, Vol. III, p. 557.

19. Quoted as note to Sainte-Beuve, *Correspondance générale*, Vol. III, p. 388.

20. Quoted in note to Balzac: *Correspondance*, Vol. III, p. 586.

34

1. February 18, 1821; *Corr.*, Vol. I, pp. 1056–57.

2. May 8, 1832; quoted by John Gibson Lockhart, *Memoirs of the Life of Sir Walter Scott, Bart.* (Edinburgh, Cadell, 1837–38), Vol. IV, pp. 307–8.

3. Barrès, *op. cit.*, Vol. XIV, p. 76.

4. Lumbroso, *op. cit.*, p. 60.

5. *Ibid.*, pp. 67–68.

6. Barrès, *op. cit.*, Vol. X, p. 64.

7. Durand, *Le Décor mythique de la Chartreuse de Parme*, p. 42.

8. *Pensées. Filosofia nova*, Vol. I, p. 13.

9. *Ibid.*, p. 16.

10. *Voyage dans le Midi de la France*, p. 206.

11. Durand, *op. cit.*, p. 162 and *passim*.

35

1. [June, 1839]; *Corr.*, Vol. III, p. 286.

2. Du Parc, *Quand Stendhal relisait les Promenades dans Rome*, p. 96.

3. August 10, 1839; *Corr.*, Vol. III, p. 286.

4. September 26 [1839]; *Corr.*, Vol. III, pp. 293–94.

5. October 1, 1839; *Corr.*, Vol. III, p. 295.

6. November 28, 1839; *Corr.*, Vol. III, p. 571.

7. January 4, 1840; *Corr.*, Vol. III, p. 319.

8. Peladan, *Ernest Hébert*, pp. 38–39.

9. *Ibid.*, pp. 13–16.

10. January 29, 1840; *Corr.*, Vol. III, p. 325.

11. *Revue des Deux Mondes*, October 13, 1923; quoted by Jourda, *Stendhal raconté par ceux qui l'ont vu*, pp. 120–22.

12. August 10, 1840; *Corr.*, Vol. III, pp. 378–80.

13. *P d R*, Vol. I, p. cxxxvi note.

14. Balzac, *Oeuvres complètes*, Vol. XXIII, pp. 737, 738, 735.

15. For the successive drafts of his letter, see *Corr.*, Vol. III, p. 393 sqq.

16. Quoted by Jourda, *Stendhal raconté par ceux qui l'ont vu*, p. 118.

17. April 5, 1841; *Corr.*, Vol. III, pp. 434–35.

18. April 10, 1841; *Corr.*, Vol. III, p. 435.

19. April 19, 1841; *Corr.*, Vol. III, p. 438.

20. June 15, 1841; *Corr.*, Vol. III, p. 450.

21. June 19, 1841; *Corr.*, Vol. III, p. 462.

22. Billy, *op. cit.*, p. 267.

23. August 9, 1841; *Corr.*, Vol. III, p. 489.

36

1. December 8, 1841; *Corr.*, Vol. III, p. 512.

2. Pinvert, *Un ami de Stendhal*, p. 16; *Armance*, précédé d'une notice biographique par R. Colomb, p. lxvii.

3. February 25, 1842; *Corr.*, Vol. III, p. 527.

4. Billy, *op. cit.*, pp. 270–71.

5. February 25 [1842]; *Corr.*, Vol. III, p. 515.

6. Du Parc, "Echos diplomatiques de la mort de Stendhal," in Del Litto, *Première journée du Stendhal-Club*, pp. 91–92.

7. Brun, *op. cit.*, p. 43.

37

1. February 8, 1843; Ollivier, p. 257.

2. Simon, *Stendhal par Gobineau*, p. 15.

3. "Monday—April 1845." Miller, p. 240.

4. Stendhal: *La Chartreuse de Parme*, Préface de F. Sarcey, p. ii sqq.

5. See Stryienski, *Soirées du Stendhal Club* (1904), p. 327 sqq.

6. Paton, *Henry Beyle*, Preface, pp. v, vi.

7. Zola, *Les Romanciers naturalistes*, p. 75.

8. *Ibid.*, p. 83 sqq.

9. Barrès, *op. cit.*, Vol. XIV, p. 92.

10. Bourget, *Etudes et Portraits*, Vol. I, p. 261 sqq.

11. Cordier, *Stendhal et ses amis*, pp. 1, 8.

12. Faguet, *Politiques et moralistes du XIXe siècle*, p. 2 sqq.

13. Brun, *op. cit.*, pp. 48, 135 sqq.

14. In 1905 the committee included Gabriele d'Annunzio, Joseph Primoli, Alfred Vallette (editor of *Le Mercure de France*), Louis Ganderax (editor of *La Revue de Paris*), Paul Flat *(La Revue bleue)* and Adrien Hébrard *(Le Temps)*. Later members included Raymond Poincaré, Gabriel Faure and Emile Henriot.

15. Mélia, *op. cit.*, avant-propos, p. 6.

16. Cordier, *Stendhal et ses amis*, p. 3.

17. Blum, *Stendhal et le Beylisme*, pp. 2–3, 4, 5, 304, 307.

18. Bourget, *Stendhal: Discours*, pp. 17–18.

19. Henriot, *op. cit.*, pp. 1–2, 4.

20. Marsan, *Stendhal célébré à Civitavecchia.*

21. Valéry, *op. cit.*, Vol. II, p. 81 sqq.

22. David, *Stendhal: sa vie, son oeuvre*, p. 14.

23. Bosselaers, *Le Cas Stendhal*, pp. 229–31.

24. Destutt de Tracy, *op. cit.*, Vol. I, p. 98; in *Ecoles italiennes de la peinture*, Vol. II, p. 8, Stendhal wrote: "Corregio brought painting close to music."

25. Ditlivsen, *op. cit.*, pp. 60–61.

26. Stendhal, *Mélanges d'art*, p. 170.

27. Collignon, *L'Art et la vie de Stendhal*, p. 41.

28. Yet Elizabeth Barrett (Miller, *loc. cit.*) wrote: "Balzac could scarcely put out a stronger hand."

29. Hazard, *La Vie de Stendhal*, p. 47.

30. Blum, *op. cit.*, pp. 273–74.

31. Sarcey, *loc. cit.*

32. Fineshriber, *Stendhal the Romantic Rationalist*, p. 54.

33. Mélia, *op. cit.*, p. 13.

34. Brun, *op. cit.*, p. 53.

35. January 4, 1805; *Journal*, pp. 550–51.

36. Quoted by Barrès, *op. cit.*, Vol. XIV, p. 71.

37. Blum, *op. cit.*, pp. 317–18.

38. Martino, "Stendhal à cosmopolis," *Nouvelles soirées du Stendhal-Club*, p. 47 sqq.

39. Brombert, *Stendhal et la voie oblique*, p. 166.

40. Boncompain et Vermale, *op. cit.*, p. 24.

41. Quoted by Boyer, *Les Lectures...*, p. 85.

42. Krutch, *op. cit.*, p. 240.

43. Stendhal, *Armance*. Préface de André Gide, p. ii.

44. Valéry, *op. cit.*, pp. 138, 139.

45. François-Poncet, *Stendhal à Brunswick*, p. 116.

Selected Bibliography

Selected Bibliography

English books are published in London, French books in Paris, unless otherwise indicated.

ANCELOT, MME., *Les Salons de Paris. Foyers éteints.* Tardieu, 1858.

ARBELET, PAUL, *La Jeunesse de Stendhal.* Champion, 1919. 2 tomes.

———, *Louason, ou les perpléxités amoureuses de Stendhal.* Grenoble, B. Arthaud, 1937.

———, *Premier voyage de Stendhal au pays des comédiennes.* L'Artisan du Livre, 1928.

———, *Stendhal au pays des comédiennes.* Grenoble, B. Arthaud, 1934.

———, *Stendhal épicier; ou les infortunes de Mélanie.* Les Oeuvres représentatives, 1926.

———, *Stendhal et le Petit Ange.* Les Amis d'Edouard, 1926.

———, *Trois solitaires. (Courier. Stendhal. Mérimée).* Gallimard, 1934.

ASSELINEAU, CHARLES, *Bibliographie romantique.* Rouquette, 1872.

BALZAC, H. DE, *Correspondance.* Textes réunis, classés et annotés par Roger Pierrot. Garnier, 1960–64.

———, *Oeuvres complètes,* Tome XXIII. Michel Lévy, 1873.

BARDÈCHE, MAURICE, *Stendhal romancier.* La Table Ronde, 1947.

BARRÈS, MAURICE, *Mes Cahiers.* Plon, 1929–33.

325

BASCHET, ROBERT, *E.-J. Delécluze. Témoin de son temps, 1781–1863.* Boivin, 1942.

BELLANGER, CHARLES, *Notes stendhaliennes.* Suivies du *H.B.* de Mérimée. Editions du Myrte, 1948.

BENEDETTO, LUIGI-FOSCOLO, *Indiscrétions sur Giulia.* Le Divan, 1934.

BERLIOZ, HECTOR, *Mémoires.* Michel Lévy, 1870.

BILLY, ANDRÉ, *Ce cher Stendhal . . . Récit de sa vie.* Flammarion, 1958.

BLESSINGTON, LADY, *The Idler in France.* Colburn, 1841.

BLIN, GEORGES, *Stendhal et les problèmes du roman.* Corti, 1954.

———, *Stendhal et les problèmes de la personnalité.* Corti, 1958.

BLUM, LÉON, *Stendhal et le Beylisme.* Ollendorff, 1914.

BONCOMPAIN, CLAUDE, ET VERMALE, FRANÇOIS, *Stendhal; ou la double vie de Henri Beyle.* Amiot Dumont, 1955.

BOPPE, ROGER, *Stendhal à Rome. Les Débuts d'un Consul, 1831–1833.* Avec une introduction par Henri Martineau. Horizons de France, 1944.

BOSSELAERS, REMI, *Le Cas Stendhal. Une mise au point. Essai typologique et littéraire.* Droz, 1938.

BOUGY, ALFRED DE, *Stendhal: Sa vie et son oeuvre.* Cherbuliez, 1868.

BOURGET, PAUL, *Essais de psychologie contemporaine.* Lemerre, 1885.

———, *Etudes et Portraits,* Vol. I. Lemerre, 1889.

———, *Stendhal. Discours prononcé le 28 juin 1920 à l'inauguration du monument.* Suivi du discours de M. Edouard Champion. Champion, 1920.

———, *Nouvelles Pages de Critique et de Doctrine,* Vol. I. Plon, 1922.

BOYER, FERDINAND, *La Bibliothèque de Stendhal à Rome (1842).* Editions du Stendhal-Club, No. 3, 1923.

———, *Logements de Stendhal à Rome (1831–1842).* Editions du Stendhal-Club, No. 5, 1924.

———, *Le Gagne-pain de Stendhal (1830–1842).* Editions du Stendhal-Club, No. 6, 1924.

———, *Donato Bucci et les dernières volontés de Stendhal.* Editions du Stendhal-Club, No. 8, 1924.

———, *Bibliothèques stendhaliennes à Civitavecchia et à Rome.* Editions du Stendhal-Club, No. 10, 1925.

———, *Les Lectures de Stendhal.* Editions du Stendhal-Club, No. 14, 1926.

———, *Stendhal et les historiens de Napoléon.* Editions du Stendhal-Club, No. 17, 1926.

———, *Giulia, ou le mariage manqué de Stendhal.* Editions du Stendhal-Club, No. 29, 1930.

BRANDES, GEORGE, *Main Currents in Nineteenth-Century Literature,* Vol. V. Heinemann, 1904.

BROMBERT, VICTOR, *Stendhal et la voie oblique.* New Haven, Yale University Press, 1954.

——, (ed.), *Stendhal. A Collection of Critical Essays.* Englewood Cliffs, New Jersey, Prentice-Hall, 1962.

——, *Stendhal: Fiction and the Themes of Fiction.* New York, Random House, 1968.

BROUGHTON, LORD (JOHN CAM HOBHOUSE), *Recollections of a Long Life.* With additional extracts from his private diaries, edited by his daughter Lady Dorchester, Vol. II. Murray, 1909.

BRUN, PIERRE, *Henry Beyle-Stendhal.* Grenoble, Alexandre Gratier, 1900.

BRUSSALY, MANUEL, *The Political Ideas of Stendhal.* New York, Publications of the Institute of French Studies, Columbia University Press, 1933.

BRUYAS, JEAN-PAUL, *La Psychologie de l'adolescence dans l'oeuvre romanesque de Stendhal.* Aix-en-Provence, Publications de la Faculté des Lettres, 1967.

BUSNELLI, MANLIO D., *Stendhal traducteur de Goldoni.* Editions du Stendhal-Club, No. 18, 1926.

CARACCIO, A., *Stendhal.* Hatier, 1970.

CHAMPION, EDOUARD, *Un Nouvel Exemplaire annoté des Promenades dans Rome.* Editions du Stendhal-Club, No. 19, 1926.

CHUQUET, ARTHUR, *Stendhal-Beyle.* Plon, Nourrit, 1902.

CLEWES, HOWARD, *Stendhal. An Introduction to the Novels.* Barker, 1950.

COFFE, M., *Chronique stendhalienne.* Milan, Coffe, 1907.

COLLIGNON, ALBERT, *L'Art et la vie de Stendhal.* Baillière, 1868.

CORDIER, HENRI, *Stendhal et ses amis. Notes d'un curieux.* Evreux, Charles Hérissey, imprimeur, 1890.

——, *Comment je suis devenu Stendhalien. Causerie.* Revue critique des idées et des livres, 1913.

DAVID, MAURICE, *Stendhal. Sa vie, son oeuvre.* Nouvelle Revue Critique, 1931.

DECHAMPS, J., *Stendhal et l'Espagne.* Editions du Stendhal-Club, No. 15, 1926.

——, *Amitiés stendhaliennes en Belgique.* La Renaissance du Livre, 1963.

DÉDÉYAN, CHARLES, *L'Italie dans l'oeuvre romanesque de Stendhal.* Société d'Edition d'Enseignement supérieur, 1963.

DELACROIX, EUGÈNE, *Journal, 1823–1863.* Plon, Nourrit, 1893–5.

DELACROIX, HENRI, *La Psychologie de Stendhal.* Alcan, 1918.

DELÉCLUZE, ETIENNE-JEAN, *Souvenirs de soixante années.* Michel Lévy, 1862.

DEL LITTO, V., *Bibliographie stendhalienne, 1947–1952.* Grenoble, B. Arthaud, 1955.

——, *Bibliographie stendhalienne, 1953–1956.* Lausanne, Editions du Grand Chêne, 1958.

——, *Bibliographie stendhalienne, 1957–1960.* Lausanne, Editions du Grand Chêne, 1962.

——, *Bibliographie stendhalienne, 1961–1964.* Lausanne, Editions du Grand Chêne, 1967.

——, *La Vie intellectuelle de Stendhal. Genèse et évolution de ses idées (1802–1821).* Presses Universitaires de France, 1962.

-——, *La Vie de Stendhal.* Albin Michel, 1965.

——, *Stendhal Club.* Revue trimestrielle. 15 Octobre 1959, 15 janvier 1960, 15 juillet 1960. Lausanne, Editions du Grand Chêne, 1959, 1960.

——, (gen. ed.), *Première journée du Stendhal-Club.* Lausanne, Editions du Grand Chêne, 1965.

——, *Album Stendhal.* Iconographie réunie et commentée par V. Del Litto. Bibliothèque de la Pléïade, 1966.

——, *Stendhal en Dauphiné.* Hachette, 1968.

DESCHAMPS, JULES, *Stendhal et De Potter.* Editions du Stendhal-Club, No. 13, 1925.

DESTUTT DE TRACY, A.-L.-C., *Projet d'éléments d'idéologie.* Didot, 1801–18.

DITLIVSEN, JYTTE WALKER, *Inspirations italiennes dans les oeuvres de Chateaubriand—Stendhal—Barrès—Suarès.* Torre Pellice, Chez l'auteur, 1962.

DOLLOT, RENÉ, *Stendhal. Consul de France à Trieste.* Editions du Stendhal-Club, No. 23, 1927.

——, *Stendhal à Venise.* Editions du Stendhal-Club, No. 25, 1927.

——, *Stendhal et La Scala.* Editions du Stendhal-Club, No. 35, 1935.

——, *Stendhal journaliste.* Mercure de France, 1948.

DOYON, ANDRÉ, ET DU PARC, YVES, *Amitiés parisiennes de Stendhal.* Préface de V. Del Litto. Lausanne, Editions du Grand Chêne, 1969.

DREVET, CAMILLE, *Le Dauphiné de Stendhal.* Préface de M. Henri Martineau. Gap, Editions Ophrys, 1954.

DUGAS, L., *Les Grands Timides.* Félix Alcan, 1922.

DUMOLARD, H., *Pages stendhaliennes.* Grenoble, B. Arthaud, 1928.

——, *Autour de Stendhal.* Grenoble, B. Arthaud, 1932.

DU PARC, YVES, *Quand Stendhal relisait les Promenades dans Rome. Marginalia inédits.* Lausanne, Editions du Grand Chêne, 1959.

DURAND, GILBERT, *Le Décor mythique de La Chartreuse de Parme.* Corti, 1971.

DURRY, M.-J., *Une Lettre inédite de Stendhal.* Editions du Stendhal-Club, No. 4, 1924.

——, *Stendhal et la police pontificale.* Editions du Stendhal-Club, No. 11, 1925.

——, *Stendhal et son travail consulaire: un échantillon inédit.* Editions du Stendhal-Club, No. 12, 1925.

——, *Une Passion de Stendhal: Clémentine.* Editions du Stendhal-Club, No. 22, 1927.

EDGEWORTH, MARIA, *Letters from England, 1813–1844.* Edited by Christina Colvin. Oxford, The Clarendon Press, 1971.

ESTOURMEL, COMTE JOSEPH D', *Souvenirs de France et d'Italie dans les années 1830, 1831 et 1832.* Crapelet, 1848.

FAGUET, EMILE, *Politiques et moralistes du XIXe siècle,* 3e série. Société française d'imprimerie et de librairie, 1900.

FARGES, LOUIS, *Stendhal diplomate.* Rome et l'Italie de 1829 à 1832 d'après sa correspondance officielle inédite. Plon, Nourrit, 1892.

FAURE, GABRIEL, *Stendhal, compagnon d'Italie.* Charpentier, 1931.

FINESHRIBER, WILLIAM H., JR., *Stendhal the Romantic Rationalist.* Princeton, New Jersey, Princeton University Press, 1932.

FRANCE, ANATOLE, *Stendhal.* Les Amis d'Edouard, No. 25, 1920.

FRANÇOIS-PONCET, ANDRÉ, *Stendhal à Brunswick, 1807–1808.* Bulletin de l'Académie Delphinale, 1942 et 1943. Grenoble, Imprimerie Allier, 1944.

GALPIN, ALFRED, *Fauriel in Italy. Unpublished correspondence, 1822–1825.* Rome, Edizione di Storia e Letteratura, 1962.

GALT, JOHN, *The Life of Lord Byron.* Colburn & Bentley, 1830.

GERLACH-NIELSEN, MERETE, *Stendhal théoricien et romancier de l'amour.* Copenhagen, Ejnar Munksgaard, 1965.

GIRAUD, RAYMOND, *The Unheroic Hero in the Novels of Stendhal, Balzac and Flaubert.* New Brunswick, New Jersey, Rutgers University Press, 1957.

GOURMONT, REMY DE, *Promenades philosophiques.* Mercure de France, 1905.

GREEN, F. C., *Stendhal.* Cambridge, Cambridge University Press, 1939.

GUNNELL, DORIS, *Stendhal et l'Angleterre.* Preface de M. Adolphe Paupe. Bosse, 1909.

———, *Sutton Sharpe et ses amis français.* Avec des lettres inédites. Champion, 1925.

HAZARD, PAUL, *La Vie de Stendhal.* Gallimard, 1928.

HAZLITT, WILLIAM, *Notes of a Journey Through France and Italy.* Hunt & Clarke, 1826.

HEISLER, MARCEL, *Stendhal et Napoléon.* Nizet, 1969.

HEMMINGS, F. W. J., *Stendhal. A Study of His Novels.* Oxford, The Clarendon Press, 1964.

HENRIOT, EMILE, *Stendhaliana.* Crès, 1924.

HUNT, LEIGH, *Lord Byron and Some of his Contemporaries.* Colburn, 1828.

IMBERT, H.-F., *Les Métamorphoses de la liberté ou Stendhal devant la Restauration et le Risorgimento.* Corti, 1967.

JACOUBET, HENRI, *Les Romans de Stendhal.* Grenoble, Drevet, 1933.

JACQUEMONT, VICTOR, *Lettres à Stendhal.* Introduction et Notes par Pierre Maes. Poursin, 1933.

JOUBIN, ANDRÉ (ed.), *Journal d'Eugène Delacroix.* Plon, 1932.

JOURDA, PIERRE, *Vieusseux et ses correspondants français.* Editions du Stendhal-Club, No. 16, 1926.

——, *Stendhal raconté par ceux qui l'ont vu.* Stock, 1931.

——, *Etat présent des études stendhaliennes.* Les Belles Lettres, 1930.

——, *Stendhal. L'homme et l'oeuvre.* Desclée de Brouwer, 1934.

KOLB, MARTHE, *Ary Scheffer et son temps, 1795–1858.* Boivin, 1937.

KRUTCH, JOSEPH WOOD, *Five Masters.* Cape, 1931.

LAMARTINE, A. DE, *Cours familier de littérature.* On s'abonne chez l'auteur, 1864.

LÉAUTAUD, PAUL (ed.), *Stendhal (Henri Beyle). Collection des plus belles pages.* Avec une notice par Paul Léautaud. Mercure de France, 1908.

LE BRETON, ANDRÉ, *Le Rouge et le Noir de Stendhal.* Etude et analyse. Editions de la Pensée moderne, 1966.

LEMAÎTRE, JULES, *Les Contemporains.* Etudes et portraits littéraires. Lecène et Ourdin, 1889.

LIPRANDI, CLAUDE, *Au coeur du Rouge.* L'Affaire Lafargue et Le Rouge et le Noir. Lausanne, Editions du Grand Chêne, 1961.

LUMBROSO, ALBERT, *Vingt jugements inédits sur Henry Beyle (Stendhal).* Recueillis et publiés par Albert Lumbroso. Florence, L. Franceschini, imprimeur, 1902.

McWATTERS, K. G., *Stendhal, lecteur des romanciers anglais.* Lausanne, Editions du Grand Chêne, 1968.

MAES, PIERRE, *Un ami de Stendhal. Victor Jacquemont.* Desclée de Brouwer, 1934.

MAQUET, ALBERT, *Deux amis italien de Stendhal: Giovanni Plana et Carlo Guasco.* Préface de V. Del Litto. Lausa...ne, Editions du Grand Chêne, 1963.

MARCHAND, LESLIE A., *The Athenaeum. A Mirror of Victorian Culture.* Chapel Hill, University of North Carolina Press, 1941.

MARILL-ALBÉRÈS, FRANCINE, *Stendhal.* Editions Universitaires, 1970.

MARSAN, EUGÈNE, *Stendhal célébré à Civitavecchia.* Les Amis d'Edouard, No. 79, 1925.

——, *Stendhal.* Editions des Cahiers Libres, 1932.

MARTIN, MARIETTA, *Un Aventurier intellectuel sous la Restauration et la Monarchie de juillet. Le Docteur Koreff (1783–1851).* Champion, 1925.

MARTINEAU, HENRI, ET MICHEL, FRANÇOIS (ed.), *Nouvelles Soirées du Stendhal-Club.* Mercure de France, 1950.

MARTINEAU, HENRI, *L'Itinéraire de Stendhal.* Messein, 1912.

——, *Le Coeur de Stendhal.* Histoire de sa vie et de ses sentiments. Albin Michel, 1965.

——, *Petit Dictionnaire stendhalien.* Le Divan, 1948.

——, *L'Oeuvre de Stendhal.* Histoire de ses livres et de sa pensée. Albin Michel, 1951.

MARTINO, PIERRE, *Stendhal: Del Romanticismo nelle arti.* Editions du Stendhal-Club, No. 1, 1922.

———, *Sur les pas de Stendhal en Italie.* Editions du Stendhal-Club, No. 7, 1924.

———, *Une Rencontre italienne de Stendhal: M. de Micciché.* Editions du Stendhal-Club, No. 27, 1928.

MÉLIA, JEAN, *La Vie amoureuse de Stendhal.* Mercure de France, 1909.

MÉRIMÉE, PROSPER, *Portraits historiques et littéraires.* Calmann Levy, 1892.

MICHEL, FRANÇOIS, *Etudes stendhaliennes.* Présentées par Henri Martineau et par Jean Fabre. Mercure de France, 1958.

MILLER, BETTY (ed.), *Elizabeth Barrett to Miss Mitford.* Murray, 1954.

MITCHELL, JOHN, *Stendhal: Le Rouge et le Noir.* Arnold, 1973.

MORGAN, LADY, *Italy.* Colburn, 1821.

———, *France in 1829–30.* Saunders & Otley, 1830.

MORLEY, EDITH J. (ed.), *Henry Crabb Robinson on Books and Their Writers.* Dent, 1938.

OLLIVIER, DAVID (ed.), *Correspondance de Liszt et de la Comtesse d'Agoult.* Grosset, 1934.

PATON, ANDREW, *Henry Beyle.* Trübner, 1874.

PAUPE, ADOLPHE, *Histoire des oeuvres de Stendhal.* Introduction par C. Stryienski. Dujarric, 1903.

PELADAN, *Ernest Hébert. Son oeuvre et son temps.* Delagrave, 1910.

PINVERT, LUCIEN, *Un ami de Stendhal. Le critique E.-D. Forgues, 1813–1883.* Leclerc, 1915.

PLANTA, EDWARD, *A New Picture of Paris.* Leigh, 1831.

PRÉVOST, JEAN, *La création chez Stendhal.* Mercure de France, 1951.

PRIMOLI, COMTE JOSEPH, *Une promenade dans Rome sur les traces de Stendhal.* Inédits de Stendhal. Les Amis d'Edouard, No. 45, 1922.

PROTHERO, ROWLAND E. (ed.), *The Works of Lord Byron. Letters and Journals.* Murray, 1898–1910.

RAITT, A. W., *Prosper Mérimée.* Eyre & Spottiswoode, 1970.

REDDING, CYRUS, *Fifty Years' Recollections, Literary and Personal,* Vol. II. Skeet, 1858.

RICHARD, JEAN-PIERRE, *Stendhal et Flaubert. Littérature et sensation.* Préface de Georges Poulet. Editions du Seuil, 1954.

ROCHEFORT, HENRI, *Les Aventures de ma vie,* Vol. II. Dupont, 1896.

ROY, CLAUDE, *Stendhal par lui-même.* Editions du Seuil, 1968.

ROYER, LOUIS, *Bibliographie Stendhalienne, 1928–1929.* Editions du Stendhal-Club, No. 30, 1930.

———, *Bibliographie Stendhalienne, 1930–1931.* Editions du Stendhal-Club, No. 33, 1932.

———, *Bibliographie Stendhalienne, 1932–1933*. Editions du Stendhal-Club, No. 34, 1934.

———, *Stendhal au physionotrace*. Editions du Stendhal-Club, No. 31, 1930.

———, *Stendhal candidat à la Bibliothèque royale*. Editions du Stendhal-Club, No. 32, 1931.

RUDE, FERNAND, *Stendhal et la pensée sociale de son temps*. Plon, 1967.

SAINTE-BEUVE, C.-A., *Causeries du lundi*. Tome IX. Garnier, 1854.

———, *Correspondance générale*. Recueillie, classée et annotée par Jean Bonnerot. Stock/ Privat, Didier, 1935–.

SAND, GEORGE, *Correspondance*. Textes réunis, classés et annotés par Georges Lubin. Garnier, 1964–68.

———, *Histoire de ma vie*, Tome IV. Calmann-Lévy, 1904.

SÉCHÉ, ALPHONSE, *Stendhal*. Louis-Michaud, 1912.

SIMON, CHARLES, *Stendhal et la police autrichienne*. D'après des documents inédits. Editions du Stendhal-Club, No. 2, 1923.

———, *Les Souvenirs du Baron de Strombeck et de Louis Spach sur Stendhal*. Editions du Stendhal-Club, No. 9, 1925.

———, *Stendhal par Gobineau*. Editions du Stendhal-Club, No. 20, 1926.

———, *Le Sillage de Stendhal en Allemagne*. Editions du Stendhal-Club, No. 21, 1926.

———, *Nouveaux inédits de Stendhal*. Editions du Stendhal-Club, No. 28, 1930.

SMILES, SAMUEL, *Memoir and Correspondence of the Late John Murray*. Murray, 1891.

SMITH, HORATIO E., *La Fortune d'une oeuvre de jeunesse de Stendhal en Amerique*. Editions du Stendhal-Club, No. 24, 1927.

SMITH, MARION ELMINA, *Une Anglaise intellectuelle en France sous la Restauration. Miss Mary Clarke*. Champion, 1927.

STENDHAL, *Correspondence*
Correspondance. Préface par V. del Litto. Edition etablie et annotée par Henri Martineau et V. Del Litto. N.R.F., Bibliothèque de la Pléîade, 1968. 3 tomes.

———, *Autobiography*
Oeuvres intimes. Texte établi et annoté par Henri Martineau. N.R.F., Bibliothèque de la Pléîade, 1966.

———, *Biography*
Vies de Haydn, de Mozart et de Métastase. Texte établi et annoté par Daniel Müller. Préface de Romain Rolland. Champion, 1914.
Vie de Rossini. Suivie des Notes d'un Dilettante. Texte établi et annoté avec preface et avant-propos par Henry Prunières. Champion, 1922. 2 tomes.

Vie de Napoléon. Introduction de Michel Wassiltchikov. Petite Bibliothèque Payot, 1969.

———, *Travel*

Rome, Naples et Florence. Texte établi et annoté par Daniel Müller. Préface de Charles Maurras. Champion, 1919. 2 tomes.

Promenades dans Rome. Texte établi et annoté par Armand Caraccio. Préface de Henri de Régnier. Champion, 1938.

Mémoires d'un touriste. Texte établi et annoté avec un avant-propos par Louis Royer. Préface de Jean-Louis Vaudoyer. Champion, 1932. 2 tomes.

Voyage dans le Midi de la France. Etablissement du texte et préface par Henri Martineau. Le Divan, 1930.

Pages d'Italie. L'Italie en 1818. Moeurs romaines. Le Divan, 1932.

———, *Novels and Short Stories*

Romans et nouvelles. Texte établi et annoté par Henri Martineau. N.R.F., Bibliothèque de la Pléïade, 1966, 1968. 2 tomes.

Romans et nouvelles. Précédés d'une notice sur de Stendhal par M. R. Colomb. Michel Lévy, 1854.

Armance. Précédé d'une notice biographique par R. Colomb. Calmann Lévy, 1877.

Armance. Texte etabli et annoté par Raymond Lebegue. Préface de André Gide. Champion, 1925.

La Chartreuse de Parme. Préface de Francisque Sarcey. Conquet, 1883.

Chroniques italiennes. Michel Lévy, 1855.

———, *Criticism*

Racine et Shakespeare. Préface et notes de Bernard Drenner. Pauvert, 1965.

Histoire de la peinture en Italie. Texte établi et annoté avec préface et avant-propos par Paul Arbelet. Champion, 1924. 2 tomes.

Mélanges d'art. Le Divan, 1932.

Mélanges de littérature. Fragments romanesques et poétiques. Le Divan, 1933. 3 tomes.

Molière, Shakespeare, La Comédie et le rire. Le Divan, 1930.

Ecoles italiennes de peinture. Le Divan, 1932. 3 tomes.

Idées italiennes sur quelques tableaux célèbres. Abraham Constantin. 2e edition revue et annotée par Stendhal. Le Divan, 1931.

———, *Journalism*

Courrier anglais. Etablissement du texte et préfaces par Henri Martineau. Le Divan, 1935, 1936. 5 tomes.

———, *Theatre*

Théâtre. Etablissement du texte et préfaces par Henri Martineau. Le Divan, 1931. 3 tomes.

——, *Miscellaneous*

De l'Amour. Texte établi, avec introduction et notes, par Henri Martineau. Garnier, 1959.

Mélanges de politique et d'histoire. Etablissement du texte et préfaces par Henri Martineau. Le Divan, 1933. 2 tomes.

Mélanges intimes et marginalia. Etablissement du texte et préfaces par Henri Martineau. Le Divan, 1936. 2 tomes.

Pensées. Filosofia nova. Le Divan, 1931. 2 tomes.

STRAUSS, ANDRÉ, *La Fortune de Stendhal en Angleterre.* Didier, 1966.

STRYIENSKI, CASIMIR, *Soireés du Stendhal Club. Documents inédits. Préface de L. Bélugou.* Mercure de France, 1904.

TAINE, H., *Voyage en Italie.* Hachette, 1866.

TILLETT, MARGARET, *Stendhal. The Background to the Novels.* Oxford University Press, 1971.

TOYE, FRANCIS, *Rossini. A Study in Tragi-Comedy.* Barker, 1954.

TROUT, PAULETTE, *La Vocation romanesque de Stendhal.* Editions universitaires, 1970.

VAILLANT, PIERRE, *Une relation anglaise, annotée par Stendhal, sur les moeurs américaines vers 1830.* Grenoble, Imprimerie Allais, 1957.

VALÉRY, PAUL, *Variété,* Vol. II. Gallimard, 1930.

WOOD, MICHAEL, *Stendhal.* Elek, 1971.

ZOLA, EMILE, *Les Romanciers naturalistes.* Charpentier, 1881.

Index